Jefferson County's
[VIRGINIA]
Fourth Estate
1840–1850

William D. Theriault

"Burke said there were Three Estates in Parliament: but, in the Reporters' Gallery yonder, there sat a Fourth Estate more important far than them all."

Thomas Carlyle, "The Hero as a Man of Letters," On Heroes, Hero Worship, and the Heroic in History, (1840)

HERITAGE BOOKS
2017

HERITAGE BOOKS
AN IMPRINT OF HERITAGE BOOKS, INC.

Books, CDs, and more—Worldwide

For our listing of thousands of titles see our website
at
www.HeritageBooks.com

Published 2017 by
HERITAGE BOOKS, INC.
Publishing Division
5810 Ruatan Street
Berwyn Heights, Md. 20740

Copyright © 2017 William D. Theriault

All rights reserved. No part of this book may be reproduced or transmitted in any form or by any means, electronic or mechanical, including photocopying, recording or by any information storage and retrieval system without written permission from the author, except for the inclusion of brief quotations in a review.

International Standard Book Number
Paperbound: 978-0-7884-5792-0

Table of Contents

List of Illustrations vii
Preface xi
Introduction xiii
Part I. The Pen and the Sword 1
   November 5, 1840, Charlestown, Jefferson County, Virginia........ 3
   April,1841, Charlestown, Virginia 6
   August 12, 1841, Charlestown, Virginia 8
   November 15, 1841, Court House, Jefferson County, Virginia.... 10
   November 1842, Charlestown, Virginia 12
   July 4th, 1843, Charlestown, Virginia 13
   July 4th, 1844, Charlestown, Virginia 17
   July 15, 1844, Jefferson County, Virginia 19
   July 17, 1844, Charlestown, Virginia 22
   December 1844, Jefferson County, Virginia 25
Part II. Manifest Destiny 29
   July 4th, 1845, Shannondale Springs, VA 29
   December 1845, Jefferson County, VA 33
   July 4th, 1846, Jefferson County, Virginia 37
   December 1846, Jefferson County, Virginia 40
   January 1847, Jefferson County, Virginia 41
   July 1847, Jefferson County, Virginia 44
   January 1848 46
   April 1848, Jefferson County, Virginia 48
   July 1848, Jefferson County, Virginia 50
   August 1848, Jefferson County, Virginia 53
   November 1848, Charlestown, Virginia 54
   December 1848, Jefferson County, Virginia 57
Part III. Seeing the Elephant 61
   January 1849, Jefferson County, Virginia 62
   February 1849, Charlestown, Virginia. 64

March 29, 1849, Charlestown, Virginia 67
April 1849 70
March, 1849, Near Cairo, Illinois 73
April 12, 1849, St. Louis, Missouri. 74
April 19, 1849, Independence, Missouri 77
May 1849, Jefferson County, Virginia 80
May 1849, St. Josephs, Missouri 83
May 6, 1849. 86
May 8, 1849, Indian Territory 87
May 11, 1849, Kickapoo Nation, Indian Territory 87
May 13, 1849, Camp Seevers 88
May 25, 1849, Shawnee Nation, near Josephs, Mo. 91
May 28, 1849, Fort Kearney 93
June 1849, Jefferson County, Virginia 96
June 1, 1849, near Chimney Rock 98
June 2, 1849, near Chimney Rock 100
Early June, 1849, San Francisco, California 103
June 11, 1849, Chimney Rock, City of the Plains 104
June 28, 1849, Rocky Mountains, east of the South Pass 109
July 4th, 1849, Charlestown, Virginia 112
July 4th, 1849, Green River Crossing, Utah Territory 113
July 4th, 1849, Sacramento City, California 115
August 1849, Jefferson County, Virginia 117
September 1849, Charlestown, Virginia 119
September 9, 1849, Sacramento, California 120
September 29, 1849, Sacramento, California 128

Part IV. Golden Shackles 133
October 1849 133
October 4, 1849, Sacramento, California 135
October 15, 1849, Upper Sacramento 136
November 1849, Charlestown, Jefferson County, Virginia 140

November 1, 1849, Weaver Creek, California 142
November 13, 1849 147
December, 1849 148
December 30, 1849, Weaver Creek (California) 150
Part V. Conflict and Compromise 153
January 1850, Washington, D.C. 154
January 20, 1850, Webon Creek, California 159
January 22, 1850 161
February 1850, Washington, D.C. 162
February 16, 1850, Webon Creek, California 165
February 27, 1850, Sacramento City 168
March 1850 170
April 1850 173
April 12, 1850, Sacramento City, California 174
May 1850, Washington, D.C. 177
June 1850, Washington, D.C. 179
June 20, 1850, Weber Creek, California 183
July 4th, 1850, Washington, D.C. 188
July 9, 1850, Washington, D.C. 191
July 27, 1850, Sacramento City, California 192
August 1850, Washington, D.C. 193
August 14, 1850, Sacramento City, California 197
August 31, 1850, Sacramento City, California 199
September 1850, Washington, DC 201
September 12, 1850, Sacramento City 204
November 1850, California 205
November 22, 1850, Headquarters, Calaveras Co. 207
December 1850, California 210
Epilogue 211
Notes 213
Index 227

List of Illustrations

Figure 1. Charles Varle, *Map of Frederick, Berkeley, & Jefferson Counties in the State of Virginia, 1809* xii

Figure 2. View of Jefferson's Rock, Harper's Ferry, Virginia, 1854. xiv

Figure 3. John S. Gallaher, ca. 1840 2

Figure 4. William Henry Harrison, 1773-1841. 3

Figure 5. *The Ladies Garland*, published by John S. Gallaher. Courtesy Harper's Ferry National Historic Park. 4

Figure 6. Charlestown, Virginia, ca. 1840, from Howe, *Historical Collections*. 6

Figure 7. Cedar Lawn. Home of John Thornton Augustine Washington and family. 11

Figure 8. Charlestown, Virginia, 1843, from sketch by Henry Howe. 13

Figure 9. Ruins of Trinity Church, west of Charlestown, 1843, from sketch by Henry Howe. 15

Figure 10. Shannondale Springs, ca. 1840, from Howe, *Historical Collections* 16

Figure 11. Rion Hall. Built by William Lucas, 1836. 18

Figure 12. Henry Bedinger, 1812 - 1858 19

Figure 13. *Spirit of Jefferson*, first issue, July 17, 1844 21

Figure 14. Clay and Polk campaign ribbons, 1844. 24

Figure 15. Shannondale Springs, Virginia, from S.H. Brown, *Map of Jefferson County, Va., 1852* 27

Figure 16. James L. Ranson, 1791 – 1868; John Blair Hodge, 1825-1896 30

Figure 17. Harper's Ferry, Virginia, ca. 1840. From Howe's *Historical Collections* 36

Figure 18. Pennsylvania Senator David Wilmot, 1814-1868 39

Figure 19. Jefferson County (West) Virginia, Court House 41

Figure 20. I.O.O.F. Virginia Lodge No. 1, Harpers Ferry, WV. Courtesy Harper's Ferry National Historical Park. 43

Figure 21. Col. J.F. Hamtramck, 1798-1858, Colonel, 1st Volunteer Regiment, Mexican War. 52

Figure 22. "Seeing the Elephant," by Wm. B. McMurtrie 60

Figure 23. Dr. Wakeman Bryarly. He served as the Surgeon in the Charlestown Company of miners. 65

Figure 24. Ezra Meeker, *The Old Oregon Trail*, postcard, 1906......... 69

Figure 25. Charles J. Faulkner, 1806-1884 70

Figure 26. Cairo, Illinois, ca. 1850.. 72

Figure 27. St. Louis, Missouri, ca. 1840's. 74

Figure 28. Independence, Missouri, 1850. 75

Figure 29. Prairie Schooler, by James M. Hutchings, *Scenes of Wonder and Curiosity in California* (1862). 76

Figure 30. Steamboat Race, Currier & Ives, ca. 1866........................ 76

Figure 31. Shepherdstown, Virginia, 1840's. From Howe, *Historical Collections.* 79

Figure 32. St. Josephs, Missouri, ca. 1840. 82

Figure 33. Ferry Crossing, Oregon Trail, by Ezra Meeker, 1906 85

Figure 34. Scene on the desert, by George H. Barker, Placerville, CA: J.M. Hutchings, 1853 90

Figure 35. Fort Kearney, ca. 1849.. 93

Figure 36. Chimney Rock; Court-House Rock (right), by James E. Wilkins, 1849... 97

Figure 37. Ash Hollow, on the Oregon Trail. Courtesy Ash Hollow State Historical Park, Nebraska. 102

Figure 38. Senators David Broderick, 1820 - 1859 (left) and William Gwin, 1805 - 1885 (right)... 103

Figure 39. Chimney Rock; Court-House Rock (right), George H. Barker, J.M. Hutchings, Placerville, ca. 1853 104

Figure 40. Fort Laramie, ca. 1845... 107

Figure 41. Devil's Gate. Courtesy of Wyoming State Historic Preservation Office. 108

Figure 42. Sacramento City, California, 1850.................................. 115

Figure 43. Fort Hall, ca. 1850. 116

Figure 44. William A. Jackson, *Map of the Mining District of California*, New York: Lambert and Lane, 1851. 127

Figure 45. The Miners' Ten Commandments (for those who had "seen the elephant") 132

Figure 46. Weaverville, California, by James Hutchings, Shasta: A.R. Ross, 1855 142

Figure 47. Jacob Engle. Charlestown, (Va.) Mining Co. 147

Figure 48. Edward W. McIlhany, Charlestown (Va.) Mining Co., 1849. 147

Figure 49. President Zachary Taylor 153

Figure 50. Sutter's Fort, ca. 1850. 161

Figure 51. Senator Henry Clay, 1777 – 1852. 169

Figure 52. Senator Daniel Webster, 1782 – 1852. 169

Figure 53. Senator John C. Calhoun, 1782 – 1850 169

Figure 54. Disunion over slavery. From *Punch*, November 8, 1856. 170

Figure 55. James Rumsey House, Shepherdstown, Virginia, from a drawing by Henry Howe, 1843 181

Figure 56. Washington Monument, Washington, D.C., ca. 1850 188

Figure 57. Humbolt River Valley, by Daniel Jenks, 1859 196

Figure 58. Servility of the Northern States in arresting and returning fugitive slaves. 203

Figure 59. Peter H. Burnett, 1807 – 1895 210

Preface

This story begins in Jefferson County, Virginia, in the early 1840's. Told chiefly through the viewpoints and voices of contemporary local journalists, it attempts to present events as they saw them. Residents' world views were shaped mainly by what they read in the press, augmented by letters and word of mouth, so the Fourth Estate exerted an enormous influence on the public's thoughts and actions.[1]

The cast of characters includes John S. and Horatio N. Gallaher of the *Virginia Free Press*; James W. Beller of the *Spirit of Jefferson*; and Henry Hardy, H.W. McAnly, and John H. Zittle of the *Shepherdstown Register*. J. Harrison Kelly and B.F. Washington also figure largely in this narrative, for they both wrote for local newspapers before becoming editors in their own right.

Like many newspapers of the time, they were political organs, founded to publicize party ideas and promote candidates seeking public office. These editors represent the viewpoints of the local Whig and Democratic parties as they struggled with major issues such as the Mexican War, Westward Expansion, the California Gold Rush, the spread of slavery, and more.

Adopting the motto that "The Pen is mightier than the sword," many editors believed they could use their skills to shape voters' opinions. The public, in turn, could use ballots, not bullets to influence public policy. Within the newspapers' pages, writers waged war with ideas, creating political discourse supported by a code of honor much like boxers who adhered to the Marquis of Queensbury rules. The public loved it. Occasionally, when an editor violated the code, he was challenged to a duel to settle the quarrel.

While some of the participants spent their entire professional careers in Jefferson County, Virginia, others followed the news and their fortunes westward, settling in California or other newly opened territories. Others, broke or homesick, returned to the East coast.

The current volume closes with the signing of the Compromise of 1850, but subsequent volumes will continue the narrative up through the 1870's to the end of Reconstruction, exploring how these journalists tried to change their world and in turn were changed by it.

A NOTE TO THE READER

The resources listed in the *Notes* section are available as verbatim transcripts and digital facsimiles in the *West Virginia GeoExplorer Project* at:

http://www.wvgeohistory.org/Search.aspx#v=69841

From there, you can explore its large collection of newspapers, images, and interviews and other information.

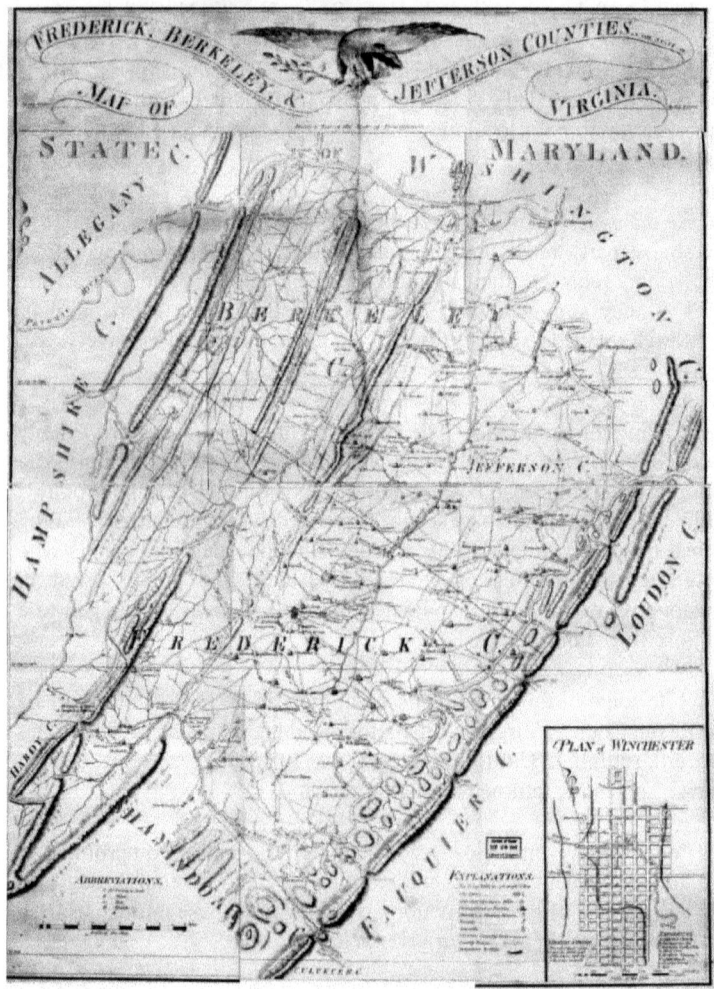

Figure 1. Charles Varle, *Map of Frederick, Berkeley, & Jefferson Counties in the State of Virginia,* 1809.

Introduction

JEFFERSON COUNTY, VIRGINIA, was formed from the southern part of Berkeley in 1801. Bounded by the Potomac and the Shenandoah Rivers, it was named for Thomas Jefferson, who declared the view at the confluence worth a trip across the Atlantic. The country was known for its fertile farmland as well as deposits of limestone and iron ore. In his *Historical Collections of Virginia* (1845), Henry Howe remarked that:

> It was settled principally by old Virginia families from the eastern part of the state; and the inhabitants still retain that high, chivalrous spirit, and generous hospitality, for which that race was so remarkable in the palmy days of their prosperity.

Geographically, it was one of the Western counties, sharing their need for improved transportation and complaining that their people were under represented in the State Legislature. Demographically, its population was almost one third slave, placing it with the Eastern counties in its concern to maintain its "peculiar institution." White citizens generally considered the small number of free back residents to be lazy and ignorant, poor examples for their slave brethren. The Legislature encouraged them to leave the State on penalty of being returned to slavery.

Politically, since the close of the 1830 State Constitutional Convention, Jefferson, like the other Virginia counties, was governed by an aristocracy, not a democracy. White male property owners or renters over age twenty-one could vote for representatives to the General Assembly. The Assembly selected the officials who served at the Federal, State, and local level, from the Governor to the county sheriff. Thus the citizenry had little direct voice in the selection of local officials.

Early in the country's history, Thomas Jefferson recognized that the press could inform the masses and shape public opinion, whether its readers had the vote or not. Newspapers were present in every pub or coffee house, passed from hand to hand, or tacked to notice boards. But to fully utilize this resource, citizens must be literate and have access to a free public education. Writing to a delegate of the Continental Congress, Jefferson observed:

> The people are the only censors of their governors: and even their errors will tend to keep these to the true principles of their institution. To punish these errors too severely would be to suppress the only safeguard of the public liberty. The way to prevent these irregular interpositions of the people is to give them full information of their affairs thro' the channel of the public papers, and to contrive that those papers should penetrate the whole mass of the people. The basis of our governments being the opinion of the people, the very first object should be to keep that right; and were it left to me to decide whether we should have a government without newspapers, or newspapers without a government, I should not hesitate a moment to prefer the latter. But I should mean that every man should receive those papers and be capable of reading them. [2]

Figure 2. View of Jefferson's Rock, Harper's Ferry, Virginia, 1854.

Part I. The Pen and the Sword

CARDINAL RICHELIEU:
True, This! —
Beneath the rule of men entirely great
The pen is mightier than the sword. Behold
The arch-enchanters wand! — itself is nothing! —
But taking sorcery from the master-hand
To paralyse the Cæsars, and to strike
The loud earth breathless! —
Take away the sword —
States can be saved without it!

Edward Bulwer-Lytton, *Richelieu: Or the Conspiracy* (1839)

Figure 3. John S. Gallaher, ca. 1840

Figure 4. William Henry Harrison, 1773-1841.

November 5, 1840, Charlestown, Jefferson County, Virginia

Editor John S. Gallaher must have felt satisfied when he proofed the day's issue of his newspaper, *The Virginia Free Press*. The early election returns looked promising for Whig candidate, William Henry Harrison. Thanks, in part, to Gallaher, Jefferson County had supported Harrison by a solid majority. [3]

The Democrats knew Gallaher was a force to be reckoned with, both as a newspaperman and as a politician. At age 14, he had been hired by John Arbutis, veteran editor of the *Berkeley and Jefferson Intelligencer*. From there he had moved to the *Martinsburg Gazette*, the *Niles Register* (Baltimore), and the *National Intelligencer* (Washington, DC). [4]

After building an impressive resume, John set out on his own, hiring his younger brother Horatio [5] and establishing the *Free Press* at Harper's Ferry, Virginia (1821). From 1824 to 1828, he also published the *Ladies Garland*, a weekly that furnished women with both entertainment and educational fare. [6]

His next acquisition was the local *Farmer's Repository* (1827), which he merged with his other paper to form the *Virginia Free Press & Farmers'*

Repository. In 1832, he focused his efforts on establishing *The Virginia Free Press* in Charlestown, Virginia.

The birth of the *Virginia Free Press* coincided with the emergence of the Whig party, led by Senator Henry Clay. It had been formed in reaction to the policies of President Andrew Jackson, and Gallaher was destined to help shape and expound Clay's vision for America — "The American System."

Figure 5. *The Ladies Garland,* published by John S. Gallaher. Courtesy Harpers Ferry National Historic Park.

In general, the Whigs favored a strong federal government and a tariff to protect American industries and generate revenue. Money from sales of public lands would help fill government coffers. Proceeds would be used to create a national infrastructure of roads and canals that would unite the country. The party sought to establish a permanent national bank that would ensure a stable currency and help offset the risk and speculation found in state and local banks.

Using his pen to support Whig candidates, John was himself elected to the Virginia House of Delegates, serving from 1830 to 1835. With the management of the *Virginia Free Press* in the capable hands of his brother, he moved to Richmond in 1835, becoming chief manager of the *Richmond Compiler*. Two years later he purchased one-third interest in the *Richmond Hawk* and continued his support of state and local Whig candidates. Most recently, Gallaher had published the *Yeoman*, a campaign newspaper that supported Harrison and Tyler. [7]

Now, at age 39, Gallaher had come back to Charlestown, looking forward to spending some peaceful time with his wife, five children, and extended family. Whether Harrison or Van Buren became president,

> In either event, we will be found supporting what we candidly approve, and condemning in the language of a freeman, what we conscientiously believe to be wrong. As for the rest, let us differ as much as we may.
>
> Ours are the plans of fair, delightful peace,
> Unwarped by party rage,
> To live like Brothers.
>
> There has been strife enough for twelve months. The nation itself requires repose, which, if Gen. Harrison is elected, it will be sure to enjoy. [8]

The country was in the midst of the major recession that followed the Panic of 1837. Unemployment was high; wages, prices and profits were low.

Many banks and businesses had closed. Harrison promised to restore economic prosperity, and the voters believed him, giving him an electoral count of 234 votes to Van Buren's 60. Jefferson County had gone to Harrison by a majority of 78, although Van Buren was able to claim all of Virginia's electoral votes.

Inauguration Day, March 4, 1841, dawned cold and windy. Harrison chose to deliver a long inaugural address without the protection of an overcoat, hat, or gloves. Three weeks after delivering his speech, Harrison developed a cold. He died on April 4th, and Vice President John Tyler was sworn in two days later.

Figure 6. Charlestown, Virginia, ca. 1840, from Howe, *Historical Collections*

April, 1841, Charlestown, Virginia

On April 9th, John Tyler assumed the office of President of the United States. He was a Virginian and a strict constructionist, with Southern sympathies. In his address to the people, he noted that, although they had elected Harrison to correct and reform past errors and abuses,

> While standing at the threshold of this great work he has by the dispensation of an allwise Providence been removed from amongst us, and by the provisions of the Constitution the efforts to be directed to the accomplishing of this vitally important task have devolved upon myself. [9]

Charlestown's tribute to the late President began on April 10th at dawn with a salute from the Charlestown Artillery and the tolling of church bells. John's brother, Horatio Nelson Gallaher, had organized the event. It was cold and wet, but by 11 AM the main street was lined with people of all classes.

The procession solemnly marched to the Episcopal Church. The Charlestown Artillery led the way, followed by the Potomac Rifles, the Smithfield Blues, and the Harpers Ferry Guards. Amateur bands from Harpers Ferry and Shepherdstown accompanied them. A white horse caparisoned with black in military style represented the absent hero. Rev. Alexander Jones [10] delivered an oration and then the public dispersed. John S. Gallaher observed:

> All political animosity seemed buried in the grave of the departed, and political friends and foes apparently mourned the occasion with equal sincerity. All feelings of partisanship were merged in those of patriotism, and every indication of respect for the memory of a President of the U. States was observable and the patriotic spirit of our citizens deserve the highest praise. [11]

Remarking on the new President's recent address, Gallaher continued,

> As an exponent of principles and policy, appropriate to the occasion, the address of President Tyler will prove highly satisfactory to the great body of the American people. On the leading points — the currency, executive power, custody of the public treasure, and appointments to office, it is all that a free people might hope or wish. And this will be the conclusion of a nation, while mourning its late bereavement, that however just and poignant the lamentation for the illustrious dead, the powers and trusts of its first office have passed into safe and secure hands.

Held at the end of April, the Virginia general elections produced Whig victories at the local level. For Congress, Richard W. Barton of Frederick County defeated Jefferson County's Democratic candidate, William Lucas, and in the House of Delegates Whig candidates Capt. John Moler and Anthony Kennedy beat out Van Buren candidates William D. North and Jacob Morgan. [12]

To the editor of the *Free Press*, Harrison's Presidential victory looked as if it were starting to bear fruit.

August 12, 1841, Charlestown, Virginia

Throughout the summer, John Gallaher had been utilizing the *Virginia Free Press* and his political clout to promote the Whig's plan to end the recession. President Harrison had made the reestablishment of a national bank one of the major planks in his economic reform platform, and his supporters assumed that Tyler would carry out the wishes of his predecessor. The Bank Bill had already made its way through the Senate and had passed the House of Representatives last week. The following day, Congress sent it to Tyler for his signature.

Gallaher worried,

> Nothing is known in regard to the fate which awaits it at the hands of the President. Much speculation is afloat upon the subject — some affirming that he will sign it, others asserting positively that he will not. Our own opinion, based upon all that we have heard, and upon the wisdom and patriotic principles of John Tyler, is, that he will give a cordial approval of the bill....

> ... President Tyler has but two alternatives. He must either sanction the Bank bill just passed, or declare openly in favor of a plan similar to that reported by the Senate's Committee on Finance. ... There must be some national fiscal system. The necessities of the country require it — the indispensable functions of the government demand it — the restoration of the currency to soundness and its regulation afterwards, cannot be accomplished without it.... [13]

The President's response came a few days later in the form of a veto. Tyler asserted that his action should come as no surprise to the country, since he had voiced his opposition to a national bank throughout his career. He concluded his message by stating:

> I regard the bill as asserting for Congress the right to incorporate a United States bank with power and right to establish offices of discount and deposit in the several States of this Union with or without their consent — a principle to which I have always heretofore been opposed and which can never obtain my sanction; and waiving all other considerations growing out of its other provisions, I return it to the House in which it originated with these my objections to its approval.
> [14]

The veto deflated Gallaher's optimism about a timely solution to the nation's economic problems and made him wary about this President's future relationship to Congress:

> The present exemplification of things is an exemplification of the immense influence of this power [the veto]. — One man can set at aught the wishes of the whole people, and defeat the most beneficial legislation. This is nothing more than the autocrat of all the Russians would do — and to this extent our institutions are monarchical. But the power is given by the Constitution — the President has the right to

exercise it, and we must submit. But we must confess, we are so much of Democrats, that we feel rather restive at the substitution of one man for the will of the whole. It is in truth an invasion of the Democratic principle. We wish the power were abrogated — that the will of the people, as reflected by their immediate Representatives, might bear away. [15]

Congress quickly modified the Bank bill and resubmitted it to Tyler for his signature, and the President responded with a second veto on August 16th, warning:

[T]he conclusions to which I have brought myself are those of a settled conviction, founded, in my opinion, on a just view of the Constitution... [16]

The Whigs' reaction to the second veto was explosive. That evening, drunken party members rioted on the White House lawn, burning Tyler in effigy. A few weeks later, the Whigs expelled him and most of his cabinet resigned. The President was without a party; the Whigs' plans for reform were in shambles; and the Democrats regarded the political confusion as an opportunity to gain lost ground. [17]

Immediately reacting to Tyler's second veto, Gallaher announced that he and John H. Pleasants (editor of the Richmond *Whig*) would carry on the fight.

They would establish a new *Whig Journal*. At the same time,

We will suppress our wrath while a doubt or hope exists. There are strong reasons why the Whigs should remain firm and united — cool and considerate. The enemy are seeking, by persevering efforts, to produce division in our ranks. If they can possibly bring about a Tyler Whig party — and an anti-Tyler Whig party — their wishes will be consummated. Let us, if possible, disappoint him. Let us continue a solid phalanx, powerful and unbroken. In censuring what we consider a most unfortunate defection in the President, we must not forget, what he says to himself, that in all other great measures, equally condemned by the opposite party, he has stood by us. [18]

November 15, 1841, Court House, Jefferson County, Virginia

Frank Washington passed the pen to his sister Sally and showed her where to sign the document which would make him executor of their father's estate. Benjamin Franklin Washington was just twenty one, younger than brothers Daniel and Lawrence, and the enormity of the task before him was starting to sink in. As the other signers took their turn, he began to realize how his father's will would affect his destiny and that of his siblings. [19]

Brothers John, Daniel, and Lawrence would each receive about two hundred acres on the Great Kanawha in Mason County, along with several slaves. They were already planning their journey west. But Frank had been charged with managing the rest of his father's property until the youngest surviving child was 18. Then the remainder would be sold and the profits divided among him and the nine other children. *Cedar Lawn*, the home place, would pass out of their hands (Figure 7). They would need to make their own way in the world.

Like his siblings, Frank had a flair for writing, and he was ready to be admitted to the bar. He came from a family of politicians — his father had been a one-term member of the Virginia House of Delegates. Uncle Henry Bedinger was a Charlestown lawyer with Democratic connections. With a new proslavery, strict constructionist President in the White House, the Democrats might recoup their losses and Frank could become a rising star in the party. All promising options. Unfortunately he was tethered to Jefferson County, Virginia, until he had fulfilled his family responsibilities.

Figure 7. Cedar Lawn. Home of John Thornton Augustine Washington and family,

November 1842, Charlestown, Virginia

The events of the past year had dashed John Gallaher's hopes that President Tyler would continue the economic policies of his predecessor. In June, Tyler had vetoed two Whig-sponsored Tariff bills. Now "His Accidency" had generated so much animosity among Whigs that they poured their energy into removing him from office. In July they had introduced a bill to investigate his behavior and potentially begin impeachment proceedings. It was tabled.

Using a quote from one of his newspaper colleagues, Gallaher bristled,

> It is unfortunately true, that the Whig party elected John Tyler — it is equally true that an American Congress appointed Benedict Arnold to a high command, but when he consummated his treason, they denounced him, and rallied for their country. As well might the Whigs of the Revolution have been asked to forgive and follow Arnold, as the Whigs of the present day to follow or sustain John Tyler. The repudiation is as strong in the one case as the other. [20]

The frustrated legislators and journalists turned their attention to gaining state and national seats in the interim elections. The Congressional elections in the winter of '42 brought mixed results. The Whigs lost their majority in the U.S. House but managed to hang on to the Senate by a small margin.

Assessing the political situation, the editor noted:

> ... the Whigs for the moment are a little chop fallen, but by no means disheartened. The bright day is a little distant, to be sure, but come it must, as certainly as that Time itself contains in its chronicles of the future the year 1844. [21]

Figure 8. Charlestown, Virginia, 1843, from sketch by Henry Howe.

July 4th, 1843, Charlestown, Virginia

Jefferson County celebrated the 67th anniversary of American Independence much as she had done last year, and the year before. The rituals anchored her citizens to their collective past, reminding the gentry and the working class and the negroes, the Whigs and Democrats, of the bonds that held them together. New faces in the processions and ceremonies alerted some that change was coming.

The day began at 9 o'clock at the Court House with a 13-gun salute by the Charlestown Artillery under the command of Capt. John W. Rowan. At 10 o'clock, Rowan and his assistants had the military units formed up. John Harrison Kelly, responsible for the Methodist and Presbyterian Sabbath Schools, shepherded his charges to their place in the procession. The whole body then marched down Main Street to the Presbyterian Church, where visitors had gathered to watch the ceremonies.

The services began with an anthem from the church choir, followed by a prayer by the Rev. Mr. Dutton. Frank Washington then read the *Declaration of Independence*, and yielded his place to R. Hume Butcher, who delivered an oration on the achievements of their patriot ancestors, the science of government, and the need for an educated electorate.

The procession then reformed and marched east to a grove, where Rev. Mr. Gere addressed them on the beneficial effects of temperance. Finally, dinner was served. Ninety-year-old Peter Haines, the area's last surviving Revolutionary War veteran, held the place of honor.

After eating their fill, the men adjourned to the outdoor stage, where Democratic legislator William Lucas, President of the Day, orchestrated the regular and volunteer toasts and the intervening volleys of artillery. Although most of the toasts were not controversial, several of the speakers inserted pointed political commentary.

> Democrat R.H. Butcher led off with "The Constitution of my Country — May Time, which moulders in its career the noblest fabrics of human genius, leave this unaltered and unimpaired — for as it is, it alone can save the Republican ship from the thousand breakers in the distance hid."
>
> Whig John H. Kelly countered with: "Our Country — May the gallant ship yet outride the storm of pecuniary embarrassments — may she ever be saved from the billows and breakers of disunion — the all engulphing maelstrom of Executive power — still keep her colors flying at the mast head, borne on the winds of heaven, and fanned by the breath of fame, with every star bright and unsullied, ages after each of us shall have ceased to gaze upon its majestic fields."
>
> Frank Washington held his own with: "Our Country — When the recording Angel shall close for eternity the Book wherein is written the destinies of Nations, may her name appear embalmed in tears, the last and mightiest of the fallen great."

Out of respect for the temperance advocates at the celebration, guests drank toasts of water or lemonade.

The evening featured a procession of the Sabbath schools, under the charge of Mr. Kelley. J.S. Gallaher described the activities that followed:

> The Schools were then addressed by Messrs. John H. Kelly, and James W. Beller, and by the Rev. Mr. Gere — the two former gentlemen confined themselves to the duties of Teachers, and acquitted themselves in a manner which arguably surprised and gratified all present, and especially edified their friends, who knew they possessed capacity that only needed culture and experience for a creditable development. The officers of the day, and others, paid but a just compliment to merit, when they congratulated these young gentlemen on the success of their efforts. [22]

Gallaher concluded "There is a freshness in these scenes which draws the mind from the every day cares of life, and diminishes the perplexities and anxieties attendant upon our ordinary pursuits."

The editor had a good eye for spotting talent. Kelly and Beller were energetic, working class men in the early twenties, active in their church and in the county temperance union. Kelly had grown up in Gettysburg, Pennsylvania, and learned the trade of compositor in his teens. An outspoken Whig, he had recently joined Gallaher's staff. [23]

James W. Beller, a Jefferson County native, had recently returned home with his widowed mother and younger brother Charles. He had been teaching school in Charlestown for a couple of years to support the family. Gallaher had known James' father — they had served in the local militia in the War of 1812. Young Beller, like his father, was a Jacksonian Democrat. The editor offered the young man a job at the *Free Press*. Beller accepted and began working side by side with Kelly, learning the trade. [24]

Another young man, Frank Washington, a gentleman, had also made his debut at the celebration. He was being groomed by local Democrats to use his oratorical skills in support of their cause.

Figure 9. Ruins of Trinity Church, west of Charlestown, 1843, from sketch by Henry Howe.

Figure 10. Shannondale Springs, ca. 1840, from Howe, *Historical Collections*.

July 4th, 1844, Charlestown, Virginia

The town did not celebrate the Anniversary of Independence, although the stores were closed and most business was suspended. Sunday schools and temperance societies celebrated in Smithfield, Shepherdstown, and Harpers Ferry, but the streets around the Court House were eerily quiet.

At Shannondale, the resort and mineral springs south of Charlestown, a group assembled without notice, determined to maintain tradition. After dinner, they selected a President and Vice President for their impromptu celebration, then hastily drew up and gave a series of toasts. The familiar speaker's stage and artillery accompaniment were missing, but a negro band supplied the music as the guests raised their glasses to the Stars and Stripes flying above them:

> The day of Independence — A day ever sacred in the hearts of the American people.
>
> The Union — Let every patriot frown indignantly upon every effort to burst asunder the ties which hold it together.
>
> The Constitution — May it ever be sacred, in spite of strict constructionists and wild latitudinarians. [25]

The quiet of the day belied the intense preparations under way for the upcoming Presidential election — less than four months away. Whig politicians had already formed Clay Clubs in each electoral precinct, with each group competing to erect the tallest Liberty Pole and top it with the largest American flag and the longest political banner. Not to be outdone, Democrats were busily constructing "hickory stalks" to show that their party still honored the principles of their hero, Andrew Jackson.

The Whigs saw the election of '44 as an opportunity to implement the goals they had set in the election of '40: a National Bank, a protective Tariff, dispersal to the states of the money that the Federal government had collected by selling public lands, and a one-term Presidency. The Democrats insisted on adding another item to the debate — the annexation of Texas.

In June, John Gallaher and other leaders of the Clay Club had convened a meeting in Charlestown, pumping Whig party members full of enthusiasm for the coming contest and passing a resolution that stated:

> ...we consider the question of the Annexation of Texas as not involved in the true issues that now divide the two great parties of the country, and that any endeavor to mingle it with them is an attempt to pervert its true nature for the purpose of making political capital. [26]

There was a rumor about that Charlestown would soon have a new newspaper — a Democratic one.

Figure 11. William Lucas, 1800 – 1877 [27]

Figure 12. Henry Bedinger, 1812 – 1858 [28]

July 15, 1844, Jefferson County, Virginia

The Democrats' Presidential campaign began in earnest at the county Court House two weeks after the muted Independence Day celebration. Party stalwart Colonel Braxton Davenport chaired the meeting and James W. Beller was appointed secretary.

Attendees passed resolutions supporting the national convention's choice of James K. Polk and George M. Dallas as their candidates for President and Vice President. As in the party platform of 1840, they were adamant about the need for "a total separation of Bank and State — an Independent Treasury — a strict revenue Tariff — and for confining the action of the Federal Government to its constitutional limits."

In addition, they warned that Great Britain's policy to abolish slavery throughout the world

> is proof conclusive of the insidious designs that Government has long entertained of dissolving the American Union, — that England desires Texas to remain an independent power in name, in order that she may be better enabled to carry on her machinations against the commercial power of the United States. [29]

To further clarify this position, they supported Polk's sentiment

> ... that Texas be reannexed, and that the authority and laws of the United States be established and maintained within the limits, and also in the Oregon Territory, and let the fixed policy of our Government be, not to permit Great Britain or any other foreign power, to plant a colony, or hold dominion over any portion of the people or territory of either.

Members of the meeting appointed representatives to attend the State Democratic convention in Charlottesville. William Lucas, Henry Bedinger, Capt. John Rowan, Frank Washington, and James W. Beller were among those selected from Jefferson County. In closing the meeting they resolved,

> That the "Spirit of Jefferson," about to be established by J.W. Beller, at Charlestown, be recommended to the support of the Democratic party generally, and that the different associations throughout the county, be requested to extend its circulation. [30]

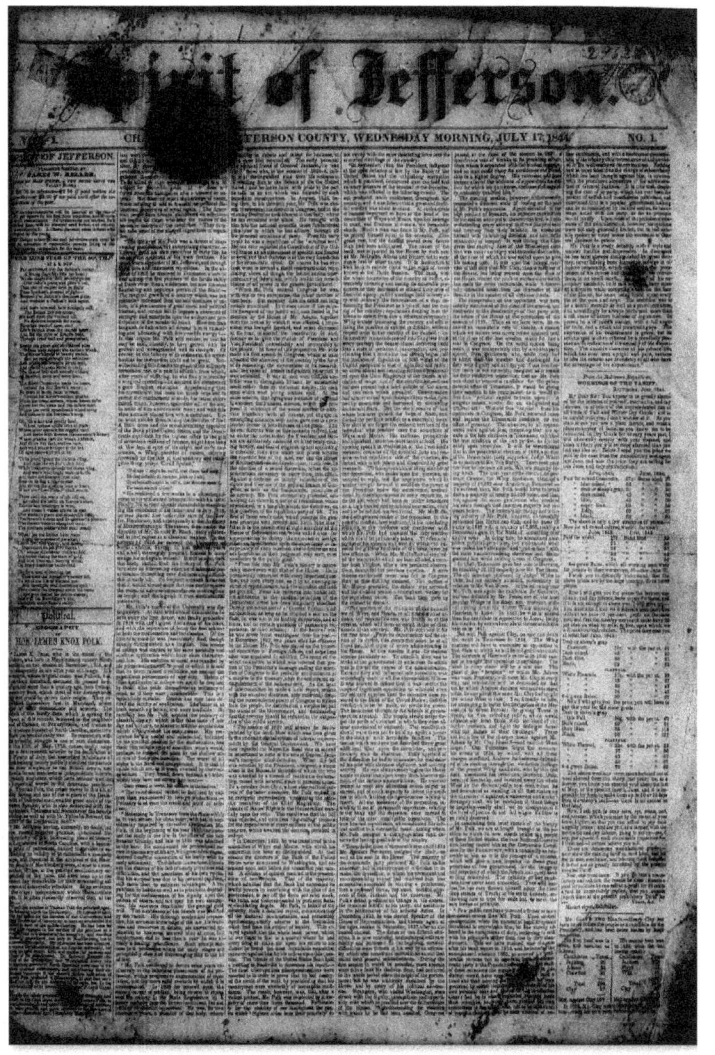

Figure 13. *Spirit of Jefferson,* first issue, July 17, 1844. [31]

July 17, 1844, Charlestown, Virginia

Democrats had tried more than once to establish their own newspaper in Jefferson County. The most recent effort, the Harpers Ferry *Constitutionalist*, was started in the Spring of 1839 to support candidate William Lucas in his bid for the U.S. Congress. Congressman Lucas had continued to bankroll the paper until he was defeated for reelection in 1841. There had been some rocky times, particularly when inexperienced editors discovered that they had bitten off more than they could chew.

Bemused Whig editor John Gallaher had chronicled most of the mishaps encountered by the editors of the fledgling press, including the brief career of William S. Smith, who

> after "nineteen weeks' experience, has (to quote his own language) "quit the scenes of turmoil, perplexities, and labors attendant upon the life of an Editor," and gone into "retirement," to seek "rest" for his "wearied frame" and "heal his broken constitution."
>
> "Here rest the remains of Icabod Crane,
>
> And here they'll rest 'till they rise again." [32]

When the newspaper finally folded, Harper's Ferry schoolteacher John J. Hickey acquired the paper's press, printing paraphernalia, and list of subscribers. The proposed new paper, named *The Jefferson Banner*, failed to appear. [33]

The first issue of the *Spirit of Jefferson* was published at Charlestown, Virginia, on July 17, 1844. Twenty-six-year-old editor James W. Beller introduced himself to his readers with both confidence and humility:

> In assuming the responsibilities that devolve upon us as the conductor of a political journal, more especially at this crisis of such momentous import to the future history of our country, we are fully aware that we take upon ourselves a task from which a stouter heart and older head than our own might well shrink from with diffidence — yet, when we reflect that we bring with us a spirit firm and unwavering in the faith that is within us, and a heart burning for the triumph of the great principles of our party, our embarrassment in this respect is in no small degree relieved. [34]

After outlining his support of the party platform, he continued,

> ... We have told you frankly on what side the "SPIRIT OF JEFFERSON," will be found, battling with all of energy and spirit it possesses. To the Democracy of Jefferson we would say, do our views upon these great fundamental questions coincide with yours? If so, may we not ask at your hands, a liberal, united and steady support! The establishment of this Journal has not been done alone at our suggestion — it is no scheme devised by us for mere pecuniary benefit. But now, that it is established, and we have at stake so much, we ask at the hand

of our friends, what is necessary for keeping our craft above water. The Democratic party in this county have felt, and that seriously, the want of a sentinel to guard the outposts of the Democratic camp. Some of our more partial friends have been induced to believe that our services would be of benefit in this arduous work, and we have most cheerfully undertaken its performance.

That you are fully able to sustain us, if you so determine, no one can doubt.... Arouse then, and give us a helping hand — make the interest of this Journal your interest — exert yourselves by all fair and honorable means to sustain it, and it will be found contending for your rights at all times and under all circumstances. You should not be discouraged because other efforts to establish a Democratic paper in this county have failed, but on the other hand, it should call forth stronger and more active exertions in behalf of this....

In conclusion, we take pleasure in stating, that as the "SPIRIT OF JEFFERSON" has been established solely with a view to the furtherance of Democratic principles, we shall have, for the present at least, the assistance of gentlemen whose experience as writers, and general acquaintance with political questions, cannot fail of proving beneficial in the cause of Republicanism, during the pending contest.

After reading the young man's first issue, Whig veteran John Gallaher noted "It is well for the party that they have found so worthy a recipient of their patronage." [35] Perhaps this time, with a crucial Presidential election less than four months' away, he would confront an opponent worthy of his efforts.

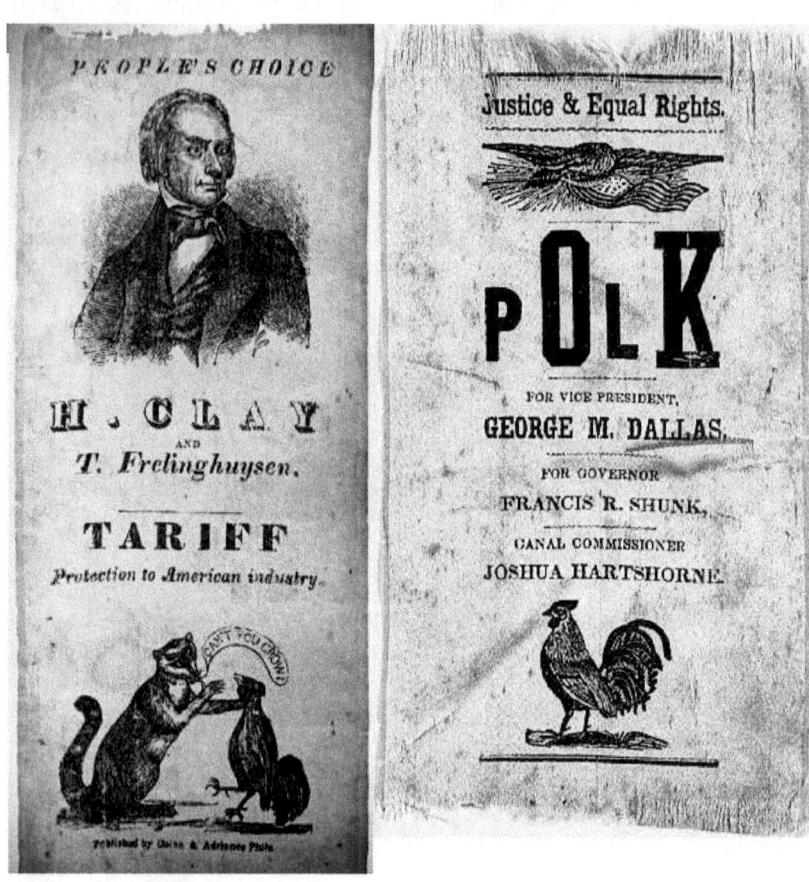

Figure 14. Clay and Polk campaign ribbons, 1844. The raccoon ("coon") was the mascot of the Whig party and the rooster ("cock") that of the Democrats.

December 1844, Jefferson County, Virginia

Voting days in the Presidential election differed with the state, all votes being cast between November 1st and December 4th.

The Whigs had wanted the election to be a referendum on the economy, a chance to set things straight after the fiasco of '40. But President Tyler, trying to improve his chances for a second term, wanted the U.S. annexation of Texas to eclipse all other issues.

He had unsuccessfully tried to push a treaty for annexation through Congress that summer. In August, he had announced that he would not seek a second term, and the Democrats readily expanded their campaign motto to "Polk, Dallas and Texas!"

Adding Texas to the Democratic platform opened a Pandora's box of other issues: Mexico warned that annexation meant war. Some advocates feared that France and Great Britain had their own plans for Texas and the territory between the Mississippi and the Pacific. Would new states be slave or free? Would abolition and expansion drain the South of its slaves, reducing its population and its clout in Congress?

The stakes were high, and even the most able politicians could not predict the consequences of a Whig or Democratic victory.

During the summer before the election, Democrats, such as B.F. Washington and William and Robert Lucas, contributed substantial, well written policy pieces to Beller's paper. The editor himself and Washington had attended several Democratic rallies in the district. The latter, now an established lawyer in Charlestown, had received glowing reviews from Beller on his presentations. [36]

The Gallaher brothers published their own verbal volleys and attended numerous Whig gatherings, often accompanied by political luminary Alexander R. Boteler. *Free Press* employee, J. Harrison Kelley, was one of the young men chosen to help with logistics at a large Whig meeting near Charlestown. [37]

Crossing party lines, both Beller and Kelley had worked together obtaining speakers for the quarterly meeting of the total abstinence society. The organization had a large following in the county, including Whigs and Democrats, Catholics and Protestants, slave owners and free soilers. [38]

Throughout the election period, *the Free Press* and the *Spirit of Jefferson* reported the fate of each state as it was added to the Whig or Democratic win column. On November 11th, news reached Jefferson County that Pennsylvania, New York, and Virginia had fallen to the

Democrats, giving them the electoral votes needed for victory. In Virginia, Henry Bedinger had succeeded Democrat William Lucas in the U.S. House of Representatives.

In Charlestown, Democrats celebrated by firing cannon and marching through the streets to the "roll of the drum and the shrill whistle of the fife." Candles appeared in the windows, lanterns on porches, posts, and fences. At 8 PM, the Smithfield delegation arrived, bringing banners, torches, and a hastily formed Glee Club. Harpers Ferry and Shepherdstown would hold similar celebrations on the 15th and 16th.

Spirit of Jefferson editor, James Beller reported:

> All in all, notwithstanding our Whig friends say the illumination was nothing to compare with what they would have had, (oh, there's the rub,) if Henry Clay had been elected, it was a very pleasing demonstration of the gratitude Democrats feel upon the great and glorious victory just achieved. [39]

Throughout the early 1840's, the war of words among political newspapers was a form of competition and entertainment. As in military conflicts, duels, and boxing, there were rules of engagement. The Gallaher brothers and James Beller (just learning) were advocates of honorable political discourse, particularly at the local level. Writers were expected to present information and opinion without distortion, using reason and clear prose. Humor and satire were fine. Sexual innuendo and *ad hominem* arguments were not.

The veteran Gallaher and the novice Beller sparred almost weekly in the pages of their newspapers, the older man often critiquing his opponent's editorial technique and the younger one energetically responding. Both newspapers tried to follow the rules, and they both bemoaned the unscrupulous tactics of the political parties at the national level and of the newspapermen who indulged in these practices.

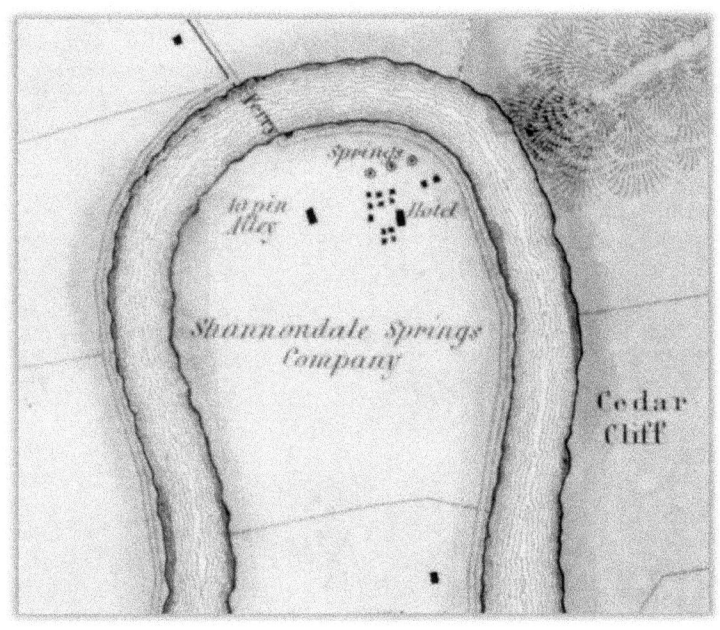

Figure 15. Shannondale Springs, Virginia, from S.H. Brown, *Map of Jefferson County, Va.,* 1852.

Part II. Manifest Destiny

> Why, were other reasoning wanting, in favor of now elevating this question of the reception of Texas into the Union, out of the lower region of our past party dissensions, up to its proper level of a high and broad nationality, it surely is to be found, found abundantly, in the manner in which other nations have undertaken to intrude themselves into it, between us and the proper parties to the case, in a spirit of hostile interference against us, for the avowed object of thwarting our policy and hampering our power, limiting our greatness and checking the fulfilment of our manifest destiny to overspread the continent allotted by Providence for the free development of our yearly multiplying millions

John L. O'Sullivan, "Annexation," *United States Democratic Review*, June, 1845

July 4th, 1845, Shannondale Springs, Virginia

Independence Day began in front of the Court House at 7 AM, with a volley from Capt. Rowan's Charlestown Artillery. Then the Captain formed up the procession and they moved through town, taking up the line of march, south to Shannondale Springs. The Shannondale Stage followed, accompanied by citizens in carriages and on horseback. Meanwhile, a large crowd from Jefferson and surrounding counties gathered at the Springs and awaited the parade's arrival. [40]

After crossing the Shenandoah River on the ferry, the procession momentarily disbanded. Rowan reformed the group, placing his Artillery at the head, and proceeded to a grove prepared for the day's services. Next came the Reader and Orator of the day, soldiers, clergy, citizens, and strangers. President of the Day, Andrew Hunter, addressed the crowd briefly and then called upon Frank Washington to read the *Declaration of Independence.*

Many in the audience already knew that William Lucas, Sr. had asked the young man to join his law practice — a sign that Frank had a powerful mentor to help launch his political career. Washington had been paying his dues to Democratic Party officials, serving as a delegate to several conventions and espousing the party platform at rallies.

Scanning the audience, Frank spotted his fiancé, Georgiana Hite Ranson. She was the 23-year-old daughter of James L. Ranson of "Gap View," in Jefferson County. A former county sheriff and War of 1812 veteran, Ranson was a wealthy farmer with a substantial number of slaves and political connections. [41]

Washington took the liberty of prefacing his reading with a lengthy explication of the phrase, "all men are created free and equal." While abolitionists insisted it clearly meant that slavery was unconstitutional, the young lawyer used history and other arguments to insist that the phrase did not affect the legality of slavery, at least as Virginia was concerned. *Spirit of Jefferson* editor, James Beller, later noted that "His remarks struck us as quite original, and forcible and convincing in their conclusion."

Figure 16. James L. Ranson (1871 – 1868); John Blair Hodge (1825-1896)

John Blair Hodge, the main orator of the day, then replaced Washington at the podium. A Martinsburg lawyer, he was about the same age as Washington and had similar political ambitions. He had, he told them, reflected on how best to address the audience on this occasion. He had first considered recounting the glories of the Revolution and the deeds of their patriot forefathers. As pleasing as that approach might be, the concerns of the day prompted him to focus on the present, so we may prepare for the future.

Although our nation has been blessed with unparalleled progress, he believed that more important, less pleasing considerations demanded our attention:

> It has been said, that the existence of two great political parties, in our government, which will watch with jealous eyes, the measures and movements of each other, must prove beneficial. This may be true, but I condemn, and I call upon every Patriot, to condemn the fierceness and bitterness of party strife, so often exhibited among our people. The

> finer feelings and the nobler impulses of our natures, are sacrificed to the spirit of party. No difference of opinion is brooked, no character is so pure that it is unassailed — no line of conduct is so free from suspicion, that it is not attributed to the basest and most unworthy motives. [42]

Everyone knew the causes of the political strife and the feelings of foreboding shared by many present: fear that the Union would fracture over slavery — that Mexico would declare war when our annexation of Texas was complete — and that war with Great Britain would also follow if we refused to negotiate an acceptable boundary for the Oregon Territory.

He continued, "should the stormcloud of war, now lowering over our heads, burst in its fury upon us," the Union must be preserved because it is the source of our freedom and prosperity.

His concluding remarks may have troubled the few Northerners in the audience who had paid attention to Frank Washington's earlier comments on the Constitution:

> We have talked of Freedom, until it has become an unmeaning name. Does not history teach us, that Education and the spirit of human liberty, have ever moved hand in hand, coworkers in the same glorious improvement? Until our people are educated, the richest treasures of the earth will lie buried in our hills, and unconnected by works of enterprise, we shall live as strangers to our brethren....
>
> Let us not boast that we are Virginians, let us not exult in the name, when thousands of our brethren, bearing the same proud title, still wear the chains of darkness — whose minds are blanks, whose vision is circumscribed, whose intellects, like untrimmed lamps, shed but a feeble, flickering light around them.

Journalists had recently lamented that Virginia had more illiterate whites than any other state in the Union, a condition that condemned them to a life of ignorance and poverty. Some listeners doubtless recognized another disturbing problem — more than a third of Jefferson County's population were slaves. For them, education was forbidden, and the "chains of darkness" were both mental and physical. In the South, in Virginia, such thoughts were best left unspoken.

Listening to Hodge's oration, editor and now State senator Gallaher reflected that the last session of the Virginia legislature had not achieved much of real importance. No great measure of public policy had been adopted. Nothing on the subject of education — nothing to improve the militia system — and very little in the way of Internal Improvement. Perhaps Hodge's speech might generate some bipartisan support for educational reform at the next session.

Closer to home, Gallaher had his own financial concerns. Getting subscribers to pay their bills was a perennial problem. Earlier in the year, he had sent brother Horatio to the Harpers Ferry Armory on payday, where he had tried to collect from the workers before they spent their earnings. In the next issue of the *Free Press*, John would lament:

> Must have a new dress during the summer, and we are devising ways and means to accomplish that object. The best method thought of, just now, is to strike off several hundred nonpaying subscribers, who have been a dead weight on us for years, — and substitute them with about two hundred new ones, who will pay in advance. [43]

One could only hope.

James W. Beller had similar concerns. His *Spirit of Jefferson* had survived its first year. Reviewing his initial venture as owner and editor, he noted in the next issue:

> In commencing this journal, we were fully conscious of the difficulties that were to be met — the prejudices to be overcome — and the open and secret opposition to be encountered. So far, we have had no cause for desponding. We have undertaken the work, and have not known, nor shall know, any such word as fail. Our whole energies, physical and mental, shall be brought in requisition, to keep our little craft above water, and to shun the breakers upon which its forerunners have stranded. [44]

At the same time, the public had a short memory when it came to supporting their favorite political organ. He continued,

> From our Whig friends, we have heretofore looked for but little support, and have not, consequently, been much disappointed. The political waters, however, are again quiet, and we should be pleased to enrol a goodly number of them with our list of patrons. When necessary, we say now, as we have said heretofore, that we shall war unceasingly against their measures, yet always regarding that it is the most glorious feature of our Government, which tolerates a free and honest difference of opinion.

Most attendees at the Independence Day celebration were oblivious to the problems of the Fourth Estate. Their minds now challenged and appetites sharpened, the audience flocked to the amply provisioned dinner table. After the cloth had been removed, President Hunter led the audience in a series of patriotic toasts, accompanied by volleys from Captain Rowan's Charlestown Artillery.

Beller's friend and Gallaher's employee, J. Harrison Kelly, had also drawn inspiration from the festivities. He had recently accepted an invitation to join Wildey Lodge No. 11 of the International Order of Odd Fellows in Charlestown. The nonpartisan benevolent society had been growing quickly during the last few years, with the first lodge in Virginia established at Harpers Ferry two years earlier. The local chapters accepted Catholics as well as Protestants and numbered in their ranks such notables as retired Indian fighter Maj. J.F. Hamtramck, Charlestown Artillery Captain John W. Rowan, and the Gallaher brothers of the *Free Press*. Many members were active in the Temperance Union and the Overseers of the Poor in Jefferson County.

Kelly's sisters, Elizabeth (age 20) and Margaret (age 15), had recently arrived from Gettysburg and now lived with him at his Charlestown residence. Now introduced into Charlestown society, they were receiving the attention of the eligible bachelors. [45]

December 1845, Jefferson County, Virginia

The month began with President Polk's annual address to Congress, announcing that, henceforth, the United States would strictly enforce the Monroe Doctrine of repelling foreign expansion into the Americas. Furthermore, it was our destiny to expand aggressively westward, populating the empty spaces and bringing the benefits of democracy to those in our path. The month ended with Texas' admission to the Union. [46]

Virginia's Democratic Governor, James McDowell, echoed the President's views on westward expansion and the annexation of Texas:

> Whatever the divided judgment of our people upon this great measure, it may be safely trusted to its own results to vindicate itself — safely trusted to its ultimate effect upon the grandeur of our country, and the extension to other lands, which it aids, of the liberty spirit of this, to dissipate all scruples and unite all hearts upon its side. The time is not distant when not a murmur will be uttered against it — when our countrymen everywhere will greet it, with a common voice, as a happy and crowning act by which this vast continent of ours will be crowded from shore to shore with a powerful and virtuous people, and the banner of our country be raised over a Republican empire as unparalleled in its extent, as unequaled in the wisdom, justice, and humanity of its rule.... [47]

Beller's *Spirit of Jefferson* enthusiastically endorsed the sentiments of the President and the Governor. Gallaher's *Free Press* was less enthusiastic, predicting pushback from Mexico, France, and England and warning that it could cost us both American blood and treasure to keep Texas in the Union.

In regard to war, the tariff, and other matters, Gallaher warned his readers,

> We can only repeat our hope that the Whigs will be quiet, and let the party in the ascendant do their worst. They should not interpose the

slightest obstacle to the preliminary movements. Let us have the plan of warfare upon the "Black Tariff," and be mere lookers on until the last moment. The power to do mischief is now more completely within the power of the Locos [Democrats] than it was in the last session — and it will be well enough to let them do their worst as speedily as possible. When the cure is more speedily performed than by tampering with the disease. [48]

Locally, both Democrats and Whigs agreed that it was time to overhaul Virginia's deplorable system of education. An Education Convention had been scheduled for December 10th in Richmond, and John S. Gallaher and James W. Beller were among the 30 local delegates chosen to attend. [49]

Gallaher was appointed one of the Convention Secretaries and reported the results upon his return: counties within the state would be divided into districts for which School Commissioners would be elected by the people, instead of being appointed by the County Court. The schools would be open to all white children, apparently the goal being "to do away with the distinction between indigent and other children — to level upward." The new system would be paid for by a county tax.

Concluding his assessment, Gallaher remarked:

> The Convention broke up harmoniously, but still I doubt, as I have done from the first, of the success of any such scheme this winter. We have too many wise men in our Legislative halls, and in the struggle to have the paternity of a scheme, every plan will be defeated. I hope I may prove in this case to be a false prophet. In the meanwhile, during the maturing of a system, let the people continue to pour in their memorials — let them march up to the difficulty and say they are ready to be taxed for this great purpose, and then the Legislature will be kept up to the proper point. [50]

Beller supported his colleague's conclusions, noting, that of all the defects of the current political system, nothing was more destructive than its "distinction, between the rich and the poor, that is so odious, that the masses of our people never will nor can, become generally educated under its workings." [51]

While his friends used the pen and the political platform to effect change, J. Harrison Kelley had pursued his own course. He had been instrumental in establishing a new Odd Fellow's hall in Shepherdstown and had risen to the rank of Deputy Grand Master of the Order for Virginia. [52]

Figure 17. Harpers Ferry, Virginia, ca. 1840. From Howe's *Historical Collections*.

July 4th, 1846, Jefferson County, Virginia

Charlestown passed up the opportunity to celebrate Independence Day, but several other locations scheduled what promised to be impressive festivities.

The Odd Fellows at Harpers Ferry planned to dedicate their new lodge hall, an affair which would include a procession and addresses by prominent members from near and far. Shepherdstown's "Potomac Rifles," a newly reformed militia company, scheduled their own parade to show off their uniforms, equipment, and marching prowess. Shannondale Springs would treat its guests to a banquet, horse races, speechifying, and patriotic music.

The country needed all the patriotic fervor it could muster. Although our dispute with England over the Oregon Territory had been peacefully resolved, we were now at war with Mexico. Congress had authorized President Polk to begin recruiting volunteers, and so far, he had asked the Governor of Virginia to supply three regiments. Captain John W. Rowan was busy recruiting members for the Charlestown Artillery.

U.S. troops under the command of General Zachary Taylor had recently defeated a Mexican force north of the Rio Grande. Now that the war had begun, both political parties and both local newspaper editors supported the U.S. effort, although their opinions on how to defeat Mexico often differed.

Democrat James Beller speculated that our recent victories may have brought Mexico to its senses and the war to a close. "But, if not, let the War be pushed into the interior. The whole country calls for a speedy, decisive, and lasting settlement of this vexed question." [53]

Whig John S. Gallaher took issue with the Democrats' criticism of those who disagreed with the Administration's military tactics. Quoting from his colleague at the Richmond *Whig*, he bristled,

> Has it come to this, that although, when war exists, the Whigs are as ready as their opponents to pour out their treasures and their blood in defense of their country, they are to be denied the right to express an opinion in regard to the character of the measures by which its peace has been disturbed? Are the taxpayers and the fighting men to be gagged, as well as to be fleeced and slain? [54]

On the Western front, American settlers in Sonoma, California, had rebelled against the Mexican authorities and proclaimed themselves citizens of the California Republic. U.S. troops were on their way to provide support. Rumors of plans for California's annexation had already started.

Large amounts of gold had not yet been discovered in California, and the immigrants heading west were generally not impressed with the discoveries reported thus far. Perhaps tongue in cheek, editor James Beller inserted the following on the front page of the *Spirit of Jefferson* to provide some incentive:

> It is stated, there are ten females to one male in California, and many of the ladies there possess large landed properties, all improved. These ladies are described as being beautiful, quite youthful, and exceeding virtuous, but anxious for good, kind and considerate husbands .— We anticipate, after these facts are generally known, that California will be taken. [55]

In Jefferson County, the month of July was ushered in with rain, which persisted through the 4th, swelling the rivers and cancelling planned festivities. Officials tried to reschedule these events for later in the month, but most of these celebrations failed to materialize. The Odd Fellows dedicated their hall at Harpers Ferry on July 25th with all the pomp originally promised. J. Harrison Kelly, age 26 and now Grand Master of Virginia, presided. [56]

There was good news about another battle being fought closer to home — the campaign for free public education. With the help of State Senator John S. Gallaher and the two local newspapers, citizens of Jefferson County had adopted the District School Bill at the last election. The County Court had appointed school commissioners, who had defined school district boundaries. To support this effort, the county formed an eleven-member, bipartisan Education Society. Horatio Gallaher, J.W. Beller, and J. Harrison Kelly were among those chosen. [57]

On July 10th, *Spirit* editor James W. Beller celebrated three years of successful operation. The number of subscribers had tripled since the paper began, and he closed the issue with an appeal for more. For Democratic supporters,

> Now is the time to be arming for the battle — gathering in new recruits, confirming the wavering and winning over the doubtful. That our paper can do all this, we are not vain enough to pretend, but of this, be assured, it will do its duty, to the fullest extent of its humble ability.... Whilst our paper shall be always moderate and respectful in its tone, it will be firm, decided and energetic in the advocacy of its principles.... Say what you may, but a man who in this day fails to take a newspaper, is recreant to himself, faithless to his family, and incompetent to discharge his duty to his country. [58]

Readers who brought in five new subscribers would get a free subscription for themselves.

Figure 18. Pennsylvania Senator David Wilmot, 1814-1868

> Provided, That, as an express and fundamental condition to the acquisition of any territory from the Republic of Mexico by the United States, by virtue of any treaty which may be negotiated between them, and to the use by the Executive of the moneys herein appropriated, neither slavery nor involuntary servitude shall ever exist in any part of said territory, except for crime, whereof the party shall first be duly convicted.

David Wilmot, "The Wilmot Proviso," August 6, 1846

December 1846, Jefferson County, Virginia

Captain John W. Rowan had been busy recruiting members for the Charlestown Artillery since last July. In November, he learned that that his company would be accepted into service as soon as it reached the minimum strength required. However, it would serve as infantry, not artillery, and additional recruits would be needed. [59] The Potomac Rifles, under the command of Major Hamtramck, were also recruiting with the hope that they, too, would be accepted.

Washington was struggling to find resources to finance the war, and it told the communities raising volunteer regiments that they must pay to feed, transport, and house their men until they were mustered into service.

Responding to this crisis, Col. Braxton Davenport scheduled a meeting at the Charlestown Court House for December 11th. James Beller and Frank Washington were among the attendees assigned to canvass the county and procure aid. [60]

The committee of aid reconvened on December 21st, this time to show the community's support for the men about to go to war. Taking the podium, the Hon. William Lucas urged everyone to discard their political differences. The causes of the war, he said, were proper matters of investigation, at the proper time and place, but now there was but one question, and every man was in duty bound to act accordingly.[61] *Spirit of Jefferson* editor and Democrat Beller observed,

> ...though the speakers embraced prominent gentlemen of both political parties, there was a careful observance to introduce nothing that would give offence to the other. All seemed to be actuated by but one motive, and the most ardent and anxious desire that the war should be prosecuted with zeal, and the honor of our Flag maintained. [62]

Recently, *Free Press* editor and Whig J.S. Gallaher had strongly condemned the war as unnecessary and immoral. It was being waged, he believed, against a weak nation, not for honor, but for territorial conquest. Stifling his strong opinions, he concluded:

> It was with the most lively intent and satisfaction that we witnessed the harmony of sentiment that seemed to pervade the meeting on the one all important question of sustaining our country's honor, and our country's flag, wherever it may float — whether on the high seas, or in the Halls of the Montezumas. All, all, seemed to be inspired with the patriotic sentiment of the lamented Decatur: "Our Country, may she always be right — but right or wrong, our Country." [63]

Figure 19. Jefferson County (West) Virginia, Court House

January 1847, Jefferson County, Virginia

On Sunday morning, the 3rd, Rowan's company marched to the Presbyterian Church in Charlestown for a special service conducted by the Reverend Mister Harris. [64]

The following morning, local citizens cheered the volunteers as they formed up in front of the Court House. Captain George W. Sappington presented them with Bibles and prayer books, and warned them:

> Let no idle difference of opinion induce you to delay at Washington, to enquire whether the war with Mexico be a righteous or an unrighteous war: stop not to enquire whether or not the President has transcended the powers delegated to him — by the Constitution of the United States, by planting the American Flag upon the banks of the Rio Grande — but fly — fly with locomotive speed to the battlefield, where I feel well assured you will, to a man, do honor to the arms you bear, and service to your beloved country. [65]

Then they marched to the Winchester and Potomac Railroad Depot and boarded a train to Harpers Ferry. From there, they took packet boats down the canal to Washington and the railroad cars to Richmond.

They arrived in the State Capitol on the 6th. J.S. Gallaher, in his role of State Senator, presented them to the mayor and Governor Smith with a brief speech. Frank Washington's brother, Lieutenant Lawrence B. Washington, was present at the ceremony, wearing the sword given to George Washington by Frederick the Great. The Governor quartered the men in the Union Hotel, along with the Berkeley company, commanded by Captain Alburtis. [66]

A week later, Lieutenant John Avis returned to Jefferson County to gather additional recruits and resources. The Secretary of War had accepted Rowan's company as a rifle corps, not as artillery, and wanted its size to be increased. [67]

The volunteers had already received several appointments: James Cunningham, pronounced the greatest fifer in the State, had been appointed Fife Major of the Virginia Regiment. James H. Baker was selected as a color bearer, and several members of the regimental color guards were chosen from the company. [68]

The company was mustered in on the 27th but did not embark for New Orleans until February 22. The food on board varied from scarce to poor and health conditions deteriorated. But they found that they would receive a pay increase and would be eligible for military land warrants when they had completed their service. Most of the volunteers were itching to "see the elephant." [69]

Once the volunteers had left Jefferson County, the political battle resumed, unabated. Both parties were already searching for Presidential candidates for the election of '48. Politicians evaluated the military performances of Generals Winfield Scott and Zachary Taylor to see if either could replace incumbent Polk or challenger Clay.

Amidst the turmoil, J. Harrison Kelly practiced his trade, serving as compositor for the *Virginia Free Press*, writing copy, and performing minor duties for the local Whig party. In his role as the Odd Fellows Grand Master in Virginia, he presided at the opening of new lodges at Strasburg, Woodstock, and Harrisonburg. In a January article published in the *Free Press*, he noted:

> The spread of Odd Fellowship in this State is becoming more and more general, as the great truths upon which it is based are spread before an enlightened and intelligent people. Based upon certain truths, which are alike axioms among all nations and creeds, it presents a nucleus around which antagonistic spirits, and men of all parties, etc., and faiths, may unite, and rally, for the diffusion of Benevolence and Charity, and the general amelioration of suffering humanity.... [The Fellowship includes] present Colonel and Lieut, Col. of the Virginia Regiment, Col. John F. Hamtramck of Caledonia Lodge, Shepherdstown, and Gen. Randolph of Front Royal Lodge, in Warren county. Beside these, there are men whose political and religious integrity are unimpeachable, and who constitute a model for the virtuous and upright. [70]

Kelly had his work cut out for him.

Figure 20. I.O.O.F. Virginia Lodge No. 1, Harpers Ferry, WV. Courtesy Harpers Ferry National Historical Park.

July 1847, Jefferson County, Virginia

Throughout the Spring and into the Summer, the *Spirit* and the *Free Press* had brought Jefferson County residents news of U.S. victories in Mexico. But the editors' coverage of one incident changed their relationship from cool and challenging to hot and hostile.

Whigs in the U.S. House of Representatives offered a resolution to present General Zachary Taylor with a medal in gratitude for his victories in Mexico. Democrats managed to amend the resolution so that the message engraved on the medal criticized some of Taylor's actions.

Jefferson County Whigs met at the Court House to register their disapproval. After the Chair proposed a resolution condemning the House's actions, Democrat Frank Washington offered an amendment supporting the Administration's position that the war had been "brought on by an act of Mexico, and prosecuted on our part to vindicate the honor and rights of our country..." [71]

Most Whigs regarded the war as an unnecessary one of territorial conquest. Countering Washington's amendment, J. Harrison Kelley rose and remarked that President Polk had promoted General Taylor to neutralize Winfield Scott's political popularity and then engineered the incident with Taylor and the medal to prevent old "Rough and Ready" from gaining political traction.

Attendees eventually adopted the Chair's original resolution, with the vote split along party lines. Had the disagreement stopped there, tempers probably would have subsided. But both editors chose to take the conflict to a new level.

In his next issue, *Free Press* editor Gallaher labeled Congress' insult of General Taylor "infamous," and castigated local Representative Henry Bedinger for supporting the action. *Spirit* editor Beller shot back, accusing Gallaher of verbally supporting the enemy's war effort. Gallaher returned fire, calling Beller's attack "disingenuous" and his coverage of the incident either incompetent or "conceived and put forth, purposely, willfully, and maliciously, to deceive, and misrepresent the action of your partizans and friends in Congress." [72]

Traitor? Malicious liar? Incompetent? Editors had dueled over lesser accusations.

Despite their differences, both editors rallied their audience to vote for Jefferson County's Free School Bill and celebrated its passage on June 3rd. [73]

Jefferson County residents celebrated the seventy-first anniversary of American Independence at Shannondale Springs on Saturday, July 3rd. The Whig party was heavily represented by the officials on stage (including Horatio Gallaher and J.H. Kelly).

Orator of the Day, John H. Cookus focused on the humanity shown by U.S. officers in the war with Mexico and on the country's philanthropic efforts to relieve suffering caused by the Great Famine in Ireland. [74]

The toasts of the day included praise of Generals Taylor ("uninfluenced by prejudice and unstained by party") and Scott, whose victories bring "imperishable honor to his name." A toast to President Polk was noticeably absent.

The Virginia Volunteers celebrated the holiday at Camp Buena Vista, Mexico, with a big, Virginia Style meal, patriotic music, speeches, and several rounds of toasts, including:

> The Declaration of Independence — May its benign influence soon spread over the benighted land of Mexico, rendering her worthy the name of Republic.
>
> The President of the United States — However divided among ourselves, we will always present an undivided front to our enemies. [75]

Several members of the Jefferson Volunteers (now designated Company "K") had formed a temperance organization they dubbed the "Spring Water Boys of Buena Vista, No. 1." They, of course, refused temptation.

Although liquor was forbidden in camp, the drinking men found a way around this restriction. Going into town with their dogs, they bought rum stored in skins and tied them to their pets' tails. The animals were trained to sprint past the sentries with their prize and deliver it to thirsty volunteers. Man's best friend, indeed!

Back at home, *Spirit* editor Beller introduced the first issue of volume four, pointing out the new four-column format and hinting that he needed new subscribers to support his bigger paper:

> ... we again throw ourselves upon the generosity of our patrons. If in our past course as editor we have given offence to any, or failed to discharge our duty to our party or our principles, [it can], we are sure, be rather attributed to error of judgment, rather than the dictates of the heart. For [the future], we promise the best we can perform [in] ...our own way, and in the manner [corresponding] with our own judgment, and proper self-respect and independence. [76]

Jefferson County's Fourth Estate, 1840-1850

In the next issue of the *Free Press*, John S. Gallaher noted: "The *Spirit of Jefferson* of last week came to us in an enlarged and improved form. It is now among the largest country papers in the State, and is edited with ability [by J.W. Beller], and its mechanical work executed with taste." [77]

A truce on the home front? Perhaps.

January 1848

The war with Mexico was all but over. U.S. forces had been victorious on every front, and now both Whigs and Democrats turned their attention to the terms of the treaty and the Presidential election at year's end. Locally, the parties focused on one of the State Senatorial seats, currently occupied by John S. Gallaher and open for election in April.

Both parties considered the April election crucial to the national contest in November. Issues brought to the local electorate in the Spring would be debated, modified, and refined through the Summer and into the Fall. In the Jefferson County area, the *Spirit of Jefferson* and the *Virginia Free Press* would be the main sources of information for the public.

Both editors and their staff were girding for battle, sharpening their pens and preparing their presses for the struggle ahead.

The Democrats held a public meeting at the Court House on January 17th. James Beller was selected as one of the delegates to the Congressional district convention and Frank Washington chosen to help draft resolutions to be presented. When the draft was completed, Washington rose and presented it to his colleagues:

> The Democrats strongly approved President Polk's prosecution of the war with Mexico and supported him for reelection — The U.S. should recoup the cost of the war by annexing land from Mexico. Since the country is "totally incapable of self-government, [this action] could work but little if any injury, while to us it would be a valuable acquisition of territory, and called for from the highest considerations of commercial policy"
>
> Congress has no right to prohibit slavery in these newly acquired territories; and,
>
> The Whig candidate, General Zachary Taylor, may be a great warrior but would not make an acceptable President. [78]

At the Whig meeting, President Andrew Hunter helped those present draft and present their own resolutions:

The war with Mexico was cruel, costly, and unnecessary.

Any "indemnity, that can be extorted from our impoverished and downtrodden enemies, would be but a miserable compensation for the innumerable evils inflicted..."

They would support either Henry Clay or Zachary Taylor for President, and

They would meet at Winchester in February to nominate a candidate for State Senator, John S. Gallaher being their preference. [79]

John's brother and coeditor, Horatio Nelson Gallaher, and J. Harrison Kelly were among the delegates chosen to attend the February convention in Richmond.

April, 1848. Jefferson County, Virginia.

Democratic party leaders in Virginia's 10th Congressional District blamed many of their losses in the last major election on Jefferson County's poor organization and lack of leadership. [80] The *Spirit of Jefferson* had been born out of this defeat, and James Beller had been selected to turn things around. Young, politically inexperienced, and new to the newspaper business, he was under pressure to perform, and the April and November elections were his chance to gain notoriety in has party and profession or to sink into oblivion.

On February 17th, James W. Beller married Jane Elizabeth Kelly, a sister of J. Harrison Kelly. (They had been courting for about a year.) The event was reported as one of the largest in the memory of Charlestown residents. The couple boarded the train at Harpers Ferry and set out for a two-week honeymoon in Baltimore, Washington, and points unknown. Recording the event in the *Free Press*, J.S. Gallaher noted, "May their after life be as joyous and free of care as the youthtime of their wedded state." [81]

The Whigs of the 10th Congressional District held their Senatorial Convention at Winchester on February 10, and nominated John S. Gallaher as their candidate. His response soon followed: he would be relieved not to endure another severe canvass, so don't let his incumbency prevent them from choosing a more electable candidate. The convention sustained Gallaher's nomination unanimously and with acclamation. He would battle it out with Democrat Hierome Opie on April 27th. [82]

Attacks from the *Spirit of Jefferson* followed in quick succession, accusing Gallaher of delaying revision of the District School Bill to gain votes, wasting Virginia's money on transportation projects, and neglecting his constituents during his campaign. The *Free Press* editor parried each thrust, but he was now on the defensive. [83]

Gallaher published his pre-election issue one day early — on election day — to get the final word before the voters:

> All we ask for is fair play, and we do not now hesitate to say, in advance, that this contest has not been conducted by our opponents in that honest, frank and candid manner, generally characteristic of Virginians. Questions have been blinked, and beaten around: Their course on the School Bill has been softened and tempered to suit this one, and then held up to suit the caprice of another, who was an opponent. Anything and almost everything, if thereby a vote could be made out of it! They have, indeed, by their insidious and fitful course on the School question, won the sobriquet of

"THE ARTFUL DODGERS!" [84]

Gallaher lost the five-county election by 22 votes, winning by over 100 votes in Jefferson and losing by a little more than 100 in Frederick. (It had voted down the education bill earlier.) In the issue following his defeat he concluded:

"USED UP." — "LAID OUT."

> The senior editor of this paper has, for the first time, in his own person, realized a political defeat. The novelty of the thing smooths the disappointment, and he feels in a mood quite as philosophic "as could be expected." It would be useless to speculate upon the causes of this disaster — the "fixed fact" is known that he was short of votes! His opponents were active, and his friends perhaps rather too sanguine. Some had "corn to plant," and did not suppose he would need their aid — some didn't like his Taylorism — some were a little "sulky" in reference to the School bill, for which they had themselves voted — and others thought him rather prodigal on the subject of Internal Improvements....
>
> He has the proud satisfaction of knowing that his defeat is no dishonor — that his escutcheon is unsullied — and that, in going down, his flag was still unfurled — there was no backing, no trimming, no dodging. Somebody had to be beaten, and the old soldier might as well take the rubbers as the young one. [85]

Responding to the election returns, Beller exclaimed:

> The great leader of the Whig phalanx (and as we honestly believe, the strongest man of the party,) has been defeated.... His political death is now a fixed fact — dead, dead, beyond resurrection! And whilst we rejoice at this event as a proud political triumph, it is in no spirit of malevolence or personal malignity that we thus rejoice. For the man and the gentleman, we have the highest personal feelings of regard, and even in the heat of political excitement, we hope we have said nothing impugning in the slightest degree, his honorable bearing as a man, or his kindness of heart and many noble qualities, as a citizen and neighbor. [86]

The battle for the Virginia Senate was now history, but there was little time for sulking or self-congratulation. The conflict between James K. Polk and Zachary Taylor would be decided in November, and both sides began to recruit and rearm for the next encounter.

July 1848, Jefferson County, Virginia

The treaty with Mexico, signed in May, ceded most of the Southwest to the United States. Before the ink was dry, Congress began arguing the question of slavery being extended into the new territories. If the Southern states didn't get some concessions on the matter, it could be a Union breaker.

In February, James W. Marshall had found gold at Sutter's Mill in California, but the magnitude of the discovery had not yet reached the East Coast. For now, Americans were focused on the great military victory.

Jefferson County residents scheduled Independence Day celebrations for Charlestown, Harpers Ferry, and Shannondale. James Beller reflected:

> It is a matter of congratulation, that there is one period, at least, when men of all creeds and all political divisions, can meet on the same common platform.... And though the signs be now inauspicious, for the perpetuity of the Union, as "one and indivisible," yet in the onward march of our Nation to glory and to greatness, there is much to cheer the heart of the patriot and the philanthropist.... [87]

In Charlestown, cannon boomed to open the festivities, and visitors packed the Presbyterian Church to hear Rev. N.G. North's sermon. Samuel J.C. Moore then read the *Declaration of Independence* and was followed by Lawson Botts, whose oration J.S. Gallaher pronounced a "brilliant production," "full of fire and animation." [88]

When the services concluded, many attendees strolled down Main Street to Col. Sappington's Hotel, where a lavish spread awaited them. After the tables were cleared, guests chose Frank Washington to preside over the toasts and J.H. Kelly as one of the recording secretaries.

Participants proposed a baker's dozen of regular toasts — all effusive but the one for President Polk. The volunteer toasts were more telling and included the following:

> B.F. Washington — The Compromises of the Constitution: Broad enough and strong enough to uphold the Union. "May we cling to them as the mariner clings to the last plank when night and the tempest close around him."
>
> J. Harrison Kelly: — Pennsylvania and Virginia: The State of my nativity and the home of my adoption — may the Keystone ever bind the "Old Dominion" in the Federal Arch, in the indissoluble bonds of a fraternal Union.
>
> James W. Beller — Our Union: "One and indivisible." Sustained hitherto by the patriotism of the people.

Compromises of the Constitution: Palsied be the hand that would mislead the one or o'erleap the barriers of the other. [89]

The crowd dispersed, full of good food and good cheer.

The Jefferson Volunteers had not yet returned from Mexico, but citizens were already planning a special celebration for the men in August. Would the Independence Day good feelings linger another few weeks, or would they evaporate in the heat of Presidential politicking?

Figure 21. Col. J.F. Hamtramck (1798-1858). Colonel, 1st Volunteer Regiment, Mexican War.

August 1848, Jefferson County, Virginia

At the end of June, residents began planning a homecoming celebration for the Jefferson Volunteers. The meeting at the Court House was chaired by Democratic leader A.J. O'Bannon, with Whig J.H. Kelly serving as secretary. James Beller and Andrew Hunter were among the speakers who urged that the returning heroes get the recognition they deserved. [90]

The committee agreed to find a suitable speaker for the event, solicit subscriptions for a public dinner or barbecue, and invite guests. The celebration would be scheduled for some time in August to give the veterans time to return to their homes. Before dispersing, the committee resolved "to conduct the arrangements for the proposed welcome as to eschew all references to the party politics of the day."

Their plans hit a snag at a later meeting, when they couldn't agree on a speaker. Finally, they agreed on two speakers: Democrat Henry Bedinger and Whig J.H. Kelly. But Democrats (probably O'Bannon and Washington) rebelled, asserting that an antiwar Whig had no place on the podium. The Democrats broke from the meeting and proceeded to schedule their own party rally, which would include honors to the veterans.

Infuriated at this maneuver, *Free Press* Editor J.S. Gallaher thundered:

> It is a most highhanded, arbitrary, and presumptuous work.... Did the brave Volunteers go to Mexico to make Democratic capital — or, was it for the high purpose of serving their country? And can they now, on their return to their homes, lend themselves as tools to wily politicians? No! while they would have had their hearts gladdened by a kind reception of their fellow citizens, they will reject with an indignant scorn this bald endeavor to render them the supple instruments of party demagogism. [91]

The Democrats held their barbecue on August 17th in a grove on Col. Braxton Davenport's *Altona*, west of Charlestown. (Both O'Bannon and Washington played major roles in the planning. James Beller did not.) Although they had invited numerous party luminaries and prepared for several thousand guests, turnout fell far short of their expectations.

Less than two hundred participants made up the procession from Charlestown to *Altona*, which was led by the Jefferson Volunteers' Captain John W. Rowan. Few of the volunteers who attended were in uniform and Col. John F. Hamtramck, commander of the First Virginia Regiment, was conspicuously absent. Responding to the Democrats' invitation, the Colonel noted:

> ... however gratified I may feel at the greetings and "welcome home" of my fellow citizens, I am constrained to decline your polite

invitation, as the "festival" seems to have in view the defeat of our old Chief [Zachary Taylor] whom the enemies of our country would never defeat, while the soldiers who served under him are complimented with an invitation to the meeting. [92]

The gathering at *Altona* numbered less than one thousand.

Reviewing the event from his Whig perspective, J.S. Gallaher noted:

> ... a more spiritless affair — considering the extraordinary exertions made — has never been witnessed in our county, How unlike the Festivals of '40 and '44, both in numbers and in enthusiasm! The speeches fell stillborn, or else were applauded so feebly as to exhibit the more strikingly the lack of all ardor, life and energy. With the demonstration, and the fruits thereof, we are content. We commiserate the conditions of the desponding, and wish them better luck when next they invite speakers of eminent ability to a party jollification. [93]

November, 1848, Charlestown, Virginia

Both Beller and the Gallahers had used their newspapers to campaign tirelessly for their Presidential candidates. The election, they believed, would determine whether slavery would be extended into the new territories acquired from the Mexican War.

Beller had warned voters that the Whig candidate, war hero Zachary Taylor, had no administrative experience and no political principles to guide him. Taylor's running mate, Millard Fillmore, had supported the Wilmot Proviso, a policy that banned slavery from the new territories.

The Gallahers warned readers that Democratic candidate, Lewis Cass, was no friend to the South. He was, they contended, a political opportunist who had enriched himself at public expense. Cass opposed the Wilmot Proviso and promoted "popular sovereignty," an approach that would allow voters of each new state to determine the status of slavery. [94]

Free Soil candidate, Martin Van Buren, wanted to ban slavery in all new territories. Southern Democrats regarded him as a traitor to their party and feared that he would lead antislavery voters out of the Democratic camp.

As November 7th approached, James Beller and Frank Washington helped organize a Democratic Committee of Vigilance, which appointed members to oversee activities in each voting district. John and Horatio Gallaher and J.H. Kelly performed the same function for the Whig cause. In their last issues before the election, both sides laid out their battle plans for Election Day: how to determine which party members had not voted, how to transport them to the polls, how to convince wavering members to cast the right vote. [95]

For the first time in our history, voters in a Presidential election had all cast their ballots on the same day — and, thanks to the wonders of the "Magnetic Telegraph," State election returns could be broadcast soon after the results had been tabulated. It still took a while for votes from the hinterlands to reach the State capitols, but the news could now reach the public in days rather than weeks.

In the November 14th issue, *Spirit* editor Beller mournfully reported,

> ... Gen. TAYLOR has been elected President of the U. States. It comes upon us like a fire bell at night, and has utterly astounded our reason, no less than excited our fears.... Our heart is sick at the contemplation. [96]

Martin Van Buren had indeed drawn antislavery Democrats into the Free Soil Party, giving the Whigs a majority. Reading the young editor's lament, John S. Gallaher responded:

> In the midst of our moderate and reasonable joy at the consummation of an event which long since we deemed certain, we are sorry to find some of our friends of the defeated party in a very gloomy mood. — They even admit that they are sick at heart at the contemplation. We would give them consolation if we could.... [T]here is a retributive Providence in all that has happened. The War so heedlessly brought on by the President has brought forth a hero and a patriot to redeem the country, and to secure peace and happiness for many years to come. [97]

On November 16th, Whigs gathered at Captain Sappington's Hotel in Charlestown to plan a Grand Illumination to be held on the 24th (Zachary Taylor's birthday). In a separate meeting, members of the Rough and Ready Club celebrated the Taylor victory and gave a vote of thanks to their president, John S. Gallaher, for his devotedness, sagacity, and foresight for his early and energetic advocacy of the President elect. [98]

When asked to put a notice of the Whig Illumination in the *Spirit of Jefferson*, James Beller complied, murmuring, "No doubt a creditable display will be gotten up, and like one of our distant contemporaries, the only consolation we can have, is that none of the powder and candles will be burnt at our expense." [99]

The celebrations over, both editors paused to take stock of their resources. Both had expanded the size of their newspaper to accommodate the political discourse they had to carry. That would need to be payed for, as well as the additional paper and ink needed for a larger operation. Beller had tried to offset some of the costs by offering a subscription that covered only the election season. Now he needed to convert some of his part time customers to full time subscribers.

Both editors threatened to drop subscribers who did not pay up immediately, but they were on the horns of a dilemma: Their newspapers were political organs — vehicles mean to carry their party's message to potential voters. Dropping nonpaying customers meant reducing their audience, something they couldn't afford, particularly in a closely contested election. On the other hand, they both had businesses and families to support. Gifts of firewood in the winter and vegetables in the summer only went so far.

Beller began a new advertising campaign, promising subscribers that the *Spirit* would carry more literature and content that appealed to children and the ladies. To the men, he went as far as to suggest that they ought to take two newspapers (one from each political party) so they could have a broader view of national and international events.

For potential readers who wished to avoid the blistering language of the political press, he urged:

> Whilst, in regard to our political course, we shall as we have ever done, sustain the principles of Democracy without fear or flinching, we shall never convert our columns into a vehicle of personal attacks or defamation. This course is most in accordance with our own feelings, and best suited to the improved temper of the age, which happily no longer countenances an evil-speaking journal as either desirable or respectable.... [100]

Now that the political contest had ended, some of the news items that had been buried on the back pages started to get attention. Although James W. Marshall had discovered gold at Sutter's Mill in Coloma, California, way back in January, the story had been a sleeper until the New York *Herald* gave it space in August.

The *Virginia Free Press* was the first local paper to cover the story in any depth. In late September, it reported that "An immense bed of Gold, one hundred miles in extent, has been discovered in California, on American Fork and Feather rivers tributaries of the Sacramento, near Monterey." Settlements had been abandoned, soldiers and sailors had left their posts, following the lure of gold. [101]

For decades, the press had scolded their Eastern readers that vast resources — timber, coal, even gold — were available right under their noses in western Virginia and Pennsylvania. Would fortune seekers from Jefferson County be satisfied exploring the natural resources nearby, or would they be captivated by the marvelous accounts reaching them from the far West?

December 1848, Jefferson County, Virginia.

Political events in December quickly percolated into the brains of both Democratic and Whig residents, igniting their imaginations and raising tempers to a new high.

On December 4th, incoming President Zachary Taylor announced that the residents of California and New Mexico would soon apply for admission to the Union as sovereign States, noting that, preparatory to their admission,

> ... the people of each will have instituted for themselves a republican form of government, "laying its foundation in such principles and organizing its powers in such form as to them shall seem most likely to effect their safety and happiness." By awaiting their action all causes of uneasiness may be avoided and confidence and kind feeling preserved. With a view of maintaining the harmony and tranquility so dear to all, we should abstain from the introduction of those exciting topics of a sectional character which have hitherto produced painful apprehensions in the public mind....

> But attachment to the Union of the States should be habitually fostered in every American heart.... In my judgment its dissolution would be the greatest of calamities, and to avert that should be the study of every American. Upon its preservation must depend our own happiness and that of countless generations to come. Whatever dangers may threaten it, I shall stand by it and maintain it in its integrity to the full extent of the obligations imposed and the powers conferred upon me by the Constitution. [102]

On December 5th, outgoing President Polk reiterated Taylor's concerns, pointing out that the next Congress must replace the U.S. military law imposed on New Mexico and California with a more appropriate form of government:

> The immensely valuable possessions of New Mexico and California are already inhabited by a considerable population. Attracted by their great fertility, their mineral wealth, their commercial advantages, and the salubrity of the climate, emigrants from the older States in great numbers are already preparing to seek new homes in these inviting regions. Shall the dissimilarity of the domestic institutions in the different States prevent us from providing for them suitable governments? These institutions existed at the adoption of the Constitution, but the obstacles which they interposed were overcome by that spirit of compromise which is now invoked. In a conflict of opinions or of interests, real or imaginary, between different sections of our country, neither can justly demand all which it might desire to obtain. Each, in the true spirit of our institutions, should concede something to the other.

Government officials had brought samples of California gold east for testing and confirmed that "these mines are more extensive and valuable than was anticipated." [103]

The two Presidents' efforts to handle the status of slavery in the new territories was undermined the following week, when Massachusetts Whig John G. Palfrey introduced a bill to abolish slavery in the District of Columbia. [104] Southern Whigs and Democrats found a common sectional issue that trumped many of their long standing party differences.

Reacting to Palfrey's proposal, John S. Gallaher fumed:

> The motion ... in regard to Slavery in the District of Columbia, and the favor with which the resolution was entertained, has created quite an excitement, not only in the District, but throughout the entire Southern country....
>
> Southern Statesmen have been alarmed and grieved by this overt act, and well they may be. They see the circles around them, in the keeping of the North, drawn tighter and smaller continuously, with no guarantee that the process will be in the least loosened! No wonder they are alarmed. This Union is one of compromises, of safeguards and balances. The North has the power to crush the South, or ruin the Union in the attempt. But ought the North to use this power? There lies the question. It should be well pondered and well reflected upon, and considered. Who is so unpatriotic, so traitorous, as to cooly calculate the value of this glorious Union? [105]

Southern Congressmen at both the State and National level immediately began preparing their response. As part of his personal effort to stem the tide of Northern oppression, Gallaher announced that he was joining the management of the Richmond *Enquirer*. He would spend the winter (and longer if needed) in the State capitol helping the newspaper promote Zachary Taylor's administration. [106]

Figure 22. "Seeing the Elephant," by Wm. B. McMurtrie

> **Miner:** Wall, how de do! put down your trunk
>   Your journey makes me puff
> You've travelled hard, I like your spunk
>   Say! have you been up the "Bluff"?
> **Elephant:** I reckon, yes, have you?
> **Miner**: "Yes Siree, I've been there too.
> **Elephant:** What saw you there? No gold I swear!
> **Miner**: I saw one chap when you was there.
> **Elephant:** Who?
> **Miner:** I saw the "ELEPHANT."

Part III. Seeing the Elephant

The Olden Time.

Having had occasion some days since to overhaul the rubbish which has accumulated in our office, we accidentally laid our hands on a number of the "Farmers Repository," a newspaper published in this town by our worthy and venerable friend, Richard Williams, Esq., more than forty years ago. Although the ravages of time were clearly marked on the sheet and its typography, we were enabled, with the aid of a good pair of *borrowed* spectacles, to decipher the following advertisement:

A Living Elephant.

To be seen at Mr. John Anderson's Coffee House, in Charlestown, on Friday the 20th instant. [1808] — She will be exposed from 8 o'clock in the morning till sun set, and will continue here until Saturday evening.

The Elephant, not only the largest and most sagacious animal in the world, but the peculiar manner in which it takes its food and drink of every kind with its trunk, is acknowledged to be the greatest curiosity ever offered to the public. She will draw the cork from a bottle, and with her trunk will manage it in such a manner, as to drink its contents— to the astonishment of the spectators — will lie down and rise at command. She is seven years old, and measures upwards of fifteen feet from the end of her trunk to that of her tail — ten feet round the body, and upwards of seven feet high.

Admittance 25 Cents — Children, half price.

May 20, 1808.

How many and varied the changes since those good old days! It would seem, that previous to this time, our ancestors never beheld the largest of terrestrial animals — and granting that such was the fact, how wonderful and astonishing has been the march of curious exhibitions! In these modern times, there is no event or transaction in life that is not sometimes connected with this "astonisher of spectators."

Many of our soldiers in the late Mexican War — brave and hardy as they were — had several "sights of the elephant" whilst treading the burning sands on the Rio Grande — and from the advices we have from Fort Independence, some of our California boys are fearful they will meet him in the Rocky Mountains....

We have had no business out of our office since the election of members to Congress in this State, and therefore cannot say, whether a stranger with a large trunk can be seen in any of the Coffee Houses in town.

John S. Gallaher, *Virginia Free Press*, May 10, 1849. [107]

January 1849, Jefferson County, Virginia

The events of December had given Jefferson Countians much to ponder.

John S. Gallaher had opted to leave the *Virginia Free Press* in the hands of his brother Horatio and help the Richmond *Republican* support President Taylor's administration.

Frank Washington, now relieved of administering his father's estate, was free to join the local political contests or head westward, to mine gold, seek political appointment, contend for an elected government position, or join the ranks of California's fourth estate.

Brothers-in-law James W. Beller and J. Harrison Kelly had many similar options. The former, with a growing family and newspaper as well as Democratic political aspirations, was tempted to stay put and prosper where he was planted. A friend of Kelly advised him, "all's not gold that glitters. When a fellow gets a good berth, in a sure boat, and a calm sea, it's our opinion he ought to snooze in it...." To which J.H. replied, "a setting hen never gets fat — and having tried that experiment, though not in the literal sense, he means to push along, keep moving, and, possibly, the wheel of fortune may yet roll him up a prize." [108]

For other local residents, the discovery of gold was a chance to start a new life out west or improve their lot at home. A few months' hard work in California might change their lives forever. And so, when the following notice appeared in the *Spirit of Jefferson's* first issue of the new year, the dreaming and the planning began in earnest:

> **Ho! for California.**
>
> It having been determined to organize a company for California whose principal pursuit shall be digging the soil for virgin gold, all who are desirous of joining the expedition will meet at the Law Office of B. F. Washington, on Tuesday the 9th instant (January 9, 1849), at seven o'clock in the evening. [109]

Depending on their resources, those who decided to go west could choose a water or overland route. Either way, they would endure an arduous and potentially dangerous journey to "See the Elephant."

They could book passage from New York, Philadelphia, or Baltimore around Cape Horn to San Francisco. Or they could exit at Panama, cross the isthmus overland, and embark on one of the ships plying between that location and San Francisco. The first option required an expensive, six-month journey, and traversing Cape Horn was often fraught by weather-related dangers and delays. The midway stop at Panama could be quicker and cheaper, but there were fewer passenger ships on the Pacific shore than on the Atlantic. Completing the rest of the trip could require more time and more money. The overland routes were the cheapest and most popular options. Easterners normally departed from Independence, Missouri, by wagon train in groups large enough to provide mutual assistance and protection.

The meeting on January 9th, led by A.J. O'Bannon, B.F. Washington, and J. Harrison Kelly, outlined the purpose of the proposed company, appointed a committee to screen applications, and began the process of determining the resources needed for the journey.

Consisting of fifty or more members, the company would be established "on the mutual assurance principle. Mining, or digging gold, is the primary pursuit, and the proceeds of each are to be held in common, or, in other words, to be thrown together, and divided equally...." They set the membership fee at $300, with $110 payable at the February 10th meeting, when officers would be elected. Industrious and enterprising applicants from other counties would also be accepted if space was available. [110]

Updates in the *Free Press* appealed to local residents' sense of pride and thirst for adventure. There was no doubt that the group would be strong enough to proceed with perfect safety to their destination:

> ... It will be made up of our own citizens — those in whom confidence may be placed, and who may be relied upon in any exigency.
>
> The route in contemplation is one of the finest that could be selected, abounding as it will be, with novelty and adventure. From Fort Leavenworth to the South Pass the route will be principally over prairies, in which the sportsman with his rifle may find sufficient game for his amusement. After leaving the South Pass, game is abundant, as the sharp and quick report of the rifle will attest. [111]

By the January 22nd meeting, the company had fifty-six members enrolled, with about forty applications still pending. Those already committed were setting their affairs in order and raising the funds needed to pay the entrance fee. Frank Washington chose not to renew the lease on the house his family occupied in Charlestown, opting to have his wife and children stay with his in-laws. [112]

February 1849, Charlestown, Virginia.

The fledgling Charlestown, Virginia, Mining Company reconvened on February 10th at the Odd Fellows Hall to elect officers. It now numbered seventy individuals, and membership was closed, even though more applicants were available.

The following were elected to office:

President — Benjamin Franklin Washington. Gentleman from a prominent slaveholding family. Age 29, married, two children. A practicing lawyer in Charlestown, he was an active Democrat and the favorite son of the elder politicians, but he had never run for elected office. After liquidating his father's estate, he had substantial financial resources but no local property to speak of. No military experience.

1st Commander — Robert H. Keeling. Age 22, married. Graduate of Virginia Military Institute (1846). Commissioned a Second Lieutenant in Col. Hamtramck's regiment, he served throughout the Mexican War.

2d Commander — Smith Slaughter Crane. Age 36, unmarried. Son of Catherine Strother and Joseph Crane of Jefferson County, Virginia. Mexican War veteran, participated in all the severe battles from Vera Cruz through the Valley to the City of Mexico. Member of Total Abstinence Society. Not a slave owner.

3d Commander — Joseph E.N. Lewis. Age 23, unmarried. Graduate of William and Mary College — studied law with Frank Washington. Democrat, slave owner. No military experience.

Treasurer — Edward M. Aisquith. Age 40, married, three children. Charlestown merchant. Democrat, slave owner, Episcopalian.

Quartermaster — Nathaniel Seevers. Merchant, Mason, Democrat, candidate for State senator.

Secretary — J. Harrison Kelly. Age 28, single, Whig, compositor and assistant editor, *Virginia Free Press*. Member, Total Abstinence Society. Grand Master of the International Order of Odd Fellows, Virginia Chapter.

Surgeon — Dr. Wakeman Bryarly. Age 29, single. Physician, graduate of Washington Medical University, Baltimore (1840). Mexican War veteran. [113]

The group's strong military background was no accident. Applicants had been screened by a committee that included Capt. John W. Rowan and Lieutenants John Avis and John W. Gallaher, all veterans of Company K, 1st Virginia Regiment. Former Lieutenants Vincent E. Geiger and Frank's brother Lawrence B. Washington had joined the mining company's rank and file.

Jefferson County's Fourth Estate, 1840-1850

Politics had also figured into who made the Company roster. Although Jefferson County's electorate was about evenly split between Democrats and Whigs, the members were mostly proslavery Democrats. (J.H. Kelly and the brother of his future wife were the only Whig members.) The admissions' committee appears to have favored members who could promote their political agenda in California. Pro-Temperance members were also well represented.

Figure 23. Dr. Wakeman Bryarly. He served as the Surgeon in the Charlestown Company of miners.

As outlined in the Company's constitution, its co-partnership ran from February 10, 1849, to April 1, 1850, with provisions for reorganization thereafter. Frank Washington's duties as President were chiefly administrative. Although he was the general commander of the company, the three military commanders would assume responsibility in times of danger. The Board of Directors controlled civil, military, and monetary operations, and J.H. Kelly, as Secretary, was responsible for keeping the minutes of Company and Board meetings and sending accounts of the journey to *The Spirit of Jefferson.*

Members were not to receive special treatment because of rank or social status:

> Each member of the Company shall be, and he is hereby bound and duly obligated, to engage in mining, washing and cleansing the ore — or such other employment as may be assigned him by the Board of Directors: and no member of the Board shall be excused from any branch of service, which may be assigned him, by reason of his office.

Moral statutes prohibited work on the Sabbath (except in cases of necessity), banned gambling *between members* of the Company, and imposed incremental fines for intoxication.

March 29, 1849, Charlestown, Virginia.

CALIFORNIA EMIGRANTS.
(TUNE — "O! Susanna!")
I come from Old Virginny,
With my wash-bowl on my knee;
I'm going to California,
The gold dust for to see.
It rained all night the day I left,
The weather it was dry.
The sun so hot I froze to death
Oh! brothers! don't you cry;
Oh! California!
That's the land for me!
I'm going to Sacramento,
With my wash-bowl on my knee!

———

I jumped aboard the Liza ship,
And travelled on the sea,
And every time I thought of home,
I wished it wasn't me!
The vessel reared like any horse,
That had of oats a wealth,
It found it couldn't throw me so
I thought I'd throw myself!
I thought of all the pleasant times,
We've had together here;
I thought I ort to cry a bit,
But couldn't find a tear.

———

The pilot bread was in my mouth,
The gold dust in my eye,
and though I'm going far away
Dear brothers, don't you cry.
I soon shall be in Franscisco,
And then I'll look all round,
And when I see the gold lumps there,
I'll pick them off the ground.
I'll scrape the mountains clean, my boys,
I'll drain the rivers dry,
A "pocket full of rocks" bring home —
So brothers, don't you cry! [ii]

On Thursday, March 29th, friends of the Charlestown, Virginia, Mining Company gathered at the railroad station to witness their departure. There was no band or parade but plenty of excitement and some trepidation. H.N. Gallaher noted that,

> ...the whole community will feel their loss. To many a family in our midst, it is the severance of ties the most endearing, and they who only have been made to feel and know the pangs of separation such as this, can properly appreciate the condition of those who mourn. May each member of the company prove eminently successful in his enterprise, and soon return again to cheer the home and make glad the hearth of those who with eager and anxious hope, look forward to the promised time. [115]

With fatherly affection, John S. Gallaher bid farewell to Kelly, who had worked for him more than seven years:

> We cannot permit the friendly and confidential relations, which have existed between us so long, to be severed, without an expression of our appreciation of his merits and worth. Mr. K. began life with but few advantages, but he has within him the elements of success which rarely fail a man in an emergency — integrity, industry, energy — and a sense of moral rectitude and an unwavering fealty to any trust confided to him. With constancy of spirits and unfaltering patience [he has] pursued the even tenor of his way, [and] deserves a far better reward for his efforts than he has been able to obtain thus far.
>
> Mr. Kelly takes with him our confidence and earnest good wishes for his most ample success — and if he should fail in gathering the glittering dust upon the banks of the Sacramento, he can rely upon his moral and intellectual resources, which are more certain to ensure happiness. Let him but bear in mind the motto, "Upward and Onward," and all will be well.... [116]

News had just reached residents that Colonel John C. Fremont's expedition through New Mexico to California had been ravaged by winter weather. Fremont and a handful of his men had managed seek help, but the relief expedition had found the survivors nearly frozen to death and reportedly eating the bodies of their dead comrades. [117]

As the train left the station, many wondered if they would see their friends and loved ones again.

For the aspiring miners who hadn't made the cut, there was still hope. Though not as grand as the Charlestown, Virginia, Mining Company, smaller companies were forming in Shepherdstown and Harpers Ferry. [118] Still time to grab the elephant's tail before it disappeared into the distance!

***

The Company proceeded to Harper's Ferry, then north by train to Cumberland, Maryland. The next day they boarded stage coaches and took the Allegheny Turnpike to the Ohio River. There they transferred to the steamboat *Niagara* to Cincinnati. Changing boats at Cincinnati, they traveled down the Ohio and Mississippi to St. Louis.

Jefferson County's Fourth Estate, 1840-1850

Throughout the summer and into the fall, the spirits of county residents rose and fell as news about California emigrants trickled in. Sublime scenery. Cholera. Fantastic fortunes won and lost. Towns razed by fire and wagon trains ravaged by Indian raids.

The fate of California's current and future residents remained unresolved. Reviewing the accomplishments of the 30th Congress, John S. Gallaher sighed, "No bill was passed providing a Government for either of the Territories of New Mexico or California. These measures fell through the inability of the two Houses to concur in any propositions for the purpose." [119] In the 31st Congress, the Senate had a Democratic majority, while there was a Democratic plurality in the House.

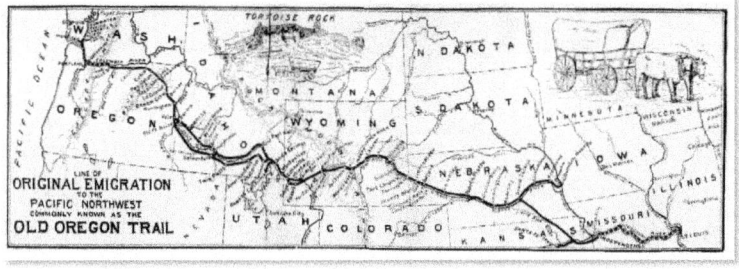

Figure 24. Ezra Meeker, *The Old Oregon Trail*, postcard, 1906.

Figure 25. Charles J. Faulkner, Sr., 1806-1884

April 1849

> "No person held to service or labor in one State, under the laws thereof, escaping into another, shall, in consequence of any law or regulation therein, be discharged from such service or labor, but shall be delivered up, on claim of the party to whom such service may be due."
>
> "Fugitives From Labor Clause," United States Constitution, Article IV, Section 2, Clause 3.

The late cold weather had destroyed all hopes for a peach crop in Jefferson County this year — the fate of the plums and apples was still uncertain. The more philosophical among the farmers opined that a year's privation would help citizens appreciate the value of fruit when it comes — an attitude some were ready to apply to the political climate.

Now that the '49ers were on their way, Jefferson County life settled back into a familiar routine. The *Free Press* and *Spirit* sparred over the best nominees for the upcoming State and local elections. Some complained that party politics rather than merit had been used to fill the Charlestown postmaster position vacated by Edward M. Aisquith. [120] The Lynchburg *Virginian* floated a rumor that both J.S. Gallaher and his son Robert would be appointed to office as a reward for supporting Zachary Taylor's candidacy.

Responding to these accusations, the *Free Press* editor fired the following salvo:

> For more than twenty years they [the Democracy] have enjoyed every office worth having under the Government, and they now have brought themselves to believe that they have a fee simple right to all the offices, and are disposed to treat as a trespasser any Whig who may get an office. It is high time that these gentry who patriotically desire a lifelong term in the service of their country should be taught the doctrine of "rotation in office" is not altogether one of theory — and if we are not mistaken, they will learn the lesson before six months have gone by. [121]

Political arguments were extended to explain the lure of California gold to Virginia's young men. The Democrats' stance against internal improvements, said the Richmond *Whig*, had blocked development of roads and railroads into the mineral rich western part of the State. Was it any wonder that youth looked elsewhere for employment? [122]

At the State level, Virginia legislators had thus far failed to develop a united position on how slavery should be handled in new States seeking admission to the Union. However, Charles J. Faulkner took a step toward mollifying proslavery Southerners when he submitted a report that examined existing legislation of Congress upon the subject of fugitive slaves and suggested some additional measures. (It would become the basis of the federal Fugitive Slave Act.) [123]

Closer to home, Jefferson County delegates followed the lead of representatives from Fauquier, asserting that it was "a matter of indifference, so far as the existence of slavery is concerned, whether Congress engraft into the forms of government of California and New Mexico the Wilmot Proviso, the Missouri Compromise, or the Senate's resolutions." J.S. Gallaher warned:

> Mr. S[cott] and the Jefferson Delegates should have remembered the relations they bore to their respective counties, Virginia, and the whole slaveholding portion of the Union — the influence attached to their opinions at the North, based upon the prominent position they occupy, as leading members of a Southern Legislature — and that a large majority if not their whole constituency disagreed with them. The evil to result from such a course is incalculable. [124]

When news from the California expedition began to arrive, residents gladly refocused their attention on dreams of gold and adventure.

Several groups from the Charlestown Company, charged with procuring mules, wagons, supplies, and other paraphernalia, set off on their missions, their goal being to rendezvous at Independence, Missouri, where the entire party would begin the journey West. Most of the '49ers proceeded by steamboat down the Ohio River from Cincinnati, Ohio, to

Cairo, Illinois, located at the confluence of the Ohio and Mississippi Rivers.

Figure 26. Cairo, Illinois, ca. 1850. [125]

March, 1849, Near Cairo, Illinois

The low lying peninsula at Cairo was surrounded by a poorly maintained levee which had been breached last Spring on the Mississippi side. Late in March 1849, the area experienced the worst flood in memory, pushing both rivers over their banks, rearranging the sandbars and other navigational landmarks, and spilling through Cairo's unrepaired levy. Although most of the city's stores and other buildings had survived, mud and water still covered the municipal area when the miners arrived.

J. Harrison Kelly and most of the Charlestown Company arrived by steamboat in early April.

> Editor, Spirit of Jefferson:
> My last letter to you was dispatched from Cincinnati. We left that place on last Saturday evening. A trip down the Ohio is full of stirring incidents, and of course I have had my share. During Saturday night, Sunday night, and Monday night, we were grounded several times, and at one time fear was entertained about our getting off. You can have no idea of the vice on the river. Gambling of every description going on all the time. When I got up this morning I found a party still gaming who were at it when I retired last evening. The heavy eye and pale countenance bespoke care and dissipation.
>
> A gentleman has just come on board our boat from New Orleans, who reports 520 deaths in that city, on Saturday week, from Cholera. We passed a boat from that place on Sunday, the *General Scott* on which thirty-five deaths had taken place — and whilst our boat was at Cincinnati, one poor fellow was lying on the wharf for an hour, in the hot sun, who had an attack — and two more cases occurred on a boat lying close by. The newspapers are all silent on this subject, and seem to be desirous of hiding the truth in regard to the ravages of this disease. — We are now on the Mississippi, about 175 miles from St. Louis. The Mississippi is a rough, muddy, and uninviting stream. It does not possess half the beauty of the Ohio.
>
> You cannot imagine the great difference between the appearance of the country along Lake Erie, (the mouth of the Ohio) and the southern part of the same State. In the north all was bleak and desolate, whilst from Cincinnati to Cairo the trees were in full foliage and verdure, and vegetation, far advanced. The apple and peach orchards were in blossom — whilst the oaks and other productions of the forest were clothed in colors of living green. I felt strongly disposed to leave the boat and ramble through the inviting groves, over beds of verdure rich and luxuriant. Our course, now, has changed. We ascend the Mississippi directly north, and shall soon again be among bleak hills and barren wastes — barren, until the genial sun shall have poured its reviving rays on the earth, and melted it from the frigid spell, into which it has been thrown by stern and inflexible Old Winter.
>
> As I cannot send this letter until after our arrival in St. Louis, I will close at this point.
>
> J. Harrison Kelly [126]

Figure 27. St. Louis, Missouri, ca. 1840's.

The Charlestown Company passed through St. Louis about a month before the "Great Fire" charred more than 400 buildings and brought river travel to a standstill. It had started on May 17th, when the steamboat *White Cloud* caught fire at the levee and then broke loose, igniting more than a score of other boats, including those carrying mail to the miners' families, anxiously waiting at home. The freight piled along the levee was next to go and then the buildings nearby.

April 12, 1849, St. Louis, Missouri.

From J. Harrison Kelly

I arrived here on yesterday evening, after a somewhat fatiguing trip. We were in hopes of going on the same boat to St. Josephs, but were disappointed. I have already witnessed scenes that would make your blood run cold, but have not now the time to give them in detail.

The Charlestown (Va.) Mining Company arrived at St. Louis on Saturday evening last in the steamer *Niagara,* from Pittsburg. All the members in good health, and a fine flow of spirits. The company left on Tuesday evening in the *Embassy* for St. Josephs.

Lieut. Lewis and Secretary Kelly leave here this evening for Dahcota [127] with a large quantity of merchandise and provision belonging to the Company. Treasurer Aisquith remains here to reship the Company's wagons from this point to St. Josephs. This accomplished, every thing will be ready for us to start early in the month of May.

I have a great deal to write you in regard to the country, climate, inhabitants, &c., but must postpone it for to-day.

Give my love to all friends and believe me yours as ever.

J.H.K.

Jefferson County's Fourth Estate, 1840-1850

Unfortunately, the men were not able to avoid the cholera which had lain dormant during the winter months and then flourished once the warm weather appeared. By the end of July, St. Louis had buried more than 4,500 victims, but many more travelers carried the disease with them on the westward migration. Graves of countless victims would be strewn along the trail as the summer wore on.

Figure 28. Independence, Missouri, 1850.

Independence, Missouri, the next major city on the river, was the furthest point to which steamboats could travel and the point of departure for emigrants taking the Oregon, Santa Fe, and California Trails. Travelers often shipped supplies to the city that they would need for their journey, and the local wagon makers specialized in building vehicles designed to survive the Oregon Trail. The "prairie schooners" manufactured in this area were lighter than the Conestoga wagons built back East and could normally be pulled by a single team of horses or mules. When filled with supplies, there was little room for passengers, so many emigrants walked alongside their wagon.

Joseph Smith and his Latter Day Saints had settled at Independence in 1831, but their religious and antislavery views angered the local citizens, who responded with violence. The Governor eventually banned them from the State. [128]

The Charlestown Company would follow the Oregon Trail from this point about 950 miles to Fort Hall in Utah Territory. Shortly thereafter, they would take the Sublett Cutoff South, to California.

Figure 29. Prairie Schooner, by James M. Hutchings, *Scenes of Wonder and Curiosity in California (1862).*

Figure 30. Steamboat Race, Currier & Ives, ca. 1866 [129]

April 19, 1849, Independence, Missouri

Thus far Kelly and his companions had witnessed disease, death, and some of the unsavory sides of human nature. They were now preparing to undertake the overland part of the journey, where they would face new trials, more challenging than the ones behind them. If a man wanted to quit and go home, now was the time.

From J. Harrison Kelly

The emigration to California is so great as to astound the stoutest heart. Many, doubtless, have supposed the larger the number the less the danger. This, however, is a very great mistake. All who migrate are dependent upon the prairie grass for forage, and the question naturally arises, will there be a sufficiency to sustain the stock? If we reason upon the information in our possession, we must be compelled in all candor to reply that the grass will not be sufficient. Those who have already travelled over the route speak of the difficulty in procuring forage, even when the number migrating were not one-twentieth when compared with the travel this Spring.

Various estimates have been made as to the number. At present no definite number can be set down. Every boat is crowded, and the road lined with migrating parties. The sturdy mechanic and the hardy farmer — the gay clerk and the assiduous professional - the grave parson and the sporting gentry — each, all, are duly represented in nearly every company numbering thirty [or more].

This place is crowded with emigrants — many are active, spirited and gay as the morning lark — whilst you can see ever and anon, a long visage, marked with care, and bearing all the traces of deep and keen anxiety. Some few companies are disbanding. They, of course, did not count the cost, and having engaged in the enterprise as a matter of pleasure, have learnt very soon, being apt scholars, that there is no fun without paying the fiddler. The fact of it is, some have seen a few stripes of the Zebra already, many a one of which has been alike, and if those which remain yet to be seen partake of the character of those already viewed, I'm not overanxious for a sight myself.

Having embarked after reflection, I am prepared to go through, and meet whatever fate awaits me. 'Tis absolute folly to meet our difficulties half way, and whilst such shall not be my case, still, I will not be altogether undisturbed when they do arise.

St. Josephs, is 120 miles from this point. We shall not get there before Saturday, as our boat happens to be the slowest on the river. We had a little brush, or rather race, about 4 o'clock this morning. The boat *Timour* came up alongside, and we had it side and side for some time. At length we attempted to pass, when the other "rounded to," preparing to run into us. This rather frightened our Captain, and he "took water," in other words, ingloriously surrendered. We had the satisfaction, however, of knocking off some twenty sacks of flour on the other boat. We are not ahead, for although I date Independence, we are two or three miles from the landing, and Independence is 3 miles from the river. It is likely

I shall get off the boat and walk to Independence, and overtake the boat at another landing, 12 miles farther up the river. Some twenty of us intend doing this.

I would not now write to you but for the fact that I presume you are anxious to hear from me on account of the prevalence of the Cholera on the river. You have doubtless learned ere this, of the death of THOMAS W. WASHINGTON, of our company. He was taken ill on Wednesday morning the 11th, and was a corpse on the next morning, the 12th. Every thing that could be done for him was done. Medical skill was baffled, and our friend and companion, who started in good health and buoyant in spirits, now lies entombed six miles below Jefferson City, Mo. The disease which terminated his life was doubtless cholera. We had a case on board our boat on the 16th. — The patient was taken off yesterday, and no new case has since occurred.

We are now at the landing and I must close. The company are at St. Josephs by this time. I met Aisquith and Lewis at St. Louis. Lewis and myself have with us the goods of the Company. Aisquith will be along in a day or two.

Write me at once, and direct to Fort Laramie, via Independence. Two weeks later, write and direct to Fort Hall, via Independence.

I will write a letter for your paper, as soon as I get a little settled at St. Josephs.

There is no cholera at St. Josephs, so far as I could learn. Indeed it is too cold. Yesterday morning, and the day before, we had right sharp falls of snow. In haste, &c.

J.H.K. [130]

A correspondent to the *Baltimore Sun* provided addition details of young Washington's burial:

> ... The boat was detained by the company until they made a neat coffin and shroud, and they buried him on the lands of Col. Ewing, some distance from the river. An engraver of the company carved his [name, residence, &c.,] upon a tombstone, and funds were left to have an enclosure erected around his grave. How different from the burial of many other victims of the cholera upon the spot, and what an alleviation will it be to the anguish of his friends. Some were thrown into rude boxes and buried at the woodyards: and others, respectable men too, who were without their friends, were rolled in blankets and covered in holes only a foot or two deep, with the bare loose earth. [131]

Of all the nightmares experienced by the emigrants on the trail or by their relatives back East, perhaps the worst was the fear of dying alone, without friends, and being left in an unmarked, shallow grave.

Figure 31. Shepherdstown, Virginia, 1840's. From Howe, *Historical Collections*.

May 1849, Jefferson County, Virginia.

A sharp frost had struck the fruit crop when it was coming into bloom, and local farmers were anxious about the results that would be forthcoming. *Free Press* editor J.S. Gallaher urged delinquent subscribers to make a partial payment in firewood – his family and his office were running short.

The results of Virginia's State and local elections were no longer a matter of speculation, and the newspaper editors' tones had lowered from warlike hyperbole to snarls. Whigs had carried the day locally: Charles J. Faulkner, Sr., had taken the Congressional seat, and William C. Worthington and Talbot S. Duke (a mechanic) won seats in the General Assembly. As for the rest of the State, it was nearly a clean sweep for the Democrats.

The *Spirit* editor focused his invective on the proscriptive policies of the Taylor administration – The Harpers Ferry postmaster, a Democrat, had been replaced by a Whig. "What words are adequate to express," said Beller, "that utter scorn and contempt, which so justly attach to an Administration who, as it were, has just stolen into power by trickery, deception and fraud, and is now perpetuating daily, a series of measures never before exampled in this history of this country." [132]

Jefferson County residents doubtless breathed a sigh of relief when they learned that the Charlestown Company had not encountered cholera at St. Josephs, Missouri. But Thomas W. Washington's death from that disease had injected this nightmarish element into their dreams of gold, exploration, and adventure.

Virginians had first encountered cholera in 1832, when it jumped from England to the major U.S. seaports and then crept up the rivers as commerce and settlement expanded westward. Reaching Harpers Ferry in the summer of that year, it killed scores of Irish canal workers and halted construction until it disappeared in the fall.

But it was hiding, not gone - merely dormant - waiting until the acquired immunity of one generation faded and was replaced by the vulnerability of the next.

Caused by a bacterium, cholera is transmitted mainly by drinking contaminated water. But these facts were not discovered until the 1880's. The poor sanitation in western towns and emigrant camps, and at river crossings contaminated by cattle and human waste, created breeding spots for the disease.

Reviewing reports from his colleagues throughout the state, editor J.W. Beller warned,

> ... progress of that fearful epidemic, the Cholera, is fast hastening to our own homes, and our own communities. ... In Virginia, accounts have reached us of its prevalence both in Charleston and Norfolk, and cases have occurred all along the Kanawha, from Point Pleasant to the Salines. In the former place, a number of deaths have occurred, and the whole community are intensely alarmed as to the progress. [133]

Responding to the warning, Charlestown officials passed an ordinance requiring streets to be cleaned, trash to be burned, and cellars to be limed. It was a start.

Although cool weather slowed the cholera outbreak in the East, the disease was already infecting travelers from New Orleans. They boarded the steamboats heading upriver and spread it along the Mississippi and Ohio River towns. In the West, it flourished in the warm, wet winters of California, attacking the settlers with a vengeance. It was already there, brought with the ships stuffed with settlers from New Orleans, from those who trekked through the Panama jungle to the Pacific, and from others approaching El Dorado from the Rio Grande.

While the Company's odds of surviving the cross country journey were enhanced by the experience, discipline, and skill imparted by its Mexican War veterans, its two physicians, and its savvy guide, most members also credited a higher power, or destiny, or just plain luck with their fortune. By month's end, fire on a steamboat docked at St. Louis had spread to the city, burning a quarter of it, incinerating much of the river traffic, and causing an estimated five million dollars of devastation. The men from Jefferson County had missed "seeing the elephant" and breathed a sigh of relief.

Figure 32. St. Josephs, Missouri, ca. 1840.

May 1849, St. Josephs, Missouri

Despite the Company's loss of Thomas W. Washington from cholera, three Jefferson Countians joined the group at St. Josephs, including two Washington relatives: Noblet Herbert, a cousin of Frank Washington, and Lawrence B. Washington, Frank's brother. When the company made camp, they named it after one of their officers, a tradition they continued throughout the journey.

May 5, 1849, Camp Aisquith

From J. Harrison Kelly

Our entire company will be here this evening, three or four having been absent in charge of the mules belonging to us. It is our intention to strike our tents on Monday morning — cross the Missouri river at this point — and get ourselves into the old trail, at an early day next week. Our guide was dispatched a few days since to select the best point for crossing the river, and he decided in favor of St. Josephs. Since my [arrival] here (22d. ult) the Ferry has been one complete jam — indeed you cannot get much nearer [than] one-fourth of a mile, at any time, unless you [go] on foot, and then you must edge between [the] mules, wagons, &c. We may make the attempt to cross on Monday, but I think we shall be at least two days unless we fare much better than those who have preceded us.

For the satisfaction of those who may have friends and relations in the Company, it may be as well to say, that all are well, with the exception of a few who have colds — indeed, a week ago, nearly every person in this place was thus attacked, [but none] of our Company, however, at this time, are confined to bed by sickness. Several of our men have been unwell, but nothing more than diarrhoea. We have connected with our train a wagon built expressly for carrying the sick, which, however we hope to have no use for. We have fifteen wagons, two of the bodies of which are built of sheet iron, and made perfectly waterproof. They are built in the shape of a boat, and are capable of bearing up some hundreds of pounds of freight, should we wish to use them as boats for crossing large streams of water. Our other wagons are strongly built, and look as though they would see us over the plains safely. Three-fourths of those going from this point drive mules or oxen — look where you will almost, and you see a yoke of twelve attached to a wagon. It is quite lively to see a dozen or twenty of these teams strung along the road, and it is more common here than a carriage is in Charlestown.

We have, in the provision way, 13,300 pounds of flour and 2,000 pounds of pilot bread — up to 8,000 pounds of bacon — lots of crushed s[oda crackers] — several barrels of molasses — beans, rice, dried fruit, coffee and tea in abundance, &c., &c. so we don't look much as though we are starving. Our wagons were loaded yesterday and today. They will contain from 2,000 to 3,000 pounds, but surely six mulês can wag along smartly with this load.

The Company had a general meeting on Wednesday morning last, when the following men were received as members: Noblet Herbert, James M. Manning and Lawrence B. Washington.

We have procured the services of a guide (Frank Smith) who is to conduct us to the Valley of the Sacramento. He has been over the route on several occasions and is respected as a man of good character.

The members of our Company have become somewhat familiarized with camp life, and while some are pleased, there are many who have no relish for this sort of life. Last night we had a perfect soaker in the way of rain. It descended in torrents and at times the very heavens seemed to be opened, and the bosom of the ground opened up. Fortunately, our position was that nothing short of a second edition of the great flood could have incommoded us seriously.

It is diverting to watch the "boys" as they pursue their different avocations: They are learning to cook in fine style, and by the time we get back we can furnish the Hotels with rare specimens. I saw some bread the other day which looked as sad as though it had lost its relatives! ....

You are aware that the provisions of the Company were on the same boat on which I came to this place. We had some difficulties procuring wagons and drays to haul it to our camp, but at length succeeded, after some trouble in hiring a couple. We had much to haul up to our encampment, but before night they quit us, and it wouldn't do to let our goods lay out on the bank of the river. Then we exhibited the genuine California spirit of the men. We had three wagons of our own at the river, two of which were loaded at once, and quickly sent off by our own boys. The third wagon was loaded with more than it could comfortably hold. However, they had the spunk, and they attached three fifth chains and hauled themselves up. I counted thirty-five of them harnessed, and they toted the wagon along with all imaginable ease. Indeed, all things considered, I do not think our Company is excelled by any, in indomitable energy and determination.

The lightning of the Old Dominion is as vivid as in this region of country — it is "brilliantly brilliant," just here. Yesterday it played many pleasing phantasms in the sky, but at night it disappeared, and the rain came down. "You'd better believe" the sentinels caught it some. Our tents are made of the very best material, inasmuch as they protect us completely from the violence of the storm without. Those who had not carefully ditched around their tents paid for their negligence in a feeling manner. How vastly uncomfortable is the cold water rolling smoothly, and a little rivulet underneath you, and there is no remedy, but you must lay there and take it coolly.

There is not half as many emigrants around us at present as there were a week ago. The large majority have made a start on the motto, "there's luck in leisure."

The Post Office at this place is overrun with business. We have a batch several times a week. Having some letters to post the other day, and finding the outside "brimming" over with letters, I told the Postmaster. He came out with a large nail keg and said to me, "Well, this makes five and half full of letters I have taken from that place this morning." This ... may give you some idea of the crowd now at this place. [134]

Figure 33. "Ferry Crossing, Oregon Trail," by Ezra Meeker, 1906

The Company hired Frank S. Smith as a guide before leaving St. Joseph. He was experienced in traversing the Oregon trail, and on the evening of May 26th, Vincent Geiger noted:

> ... we had a general meeting of the company, and by a unanimous vote, we took our Guide in as a full member of our company. Our Captain & Lieutenants [First Commander, Robert H. Keeling; Second Commander, Smith Crane; Third, Joseph E. N. Lewis] then resigned and placed the entire command & supreme control of our company in the hands of Mr. Smith, and declared him our leader & Captain. He appeared and, in a suitable manner, thanked the company for what they had done. [135]

Travelers setting out from St. Josephs were warned to join a wagon train and avoid lagging behind — there was safety in numbers. Those who ignored the warning were lucky if they just lost their livestock and not their lives.

May 6, 1849

> From J. Harrison Kelly
>
> This morning we struck our tents and had our "plunder" removed on to the steamer *Sacramento*, for the purpose of crossing over the river. There are some 3,000 oxen lying at the river awaiting their "turn" in the ferryboat. There has been such a jam ever since my arrival, and ferries above and below are crowded to such an extent, we shall have teams for hundreds of miles in length.
>
> There is no Sabbath here — business goes on with the same regularity as though no day had been set apart. A merchant admitted that he sold goods to the amount of $___ on Sunday — indeed, there is no credit done in this place. The merchants and mechanics are "coining money" here. It is impossible to get any article made [in less than] a week.
>
> It is reported in camp that the Pittsburg Company had an engagement with the Indians. There are so many conflicting accounts that I scarce know which to believe.
>
> I give you two of the reports: the Indians buried a chief and placed some memorials on the tomb of the deceased. Some of the Pittsburg Company laid sacrilegious hands on these mementos and destroyed them. The Indians became infuriated, attacked the Company, and carried off their mules. Subsequently they were recaptured by the Company. Another story is that the Indians stole the mules, and then a fight ensued in which six Indians were killed and the mules were taken by the Company. The fight took place nine miles above. As there are so many versions to the story, in what form will it be when it reaches the border of the Atlantic? The report generally believes that the Pittsburg Company were the villains — that they stole forty mules from the Indians — the Indians stole their own back and those of the Pittsburg Company. Next day the Company collected themselves and pursued, had a fight and killed half a dozen Indians, and got their mules back. [136]

May 8, 1849, Indian Territory

The effects of our Company are now in Indian Territory. [137] We shall start in a day or two, and camp again in a few days. We have met with no other serious inconveniences by the way, although some have had some difficulties. Courage, ... and we'll go through.

It is more than probable that Daniel M. Moler takes the place of Mr. James Mc Curdy, going to California. Mr. McCurdy [leaves] after "sober second thought," and Mr. Moler is anxious to join our enterprise....

Your friend,

J.H.K. [138]

May 11, 1849, Kickapoo Nation, Indian Territory, Camp Keeling

From J. Harrison Kelly

The Charlestown (Va.) Mining Company crossed the Missouri River on Monday and Tuesday last, and encamped on the beach for several nights. The "b'hoys" stood it admirably — no tents erected — all took it on the sand, with the blue sky above, except those who were compelled to stand as sentinels, who had no where to lay their weary heads. Had you or your readers seen us lassoing the mules, and dragging them on board the boat, you would have had an agreeable treat. We have reduced the art of lassoing to a perfect science, and we make considerable display of this dexterous art.

On Wednesday morning one-half of our train started for a camping ground seven miles distant. Of all miserable roads, the one from the river to this point takes the lead. For miles the wagons were sunk up to the hubs, and none of your regularly broken teams to help us out of the lurch, but instead thereof, the wildest sort of cattle — mules that had never smelt leather before — they were everlastingly jumping Jim Crow, "first upon the heel taps, then upon the toe." As the shades of evening set in we arrived at this point, with no other mishaps than a wagon, midway, with a broken axle tree, and several "bounds" for the same fix. On the next day, the other half of our train joined us. The unfortunate wagon had been "righted" but was soon in distress again, caused by the breaking of the tongue. Although we have our mules well picketed, it seems almost impossible to keep these wiry creatures — they are like the eel, as soon as you think you have them securely, that's just the time you have'nt them! The other night we had a stampede on the small order — some twenty of our critters pulled up the pickets, and went "kiting" over the prairie. After hard labor, and the loss of no small quantity of temper and sweat, they were secured. During night, mules will escape, do as we may — but we have been fortunate enough to secure all, except probably three of four.

> We are already in the land of "snakes." We have killed rattlesnakes, moccasins, copperheads, &c. It is now with us "wake snakes, Junebugs about."
>
> I have been in no section of the country that presents half the inducements for locating, so far as nature is concerned. We are just on the bluff, overlooking two most beautiful and attractive prairies, rich with herbage — a clear rivulet sends the gentle murmurings on the wings of the wind, and at eventide, when all nature seems to be enjoying repose, it thrills upon the ear with a soft and charming cadence. [139]
>
> **May 12, 1849**
>
> On yesterday afternoon we had a "shower," — It did no other damage than swim off some of our fifth chains and such other light gear! After the cessation of the rain I went a visiting to my neighbors to see how they had fared. Their houses presented scenes of desolation — the rich marl being worked ready for the potter's hand — beds, sacks, ovens, &c., towering up to keep them from the effects of the flood below.
>
> We leave in an hour for a camping ground six miles distant.

Members of the Charlestown Company took to the Trail with various degrees of enthusiasm. The Mexican War veterans and most of the working class men had few problems sharing domestic duties with the others in their mess. However, some of the gentlemen in the group took longer to acclimate without their servants (i.e., slaves) to cook, wash, dig latrines, and complete the other less glamorous tasks of the emigrant.

May 13, 1849, Camp Seevers

> From J. Harrison Kelly
>
> The Company reached this point early on yesterday afternoon, designing to remain here until Monday morning. I started off, mounted on a Spanish mule, with a "cow bell" around the neck of a horse I was leading, and some thirty or forty mules following — so you see I was sort o' bellwether for the flock. The country through which we passed has prairie extremely undulating. — Some of the boys shot prairie hens, which make a most delicious fry.
>
> Last night I was on guard, stationed about one-fourth of a mile from camp. Early in the night the wolves broke out in most dolorous cries, sufficient to awaken the sympathies of the hardest heart! Several of the most forward were much nearer me than I was to camp. If they had only come a little nearer I should have given them some gunpowder symphony....
>
> I sent you parts of a rattle from one of our prairie beauties. It was fourteen inches with several rattles had been broken off.
>
> The mules belonging to our Company are branded V.C. — Virginia Company. They do not take this mark of regard very

kindly, but kicked up their heels and went at it some, dragging those who had hold of the lariats down the ravines and up the hills.

The members of the Company are all in the most excellent health, with the exception of the three or four who have diarrhoea, which is inseparably connected with camp life — though none of them are ill enough to be on the sick list. All, thank Providence, are able to do duty.

We strike our tents tomorrow morning and go it in earnest. It is high time, too, that we were off. The road is lined with teams of oxen and mules. Men, women, and children, seem to be all bound for the gold region.

We passed quite a curiosity yesterday, en route to the Sacramento — it was a regularly built house on a wagon, with doors, windows, chimneys, &c. As I passed, I glanced inside, and found every thing snug and trim. Two young ladies were at the window, with whom I passed salutations, and passed on.

The roads on the prairie are in good order, although the deep ravines and high hills make it difficult for us to get along with any thing like rapidity. We must take it slowly and surely, and all will be well. Those who have examined our fixtures pronounce us better "fitted out" than any Company now going over the plains.

The Pittsburg Company that I referred to in a previous letter, have been arrested by the commanding office at Fort Kearney. It appears that they wantonly desecrated the burial mound of the Indians, and being remonstrated with, fired upon and killed quite a number of them. If the account be correct, it is a matter of gratification that they are in custody.

The bill of fare for dinner today, was "bean soup" — meats, salt pork — desert, short cake. If we fare as well, all the time, we shall come out No. 1.

I spoke in a former letter of Mr. McCurdy's determination as a member of our Company. He told me today, that he believed he would continue his membership, and go with us to the Sierra Nevada.

We have some hundred and thirty horses and mules, and one of the best mountaineers for a guide, that ever crossed the plains. Today we shall only go twelve miles, then fifteen, twenty, twenty-five, and thirty, which will be about our regular drives. We hope to pass all the oxen teams between here and Fort Larame. There is a point near the Fort, of seventy-five miles extent, nearly barren, and the sooner we get over that, the better for all concerned.

I hope to give you an occasional "inkling" by the way, and to keep your readers apprised of our doings.

My kind regards to all friends in the Old Dominion, for many of whom I shall always entertain feelings of the warmest attachment.

In haste, Your friend, &c.,

J.H.K.

On May 15th, the company camped at Iowa Point, [140] near an Indian station under the charge of Col. Alfred J. Vaughan, Jr. Like First Commander Robert Keeling, he had attended Virginia Military Institute, but he had moved to St. Joseph in 1848, where he landed a job as a surveyor for the Hannibal and St. Joseph Railroad. He had just been appointed Indian agent the March before the Virginians arrived. Frank Washington (and probably Keeling) visited the station, where Vaughan showed them the Indian school and farm. Not long after their meeting, Vaughan headed West, where he was appointed a Deputy U.S. Land Surveyor for Southern California.

Figure 34. "Scene on the desert," by George H. Barker, 1853

Two days and about 75 miles later, the Company encountered several graves of emigrants buried along the trail. Clothing, boxes, and other goods lay abandoned, where emigrants had tried to lighten their loads. Sickness, diarrhea, perhaps cholera, infected all of the encampments they passed. As the days and miles on the trial accumulated, these tragedies would come to seem commonplace.

May 25, 1849, Shawnee Nation, 250 miles from St. Josephs, Mo.

From J. Harrison Kelly

The Charlestown Mining Company have reached this point without any attack from their red brethren, although rumor has been busy at work in circulating all sorts of stories. The fact of it is you cannot rely on any thing you hear from this quarter in regard to the ferocity of the different tribes of Indians through which we have to pass.

We have had one death in our Company since I last wrote to you. Mr. Joseph C. Young, of Poolesville, Montgomery county, Maryland, died on the evening of the 22d instant. Mr. Y. had an attack of diarrhoea, which weakened and laid him prostrate for more than a week. After checking the diarrhoea, he was taken with the typhoid fever which terminated his existence. His remains were interred near Little Timber Creek.

The health of our Company is now good — though for two weeks past one-half of our men were more or less ill with the diarrhoea. Several of them had the symptoms of cholera, but all are now on their feet again, and the Surgeon reports to me this evening only two men unfit to stand guard — (Messrs. Hamilton C. Harrison and Benjamin Hoffman, both of this county.) They, however, are recovering rapidly and able to walk about.

Several of the men made narrow escapes with their lives within the past week. One of the teams, under the charge of Noblet Herbert, ran off — the saddle turned and threw him between the mules and under the front axletree. He held on for a minute and then released his hold, when one of the wheels passed over his hair, but without touching his head — this may be truly called a hairbreadth escape.

Daniel Fagan, of Winchester, was riding the off saddle mule, when it became frightened, and the saddle turning, the team ran off. His foot was fastened in the stirrup, and before the mules could be stopped he was dragged some 30 yards. Providentially he was uninjured, not having even a bruise. He remarked to me than he was frightened only once while in this perilous situation, and that was when he was being dragged along he looked back and saw one of the front wheels of the wagon within a foot of his head.

The mules attached to W.J. Burwell's team ran off, unseating the wagon, and presenting a most perfect wreck to all appearances, but things were not quite so bad when we came to make an examination. E.M. Aisquith and Thos. C. Moore were riding in the wagon at the time, and serious apprehensions were felt for their safety. Fortunately the wagon was loaded with bacon, soft and greasy, which neither broke their limbs nor injured them otherwise — though I don't vouch for their not being frightened.

We are now some forty miles from Fort Kearney, formerly known as Fort Childs, and are averaging about 20 miles per day. Several times we have travelled 28 miles, and then again as low as 12 miles per day. Our guide says he will put us through in 100 days, or by the 1st of September. We are now where Bryant was some twelve days later last season, and still he reached California on the 1st of September.[141] Bryant is only some four or five days in our advance at present.

Within three days we have passed some three hundred teams, and our guide supposes that we cut off at the junction of the St. Joseph and Independence trail not less than 1000 teams.

It is utterly impossible to make a rational conjecture in regard to the number who are ahead, or how far they are in advance. Probably about 1000 wagons, some of whom are reported to be five hundred miles ahead, but I don't believe a word of it.

This is the strangest climate in all creation — the wind as keen and searching, as the search warrant of a magistrate. It seems to enter into and chill the very heart strings. Yesterday we had the coldest kind of thunder gust I ever experienced. It rained and blew like a regular March storm, and the way things looked squally was a caution to those who expected this to be a trip of sport and pleasure.

We meet very few returning — not half as many as I expected.

There is much of interest to note, but in truth I have not five minutes time to write. It is raining like "flugeons," cold as December, wind piercing, bread to bake, coffee to make, meat to fry, mules to pickett, the guard to station, and a "mighty sight" of other things to attend to, so I cannot write you more.

Capt. Keeling has resigned his office as captain of the Company.

Yours, with respect,

J.H.K. [142]

The Company's next major stop was Fort Kearney, built by the U.S. Army in the Spring of 1848 to protect emigrants from Indian attacks. It was located on the Platte River, near the point where the trail from Independence, Missouri, joined the westward trail from Omaha and Council Bluffs. This military outpost, then consisting of a few frame and adobe structures and a number of tents and sheds, served as a resupply station and post office. After stopping here for rest and resupply, most travelers followed the trail along the Platte River 330 miles west to Fort Laramie. [143]

Figure 35. Fort Kearney, ca. 1849

May 28, 1849, Fort Kearney

From J. Harrison Kelly

The Charlestown Mining Company reached this point early today, and camped for the purpose of examining the several loads in the wagons, in order to see what articles might most easily be dispensed with. We are now 320 miles from St. Joseph, and 390 from Fort Independence. — Formerly, a fortification existed at the mouth of the Platte river, bearing the name of Fort Kearney, which has lately been evacuated, and the name transferred to the present fort, known heretofore as Ford Childs.

The Commandant at the Fort reports that thirty-one hundred wagons are in our advance. — Each of these teams average eight oxen, which makes twenty-five thousand head of oxen ahead of us! This is enough to startle the stoutest heart, for all who have passed over the road state that it is impossible for so great a number as this to subsist on the plains!

We intend either selling or throwing away, several thousand pounds of Bacon, Flour, &c., in order to lighten our wagons as much as possible, for we find that no headway can be made with our present loads. Our guide, Mr. Frank Smith, one of the best that ever travelled over the road, says that he will take us through in sixty-five days from this point, if our wagons have not more than fifteen or eighteen hundred pounds. — Our object is to get to California, and we must part with a good many things we would not, were it possible for us to take them along. We must dispense with our tents, among other things, and take it in the open air. Last night I made a trial of this kind of rest, and I found quite a sweet repose.

Yesterday and today, we saw quite a number of antelopes, but our boys couldn't get within "a gunshot" of them, so we didn't bring them down. The only game is prairie hens, plovers, larks, and other small birds.

Fort Kearney is situated on Grand Island, in a most beautiful location. The waters of the Platte surround it, whilst in front is a vast plain of almost illimitable extent — the eye wanders for some object of relief, but nothing presents itself save the vast plain, clothed in most luxuriant herbage.

Those who have never passed through this country can have no idea of the dull and monotonous life the emigrant lives, or rather drags out — for as to living, we don't do that, so we don't — we only exist on very poor subsistence! All along, it has been bacon and short cake, until yesterday, when it was determined that our wagons should be lightened. We then "dipped" into the molasses, sugar, vinegar, raisins, cheese, tobacco, and a few other nicknacks — delicacies which liked to have turned the heads of some of the boys.

In consequence of this general distribution, there was good living in camp for a day or two. We had fritters, raisin pudding, &c. The fact of it is, we are "some," when it comes to making nice things!

I have been much disappointed in regard to the weather we have on the plains. I calculated on weather hot enough to bake bread in the sun! but instead of that the stormy west wind makes a thick heavy coat entirely comfortable.

Whilst in camp, on several occasions, we were assailed by a swarm of bugs, numbering as many as the locusts of Egypt. We were compelled to turn out, and surround our mules, fearing a stampede.

I have spoken of the number in our advance — as to how many are in our rear, I cannot say with any accuracy. We have passed as many as a hundred wagons in a day, and the whole road seems to be swarming with emigrants.

The members of our Company have all been restored to good health, and there is not one on the sick list. We have good cause to be thankful for this, as many companies have suffered much, and many died. Scarce a day when we do not pass the grave of some one who started as buoyant in spirits, and with as fair prospects as ourselves — but we have been made to differ with them in this respect. Man is truly ungrateful — for although we have been blest, we fail to render that praise and thankfulness which grateful hearts should offer up.

We have understood that flour and bacon will not bring over a cent a pound at the Fort — we shall probably leave ours to perish on the wayside.

Mr. Frank Smith, our guide, has been elected our Captain, with supreme authority. Under his direction, I think we will get along in perfect safety.

Fort Kearney consists of some half dozen long, low houses, built of sod cut square, piled up, and covered with the same. It presents quite a novel appearance. The houses are lined with heavy osnaburg, and said to be very comfortable.

I expected to write to many of my friends whilst on my route but really the thing can't be done. There is something to do every moment during the day, and at night all are so much fatigued that they go to their beds with a perfect rush.

The trip over the country is entirely free from danger, so far as Indians are concerned. There has not been an hour since we left St. Joseph that we were not in sight of other trains of emigrants.

I am blessed with most excellent health, and believe I will get through safely. I will write to you whenever I can, but presume my next will be from Fort Laramie, some 300 miles distant. — There are monthly mails from the Fort, and you may not get this one for more than a month.

May 28, 1849, Monday Evening.

We disposed of most of our surplus articles at the Fort — though at about one-fourth what they cost us.

I find that Fort Kearney is not on Grand Island, but on the border of the Platte river.

My respects to friends,

J.H.K. [144]

> It may be sir, that the politicians of the United States are not so fastidious as some gentlemen are, as to disclosing the principles on which they act. They boldly preach what they practise. When they are contending for victory, they avow their intention of enjoying the fruits of it. If they are defeated, they expect to retire from office. If they are successful, they claim, as a matter of right, the advantages of success. They see nothing wrong in the rule, that to the victor belong the spoils of the enemy.

Senator William Learned Marcy, remarks in the Senate, January 25, 1832, *Register of Debates in Congress*, vol. 8, col. 1325., vol. 8, col. 1325.

June 1849, Jefferson County, Virginia.

As the weather grew warmer, residents' concerns about cholera escalated. Harpers Ferry citizens added their voices to the growing chorus who insisted that sanitary regulations be put in place. Persons living along the canal in South Bolivar were warned to keep their hog pens clean. The stench was almost unbearable, and they would be the first to be visited by the scourge. Doctors Nicholas Marmion and James Garry used the columns of the local newspapers to debate whether cholera had already arrived. [145]

The argument between J.S. Gallaher and J.W. Beller over appointments to office had also gone from a simmer to a boil. Beller, who had campaigned for a spot on the County Court, claimed that he and several other Democrats had been denied seats by the Whig majority already in office. Gallaher retorted that party politics played no role in the selection. There was a surfeit of qualified candidates, and those not chosen should try again later.

The "patronage" or "spoils" system had been government policy since Jefferson's administration, although it truly came into its own during the reign of Andrew Jackson. Democrat Beller predicted that "A day of reckoning will soon come, and those who now set in high places will be driven by the indignation of an insulted and outraged people, like stubble before fire, until the last lingering vestige has been swept into the depths of obscurity."

Gallaher, defending the Whig administration's replacement of Democratic office holders with Whigs remarked:

> Thus things have been managed for the last twenty years. And now that an honest old Hero has taken the reins of government in hand, and is displacing a portion of those who have been at the public crib all their lives, the cry is raised of "proscription," "Disgraceful Outrage,"

&c. They talk of Democracy and Republicanism, and yet desire that their spoilsmen should remain in office during their lives, and that their children should succeed them. Away with such hypocritical cant! [146]

Both editors, no doubt, realized that the battle over patronage went far beyond the appointment of a local postmaster or county justice. When California joined the Union, thousands of State and Federal jobs would be created. Sacramento (if it became the capitol) would become the Tammany Hall of the West. A man heading West might make a fortune with a pick and shovel, but there were other ways to get rich.

Figure 36. "Chimney Rock," by George H. Barker, J.M. Hutchings, Placerville, Ca., 1853.

June 1, 1849, near Chimney Rock [147]

The Company went into camp near the river, where there was good grass for the mules. They had filled their casks with good, pure spring water and cut firewood a few miles distant and now were settling in for the night. Sentries had been set, for hostile Indians prowled the area, waiting to take advantage of poorly defended wagon trains.

About sundown, a small party went to the river on a fishing excursion. According to diarist Geiger, an hour or two later,

> ... one of them returned stating that a party of Indians were crossing the river. Immediately all hands were preparing their guns, pistols, &c. to give the red-men a warm reception. Capt. Smith with a small party went to the river expecting to encounter the enemy. Sure enough, some objects could be discerned in the river making for the shore. Every man

was excited. They fell flat to the ground in order to conceal them selves, the better to give a fire. Every gun was charged & every eye gazed eagerly at the Indians, who in a few moments advanced nearer, when, lo, & behold, the Indians proved to be six large elk crossing the river. The men imprudently left their hiding places & drove the elk back — thus losing the chance of a good roast.

The next day, the Company laid up to rest their stock. Some of the men were busy washing and cooking. Others spent their time writing, reading, cleaning their guns, or fishing. One or two were singing and fiddling. The men were living high, feasting on lambs quarter greens, stewed peaches, rice, and molasses. Some even had peach pie. Elk had been dropped from the menu.

Frank Washington took the opportunity to write a poem:

TO MY NATIVE STATE

Virginia, Virginia, still thy valley fair I see,
While each hour with "weary step & slow" I'm wandering from thee;
   As visions of departed years come swiftly o'er my mind,
They bring to me each hallow'd spot which I have left behind.
   Tis not because thy hills are green, thy valleys fair to see,
Thy forests clothed with varied tints & fill'd with harmony,
   'Tis not because thy skies are bright as Italy's in hue,
Or on thy distant mountains rests a veil of shadowy blue,
   Tis not that thou hast ever been fair Freedom's dwelling place,
Whence warriors brave & statesmen too, a noble lineage trace,
   Nor is it that the fire first burned, thy sacred hills upon,
"Whose light with hallow'd radience now to all the world hath gone.
   Ah no, not these, nor other charms my muse might well proclaim,
Which throws while now I think of thee, a magic round thy name;
   There's something more enchanting still that bids my Spirit flee,
O'er all the weary waste of miles betwixt myself & thee.
   Just where a smiling landscape looks upon thy mountains blue,
Where met the waters on their way and swept their barriers through,
   There dwelt a maid whose sunny face, & soul of guileless love,
Around my youthful heart a chain of sweetest bondage wove.
   I woo'd her & I won her & it boots not now to tell,
The shadow after shadow that upon our pathway fell;
   We stood beside the altar & the priest pronounced us one,
And I felt that I had all the world in her whom thus I won.
   And now four years have nearly passed since on that happy day,
My stormy youth subsided to the peaceful calm of May;
   And cherubs two have bless'd my home as noble boys I ween,
As ever round the alter of domestic love were seen.
   And thus I thought my cup of bliss was full & I would glide,
With sweet contentment, peace & love, upon life's onward tide;
   But ah! a change came o'er me & I have left my home,
A wanderer to a stranger land, mid howling wastes to roam.
   Upon Pacific's distant shores is heard a startling cry,
A sound that wakes the nations up as swift the tidings fly;
   An El Dorado of untold wealth a land whose soil is gold,
Full many a glittering dream of wealth to mortal eyes unfold.
   O gold! how mighty is thy sway, how potent is thy rod!
Decrepid age & tender youth acknowledge thee a God;
   At thy command the world is sway'd, as on the deep blue sea,
The Storm King rules the elements that roll so restlessly.
   And see, the crowd is rushing now across the arid plain,
All urged by different passions on, yet most by thirst of gain;
   And I, my home & native state, have left thy genial shade,
To throw my banner to the breeze where wealth, like dreams, is made.

June 2, 1849, near Chimney Rock [149]

While most of Virginia Company used the rest stop to catch up on chores, Frank Washington and a few companions set out for Chimney Rock. Writing to his wife, he described the view from near the top of the formation, where he had scratched his name among the emigrants who had preceded him.

From B.F. Washington:

My letter is not off yet. As soon as I had finished the above, I started off in advance of the wagons to visit "Chimney," or as it should more properly be called "Monument Rock." It was about three miles distant. When I reached it I climbed up with considerable difficulty to the top pyramid, and had a splendid view of the surrounding butts or bluffs. There are two or three landings after you reach the apex of the pyramid, to which, however, you are compelled to ascend with the assistance of artificial steps cut in the soft sand rock. The striking originality of this natural mountain does not at all diminish your appreciation. The distance that lends enchantment to the view in ordinary cases, here falls short of the reality. By what strange freak of nature, this great monument of the plains, should have been revealed in its present form (for it has been the result of the action of the elements) it is impossible to say. The material of which this monument is formed, is almost entirely very compact sand, yet there are intermixed horizontally, strata of sand rock. This whole formation, both pyramid and column, was doubtless at one time a high and abrupt hill. Thuswise cut from its peculiar orientation, it has assumed, under the effect of wind and storm, its present shape. This column is so high that when you are at the base, the multitude of swallows that infest its hoary top, appear no larger than bees.

I ascended to the third landing by means of the above mentioned steps, but there was one still higher and of so precarious a nature, that I thought it prudent not to adventure it, even with the incentive in view, with the aid of my height, of inscribing my name higher up than any else. I contented myself with a somewhat lower feat, and there high up on the great monument of the plains stands our names in bold relief. If I shall never be fortunate enough to occupy a position in the Temple of Fame, my immortality shall at least be secured, here in the wilderness, until the first or second storm, shall obliterate its frail record forever. Yes, in fact, the very column that excites the wonder and admiration of the passer by, shall itself pass away, and perhaps in another year, this noble monument, which has so long stood as a landmark to the wayfarer, and doubtless the wonder and admiration of the rude and uncultivated intellect of the savage will crumble before the storms of a very few more years. Already its proportions have diminished more than two-thirds since its first discovery, and its dissected fragments scattered at its base, and the numerous crevices in its columns, show plainly that the day of its destiny will soon be over.

After you leave "Chimney Rock," and continue up the North Fork of the Platte, the scenery assumes the most strikingly original and romantic appearances you can possibly conceive of. You cannot divest your mind of the idea that you view, in the numerous butts or bluffs, on either hand, the remains of some magnificent city, built by a race long since passed away. Whose lofty columns and domes, mouldering under the effects of time, while they manifest an architectural taste differing from our modern notions, yet still adheres to the great rules governing that art. As I passed along between these immense structures, it was hard to divest my mind of the idea that the spirit of some departed giant, (or the proportions of these great castles suggest such tenants,) would rise up before me and reproach us for invading the silent streets of their deserted and mouldering city. I never saw scenery as truly romantic and as well calculated to inspire feelings of the sublime.

If I had space and time it would be my aim to enter into a scientific discourse as to the causes which have produced these singular and fantastic objects, for I have never read any thing on the subject, nor do I know what Fremont says about them, but the limits of a letter will not suffice for this. It is enough in general terms to say that at some distant period in the history of this continent, the whole valley of the Platte and its branches, and in fact the same will apply to almost all the surrounding country, were covered by a large body of moving waters, whose depth correspond to evidences legibly written upon the surrounding bluffs. This is evinced by large quantities of river stone and pebbles as well as heavy deposits of carbonate of lime, only to be found in the beds of streams, being every where found upon the highest of these elevations.

My idea, then, is that this immense body of moving waters, these ancient towers and solitary monuments, were numerous Islands, made by the sand which when the water receded and passed off by some change in the physical features of this continent through the great channels — the Missouri and its tributaries, as well as other streams — were left in the present position, rising from the bed (or as it is now a valley) of this stream. You can even see distinctly where the water came to on the Islands, and the gradual layers, one above the other, extending with peculiar exactness from one bluff to another, showing the gradual process of their formation. But enough of this. I have no doubt you are tired of my excessive learning.

Remember me affectionately to all inquiring friends.

B.F.W.

Figure 37. "Ash Hollow," by George H. Barker, J.M. Hutchings, Placerville, Ca., 1853.

On June 8th, the party reached Ash Hollow, where they found several springs of good water and a large number of ash trees. There they encountered several emigrant camps as well as a small party of Sioux Indians. The trail dropped sharply from the high bluffs to the south bank of the North Platte. [150]

Before leaving St. Louis, the Company had been divided into several messes, each with its own leader and wagon. Although this military style organization had command advantages, it was also a source of competition and friction. On June 9th, Tom Moore refused to let Pilot McKay have a mule for his team. Geiger observed, "Evident signs of dissatisfaction appeared, & many spoke of a general 'bust up.' " Another incident occurred on June 11th, when William Davidson from another mess killed a deer and brought it into camp. Geiger recorded that "In the partial & prejudiced distribution of it, our mess was left without. " [151]

In contrast to Geiger's record of discontent among the Company, J.H. Kelly's reports to the Charlestown newspapers rarely hint at internal strife.

Jefferson County's Fourth Estate, 1840-1850

Early June, 1849, San Francisco, California

About the time that Frank Washington was penning his letter home, Dr. William M. Gwin and David C. Broderick were arriving in San Francisco by separate steamers. The former, a slaveholding ex-Senator from Mississippi, had vowed that he would take charge of writing the California constitution, become one of her U.S. Senators, and return to Congress to promote a proslavery Democratic agenda. The latter, a blue collar Tammany Hall politician, had come west to oppose the proslavery faction of the party and to fight for California's entry into the Union as a free state.

Both would become U.S. Senators and enemies in the process of doing so. Each would draw hordes to their causes and would have a profound effect on several Jefferson County '49ers who had come west, ostensibly to find gold.

Figure 38. Senators David Broderick, 1820 - 1859 (left) and William Gwin, 1805 - 1885

Figure 39. Chimney Rock; Court-House Rock (right), George H. Barker, J.M. Hutchings, Placerville, ca., 1853.

June 11, 1849, Chimney Rock, City of the Plains

From Benjamin F. Washington to his wife, Georgiana

As I shall probably have an opportunity in a day or two of sending a letter back to the settlements, having already missed several by not having one in readiness, I avail myself of a few hours tarrying here, to prepare for you a few hastily thrown together lines. I am pleased to inform you that I continue to be blessed with perfect health, and am still progressing on my way without accident or difficulty. We have seen very little indeed so far worthy of note, and I supposed it impossible that any country in the world, of the same extent, could present features of such sameness and little variety. From St. Josephs to the Platte Valley, a distance of near 300 miles, there is one continued succession of hill and valley, or, in other words, one immense and rolling prairie, with frequently no tree visible for miles of travel, and here and there a trifling stream meandering among the hills. Occasionally, however, upon these streams you see some beautiful bottom land, and the trees, which grown along in such places, gives it quite an inviting and interesting appearance. Yet generally the journey of one day is like that of the day before, and the wayfarer, with teams, finds himself more interested in the conditions of the roads than in the scenery.

After we reach the Platte the immediate country around us changes its appearance. Here we enter on a low flat sandy bottom, with the Platte on the right and a continuous range of bluffs on the left, supposed by some to have been formed by the action of the wind blowing up the sands of the valley, as they resemble very much in formation snow drifts. This, however, is doubtless an erroneous view, as we find upon the tops of the highest of them large quantities of river stone and pebbles, as well as heavy deposits of carbonate of lime.

Our course up the Platte valley for 120 miles to the lower crossing on the South Fork is about 3 miles above the junction. — This distance too is characterized by the like sameness of scenery, the same flat plain shut in by bluffs. The Platte River is peculiar in its characteristics, compared to rivers with which we are familiar. Its prominent features is that it is without banks — totally devoid of trees, generally along its shores, and of rocks it has none either there or in its bed. In most places it is more than a mile in breadth, and from the road along its course the traveller sees it rolling with even and unchanging gate, its turbid and muddy waters onward, apparently on a level with himself.

We crossed the Platte as I said about 10 miles from where we strike the valley. Here we had a tall time. The place where we crossed is at least one mile and a quarter from shore to shore, the current compelling us to take a diagonal direction with the stream. The mode of proceeding was thuswise: Every man was called up to be prepared for wading. Long ropes were then attached to the fifth chain of each wagon, and in addition to the six mules, about twelve or fifteen men were hitched up and thus they set off. We took over in this way, 3 or 4 wagons at a time and succeeded during the evening in getting them all safely over. The river is fordable, as far as depth is concerned, almost any where, but the quick sands render it safe in but two or three places.

Shortly after we left the crossing we passed an encampment of about 1500 or 2000 Indians, men, women and children. They were of the Sioux tribe, a handsome and comely race of Indians. — they have no local habitations but go about in companies from place to place, sojourning as long as they see proper wherever fancy or interest or something else suggests. They appear to be very friendly offering their hands to us and asking "how." The boys traded with them for a good many small articles, such as moccasins, &c., and we also procured some ponies from them, of which, and mules, they have a goodly quantity. I saw several squaws very richly dressed in their own mode, who were really handsome, the innocence of their look and the grace of their manner little comporting with the savage wildness of their natures. The children, also, of which there seem to be an inexhaustible stock, were quite handsome and goodly looking. They live in tents made of raw Buffalo hide — they pitch and strike them with remarkable facility, and they present an air, to one leading a prairie life, of considerable comfort.

As I have dated my letter above, you will perceive we are in the vicinity of the great Chimney Rock, certainly as great a natural curiosity as any of the general objects of attraction of which our country boasts. But this is not all — the surrounding bluffs, at a distance of some five or six miles, the work of the same process by which Chimney Rock was formed, present, in a remarkable and striking degree, the time worn ruins of some vast buildings — I have thus called it the City of the Plains, from the striking resemblance. Chimney Rock is a tall symmetrical column of some hundred feet, rising perpendicularly from the apex of a pyramid. The formation is principally of sandstone and sand, and is a striking landmark to the wayfarer, for a distance of some 40 miles before he reaches it. — Fremont and Bryant, I think, give an account of it, so I refer you to them.

The Solitary Town or "Court House," as it is sometimes called, is also a most striking natural curiosity. This is in sight of Chimney Rock, and presents the appearance from the road, in the most remarkable degree you can imagine, of a magnificent Temple in ruins. It rises from the top of a beautiful and grass covered hill to the height of some four or five hundred feet, and covers about four acres of ground. I did not go up to it as I was afoot, yet several of the company did. They represent it as being striking in formation. They succeeded by means of artificial steps in some places in reaching the tops and found the view very fine.

We had last night one of the most terrific thunder storms, accompanied with very heavy hail, that I ever witnessed. The whole black-curtained heavens and earth shook with one prolonged thunder for the space of upwards of an hour. I hit a mule on the head with my hat to keep him from breaking out of camp, and my whole hat, hand and arm glittered with a blaze of electricity. These matters are, however, but little incidents on the Plains, and we receive them as small affairs. Winds and storms are received by us, in the open air, with as much philosophy as if we were home in our tenements.

The quantity of rain on this route is said to be unheard of in the history of the Plains. This has been the case for hundreds and hundreds of miles ahead of us, and consequently the grass is very fine, even in places heretofore represented as barren. We have met Mormons coming in who give us these accounts. This is regarded as providential, otherwise, as in ordinary seasons, it would be impossible for so many cattle to be sustained. In this event there must have been dreadful suffering and mortality among the emigrants. It is now ascertained that there are at least 5,000 teams on this route alone, numbering about 45,000 oxen, mules and horses, and 20,000 human beings. How many there are gone by Santa Fe I have no means of knowing, but presume the number is not small.

We are now within two days march of Fort Laramie, when we reach which we shall have arrived at the point which places us, according to calculation, one-third of the distance to our destination, it being 650 miles to St. Josephs. Well, this sheet is full — so as I have some time left before starting I will begin another. [152]

Figure 40. Fort Laramie, ca. 1845. [153]

Built on a bluff overlooking the Laramie River, Fort Laramie had started life as a trading post in the 1830's. It was purchased on June 6, 1849, by the U.S. Army and turned into a military outpost. In April of that year, the Regiment of Mounted Rifles occupied the site, from which they patrolled part of the Oregon Trail, providing security for emigrants against the increasingly hostile Northern Cheyenne and the Lakota Sioux tribes. [154]

Figure 41. Devil's Gate, ca. 1849, by George H. Barker, J.M. Hutchings, Placerville, Ca., 1853.

About a day's travel west of Independence Rock, they encountered Devil's Gate. It got its name from the Shoshone and Arapahoe Indians. Their legends recorded that an evil beast with large tusks roamed the area, preventing them from hunting and camping in the area. Determined to rid themselves of this menace, they shot at it from the passes and ravines. The angry beast tore the V-shaped opening in the ridge with its tusks and escaped. [155]

About 6 miles after breaking camp, the Company spied a cool spring about 50 yards from the trail. There they met a party of trappers who were returning to the States. The men were carrying mail back, charging 50 cents per letter. Kelly, Byarly, and several others hurriedly composed several letters and sent them on their way.

June 28, 1849, Rocky Mountains, 20 miles east of the South Pass

From J. Harrison Kelly.

Our Company has now passed over at least one-half of the road from St. Josephs, Mo., to California, and all members are in good spirits and quite buoyant in feeling, when all things are taken into consideration.

The members are all in good health, and endure the fatigue of the journey far better than anyone could have supposed. Indeed, those who know us best would be astonished were they to witness the general vivacity of spirit after undergoing the fatiguing marches of the day in the broiling sun, and scorching sand.

I wrote you from Fort Laramie, detailing most of the leading incidents of our journey up to that point. After leaving the Fort we took up the line of march over the "Black Hills," a distance of seventy-five miles, a region of country much dreaded by old mountaineers, on account of the sterility of the soil. We found the country to be much broken and grass somewhat scarce, though our stock looked in tolerable condition after passing these narrows. After leaving these hills we came again to the North Fork of the Platte river, which we crossed after a few days travel up stream, just above Deer Creek. We found the Platte to be about one fourth of a mile in width, and in many places 20 feet deep, so that fording was out of the question. We accordingly took off our two sheet iron wagon beds, made in the shape of boats, and launched them. Quite a number of emigrants were hastily engaged in preparing rafts, by digging out large trees, but our fix was decidedly the best we saw. We commenced crossing about 11 o'clock A.M., and finished the same evening about ten. Just above us, I saw an emigrant from St. Clairsville, Ohio, attempt to swim a mule over, but by some mishap he fell off, and although an expert swimmer, he found a watery grave. I saw several other emigrants make narrow escapes, but we got over without the loss of a single article of property, or accident of any kind. No one who has never seen boating in the West under all the disadvantageous circumstances, can form any idea of the danger and fatigue incident to crossing the Platte. The stream was so swift that we were compelled to start in about half a mile above the point we designed coming out, and then it was necessary to draw the boats up stream again, so that they might be brought out near the right point. It was worse than "confusion confounded" to see the state of things on the west bank when I crossed, about ten o'clock at night. Here laid a wheel, there a wagon body, with our baggage, goods and chattels, scattered over some five or ten acres.

The country through which we have travelled since crossing, is mostly of a barren character — indeed, I have not seen a single acre worthy of cultivation — it is a perfectly barren and mostly sandy waste, and a fall of rain at this season of the year, quite a rarity. From ten to four o'clock the sun is scorchingly hot, whilst the nights are decidedly cold. We are along the Wind River Mountains, a span of the Rocky, which is about the highest point. The mountain is covered with snow, and a day or two since it looked like a large fleecy cloud hung in the Heavens, and from this point presents a most beautiful appearance.

Our ascent has been so gradual and regular that we can scarcely realize the fact that we are fast verging the crossing point of the great mountain in North America — the Back Bone of the Western Continent. No one can have any clear idea of the vast masses of rock, piled high into the very clouds, which surrounds us on either side.

[We have been] travelling along the Sweetwater river, a beautiful stream [with its] head in the mountains — the water is pure and limpid, and quite refreshing. It is the most tortuous a water course I ever saw, and must have started some dark night and lost its way. I think, however, that [the stream has] an additional charm, whilst on its banks is found good herbage for the stock.

A few miles after we struck the Sweetwater, we came to Independence Rock, being a rock of gigantic proportions standing between Rattlesnake Hills and the river. Its name is taken from the fact of its being in an independent position, and a celebration of the 4th of July being held here by an emigrating party some years since.

The most interesting point in the route is the "Devil's Gate," a point in the mountain where the Sweetwater breaks through. The mountain is of solid stone, about three hundred feet in height, through which a perfectly straight cut, from top to bottom, about thirty feet wide, has been made by the rushing of the waters. The "Narrows" is also another point of interest. — There is just enough room for the stream and sometimes a road. Being hemmed in, the water is deep, and as we crossed twice in fifty yards, we have some knowledge of its depth and the difficulties attending its fording. Our folks have got so used to going to bed with their clothes soaking with water, that you need not be surprised when we return, if on every evening you see us wending our way to the Town Run, in order to get a comfortable ducking before we retire.

You may travel for days in this country, and still you have no fuel for cooking purposes save buffalo chips and wild sage. The latter is a small shrub which contains a good deal of turpentine, but take care when it comes down to cooking, and baking bread with willows, about as thick as rye straw — it requires more patience than most of us possess.

Occasionally we come across a train in which we find a number of the fairer portion of creation. Then it is that all the lively recollections of home, and early associations are brought to mind, and we bask in the Elyseums of female society, with peculiar fondness, and long for that period which will return us to our homes and our friends. I have just seen a gentleman who left St. Josephs on the 24th May, who is packing through. He informs me that he passed nearly four thousand wagons, which average at least eight oxen to the team. That makes thirty-two thousand oxen yet to cross where we could barely get a subsistence for our teams. That large numbers will be compelled to turn back or perish on the road, there is no room for doubt. It is a deplorable state of affairs when we reflect that a great portion of those in the rear are women and children! You would be astonished were you to know the number of oxen that have already died — almost every hour we pass them with their heads turned up to the sun.

I also learn from some traders — by whom I shall send this letter — that there are only about fifteen hundred wagons ahead of us. Out of this number there are six hundred ox teams, which we will no doubt head off quite easily in less than a week, so that our prospect is bright.

There has been a great deal of cholera in our rear, and many who left their homes with stout hearts and bright expectations are now entombed on the broad and expansive prairie.

We expect to reach Sutter's Fort in California, the middle of August — about forty-five days from this time, at which time you will again hear from me. If, however, a Government express will carry letters from Fort Hall, I will write from that point — but I have no expectation of that being the case.

We have had fresh meat in camp for several weeks. Mr. James Cunningham and Wm. S. Davidson each killed a buffalo at different periods, which, with antelope, prairie dogs, birds, &c., makes us quite comfortable in the meat line.

My kindest regards to all friends in the Old Dominion.

J.H.K. [156]

July 4th, 1849, Charlestown, Virginia

Independence Day was ushered in by the thunder of canon — then Captain John W. Rowan formed up the procession and marched them from the Court House to the Presbyterian Church, where Rev. Septimus Tustin led the group in prayer. Reader of the Day, Henry Clay Hunter, read the *Declaration of Independence*, and Orator Charles H. Stewart regaled the crowd with patriotic eloquence.

The celebrants reassembled out of town at Burn's Grove, where they feasted on a meal prepared by J.F. Blessing. Then they raised their glasses for a series of toasts:

> Our Union: Cemented by the blood of our ancestors, their children will ever sustain it.
>
> The Old Dominion: The first in the formation of our glorious Union, she will be the last in its dissolution.
>
> The Editor of the *Free Press*: May his fount never run dry.
>
> James W. Duke:
>
> Here's to the health of friends we love,
>
>   I care not in what sphere they move,
>
> Or whatsoe'er their mode may be,
>
>   May they have dined as well as we.

The company returned to Charlestown at an early hour. John S. Gallaher pronounced the event "one of the most agreeable and pleasant jubilees, ever had in our neighborhood — not a single incident occurring to mar the hilarity of the day."

As they watched the sun sink in the west, many residents doubtless said a prayer for their friends and relatives on the Oregon Trail and wondered how they had spent the day. [157]

July 4th, 1849, Green River Crossing, Utah Territory

The Company awoke to a chorus of coyotes. They were encamped in a beautiful valley on the west bank of the Green River, along with hundreds of other pioneers who had recently made the crossing. The Virginians had squeezed through the multitude of encampments on the east bank and used their two sheet iron wagon beds to ferry wagons and goods to the other side. Emigrants without river transportation queued up and paid the Mormon ferrymen $10 per trip. Graves dotted the riverbanks, a mute testimony to the treacherous waters.

Once across the river and settled in, the Virginians put their entrepreneurial skills to work, hiring out their boats at $5 a trip to others who needed to cross. They cleared $175 for their effort.

Tall cotton trees shaded the party, providing reconnaissance points for eagles and ospreys to spot and snatch fish among the river willows. Having drunk their fill, deer, pronghorn antelope and sage grouse retreated to safer ground.

Being the Fourth of July, quartermaster Nat Seevers issued whisky rations. Some had more or less, and the temperance men stuck to water.

They unpacked their little six-pounder canon for the first time on the trip and chained it to a stump. Tom Moore from Harpers Ferry was voted Orator for the Day. Feeling pretty good from his ration of old tanglefoot, he mounted a large tree stump. Steadying himself with an Indian pole, he launched into a patriotic discourse, providing emphasis with blasts from the canon. The noise bounced up and down the valley, rousing cheers from the emigrants and scattering the Indians.

Recalling the experience years later, '49er Ben Hoffman mused that the holiday cannonade "reminded us of home and the endearments of civilization."

The excitement continued into the evening, when a group of soldiers and a posse from Fort Laramie returned to camp from their pursuit of a murderer named Brown. What followed was recorded a by '49er from another company, Alonzo Delano:

> The volunteers had returned, without being successful in capturing Brown, but they had overtaken Williams, who had killed the rascal at the Devil's Gate, and thinking that some example of justice was necessary, they intimated that his presence was required to stand trial before a Green River jury, and he willingly returned — but his companions, dreading delay, would not accompany him. Upon his return it was resolved to try him. As his witnesses would not come, he feared a true representation of facts would not come out,

and he employed B. F. Washington, a young lawyer from Virginia, to defend him. Had he known it, there were witnesses enough in the crowd to have justified him, but as he did not, he was disposed to take advantage of any technicality, and therefore employed counsel.

A court of inquiry was organized — General Allen elected chief justice, assisted by Major Simonton, who, with many of his officers, and a large crowd of emigrants, was present. A jury was empaneled, and court opened under a fine clump of willows. There, in that primitive courthouse, on the bank of Green River, the first court was held in this Godforsaken land, for the trial of a man accused of the highest crime. At the commencement, as much order reigned as in any lawful tribunal of the States. But it was the 4th of July, and the officers and lawyers had been celebrating it to the full, and a spirit other than that of '76 was apparent.

Mr. Washington, counsel for the defendant, arose, and in a somewhat lengthy and occasionally flighty speech, denied the right of the court to act in the case at all. This, as a matter of law, was true enough, but his remark touched the pride of the old commandant, who gave a short, pithy and spirited contradiction to some of the learned counsel's remarks. This elicited a spirited reply, until, spiritually speaking, the spirits of the speakers ceased to flow in the tranquil spirit of the commencement, and the spirit of contention waxed so fierce, that some of the officer's spirits led them to take up in Washington's defence. From taking up words, they finally proceeded to take up stools and other belligerent attitudes. Blows, in short, began to be exchanged, the cause of which would have puzzled a "Philadelphia lawyer" to determine, when the emigrants interfered to prevent a further ebullition of patriotic feeling, and words were recalled, hands shaken, a general amnesty proclaimed, and this spirited exhibition of law, patriotism, "vi et armis," was consigned to the "vasty deep." Order and good feeling "once more reigned in Denmark." Williams, in the meantime, seeing that his affair had merged into something wholly irrelevant, with a sort of tacit consent, withdrew, for his innocence was generally understood, and no attempt was made to detain him. The sheriff did not even adjourn the court, and it may be in session to this day, for aught I know. [158]

Figure 42. Sacramento City, California, 1850

July 4, 1849, Sacramento City, California

Military vessels in port fired a salute at midnight to announce the arrival of Independence Day. No parade was organized or fireworks detonated, except for a few Chinese rockets. The streets were filled with the noise of firecrackers. Window glass shattered and crockery cracked from the reverberations of guns and pistols big and small.

At 1 PM, a sizeable collection of citizens gathered in an oak grove at the rear of the city hall. Rev. Mr. Deal, recently from the Sandwich Islands, opened the exercises with a prayer, followed by Mr. McClennan, who read the *Declaration of Independence*. The Honorable William M. Gwin, former Democratic U.S. Senator from Mississippi, made the closing remarks, urging the citizens of California to immediately organize a State government. [159]

Last year, chatting with Stephen A. Douglas in Washington, Gwin predicted that, since Congress had failed to give California a territorial government, it would be forced to make itself a State. He would go to California, he said, urge residents to adopt that policy, and return within a year as one of its U.S. Senators.

Broderick, Gwin, and Frank Washington would cross pens frequently in the years to come.

Less than 90 miles away, Robert B. Semple, the owner and editor of the *Weekly Alta California*, was firing up his new steam press for the first time. In his last issue, he had voiced the political opinions of many readers:

> Every person appears to be convinced that the Slavery question under the complexion that it now wears in the Atlantic States, defeated the numerous attempts made in the

last congress to give to California a territorial organization, and all men ought to be as firmly assured that unless the citizens of California settle that question for themselves, and do so at once, that it will prevent, defeat or at least protract for years to come, the establishment of any government in the country. Independent of the moral considerations which weigh so heavily in the balance against slavery, and which we have neither time or room to repeat, as a matter of expediency, — as a means of giving to this country a government — it is necessary that the people should insert in their constitution a clause forbidding the introduction of negro or other slavery. [160]

Many Californians celebrating America's Independence were satisfied to exclude black slavery and admission of free negroes in exchange for statehood. However, others saw this maneuver as just the first step in the process of ensuring their dominance over inferior parts of the population. They set to work drafting legislation to weaken the status of Indians, Mexicans, and Chinese in the new State.

Figure 43. Fort Hall, ca. 1850

The Company reached Fort Hall on July 14th. Built in 1834 as a fur trading post, it became part of U.S. Territory in 1846, as part of the treaty with Great Britain over Oregon Territory. Serving as a supply station near the point where the trail to California branched off to the southwest, it was also frequented by Mormons on their way to the Salt Lake. By the time the Charlestown men arrived at the site, it was still being run by Captain Richard Grant, who had been there for a quarter century.

At this time, the Fort's importance as a fur trading town was declining and a U.S. Army post was being established to monitor Indian activity in the area. It was ringed with Indian lodges and still populated by French fur traders. The men from the Charlestown Company bought some skins and a couple of ponies. They purchased some fried chicken that reminded them of home. [161]

August 1849, Jefferson County, Virginia

The months of July through September were known as the "sickly season," because the incidence of diseases like typhoid and cholera tended to rise with the temperature. City dwellers fled their homes for places like Shannondale Springs, where the mineral waters were thought to prevent, or even cure various illnesses.

Jefferson County residents, like many people throughout the country, had observed President Taylor's call for a national day of fasting and prayer. James Beller noted that

> Many who, heretofore, had been but irregular attendants on divine service, were present — giving earnest attention to the words of warning that came from the pulpit. All seemed to appreciate the occasion which had called them together. The heartfelt thanks were offered up to a benificent creator for the blessings which we, individually and in a national capacity, enjoy through His kind providences, as well as the fervent appeals for His continued protection, and for His special interposition to avert the scourge which has already inveloped many portions of our country in gloom, met a sincere response in the heart of each hearer. [162]

Both local editors saw other ominous signs — caused not by cholera, but by the battle over slavery in the new territories. Beller predicted that Congress would not attempt to abolish slavery throughout the States directly. First, it would apply the doctrine of the Wilmot Proviso to prevent the extension of slavery in the new territories. Then it would abolish slavery in the District of Columbia. Next it would outlaw the slave trade among the states. Finally, after several new nonslave states had been admitted, it would pass an amendment abolishing slavery throughout the nation. He concluded:

> ... who cannot foresee the degradation to which the South must be reduced by the course of such legislation? We are not the advocate of slavery in the abstract. But we are the advocate of the rights of the States guaranteed by the Constitution. And these rights all good citizens are called upon to maintain whatever their predilection or prejudices may be on the particular subject involved. We therefore go for resisting the encroachments of the North at the very threshold.

Watching the political turmoil among the Democrats, J.S. Gallaher noted that some believed their party was dissolved, with many of the Northern members now following the Free Soil banner. Others were convinced that their faction was neither dead nor dying. "It certainly has the trembles, said Gallaher, "though its voice is somewhat lusty yet — judging from the noise that it makes when a "head is taken off" by the instrument of its own invention — the "guillotine." [163]

Adding to the residents' worries, none of them had received news from the California Company since June 1. The steamboat *Algonia*, one of many destroyed in the great St. Louis fire, had been carrying thousands of letters from migrants. One letter, partially burnt, said Beeler, reported that "The emigrants were generally getting on well. The cholera had broken out among the Indians, alarming them so much that they had fled from the trail of the emigrants. The Sioux, Pawnees, and Obeyness had all disappeared."

He continued:

> As to the numerous reports that have been in circulation throughout the county as regards this company, we do not believe that there is one shadow of foundation. They are the inventions of depraved imaginations, who find pleasure in doing violence to the feelings of those in our midst, to gratify either malice or malignity against those who are absent. Some of these reports are so preposterous, that they carry with them their own refutation — others again are more plausible, but it is quite soon enough to give them credence, when some authority can be found to give truth and color to their substance. At the last accounts our company expected to reach California by the 10th or 15th of August, and we hope such may be the case. [164]

Actually, the Company was camped on the Salmon Trout River on August 15, where they were overtaken by William S. Long, a friend of B.F. Washington from Berkeley County, Virginia. Traveling by pack mule, he was able to move faster than the wagons. He offered to take Washington with him so they could arrive in California about a week ahead of the rest. Washington borrowed Dr. Bryarly's horse, and the two men left. [165]

Meanwhile, safely in California, William M. Gwin was busy wrangling a seat in the September California Constitutional Convention. [166] He had the ego to believe he should chair the event — others thought he was vain and deluded. But California was a land where men with outlandish schemes and large egos often flourished.

September, 1849, Charlestown, Virginia

The *Virginia Free Press* had finished moving its operation into the second floor of the Market House, and John S. Gallaher was delighted:

> We are now "operating" in the most pleasant printing office in Virginia — whether we refer to the indispensable requisites of light, space, or arrangement. It almost makes us feel like sending out the "old family journal" daily, if we thought we could stand it for six months. [167]

They had first occupied the old Market House in 1833, refurbishing the crumbling building to make it usable. They had moved when the Odd Fellows pulled down the old structure and built a new one.

The county's free public schools had now been in operation for almost two years. They still needed to build more school houses. Until recently, children from indigent families still needed more assistance. "Now," said Gallaher, "it embraces ALL — the high and the low — the rich and the poor." [168]

The partisan battle over government appointments to office had escalated, spreading to every level of government, from the job of the local fish inspector to the federal judiciary. Both Beller and Gallaher had waded deep into the fray, trading blow after blow. [169]

Sacramento, California

Frank Washington arrived in Sacramento a couple of weeks ahead of the former members of the Charlestown, Virginia, Mining Company, who would vote to dissolve the organization on September 16th. While many of the Company would begin mining almost immediately, Washington intended to spend some time scouting out the best location for his own gold mining efforts. In the letter to his wife that follows, he speculates that he intended to mine for three or four months and then return home with a respectable amount of gold. Then he would probably return to California and continue mining for the next few years.

On August 1, California residents elected members to the Constitutional Convention, including Robert Semple as President and William Gwin as one of the members. The Convention opened on September 1, and 45 days later it adopted a Constitution.

The information gained from Frank's fact finding trip, as well as the results of the Convention, would make him reevaluate his goals and send him off in a new direction.

September 9, 1849, Sacramento, California

B.F. Washington to his wife, Georgiana:

A day or two after my arrival here, my Dear Wife, I wrote you a hurried dispatch, in order that I might be in time for the mail by the monthly steamer, simply to advise you of my safe arrival in this land of golden promise, and that my continued enjoyment of that greatest of all blessings, the same perfect health of which you have been hitherto advised. Since that time, I have received your long and melancholy journal. and now having leisure, commence you a more extended account of my journeyings, my movements and prospects, and finally of matters and things in general.

And first, since you speak of those "beautiful rolling prairies" over which you imagine me winding my way, let me simply remark that like a great many other things of which we read, they appear to much greater advantage and clothed in more attractive colors upon paper, than when viewed with the eye. And as for Bryant and Fremont, whom you say you have been studying, the first is a humbug, too ridiculous to speak of to cunning ears — the second is more of a humbug still, for his puerilities are interwoven with a profession of much learning — and as for old Tom Benton, of whom, you do not speak, he is the most miserable humbug of the three, for professing to be learned on a subject which no man can possibly understand intelligently, except of his own observation and experience. [170]

And yet these men (Fremont especially, I mean, for Bryant is too ridiculous to comment on,) have built up a world wide fame, by publishing works giving utterly unfounded descriptions of places, which either from an absence of all practical sense, or some design for misrepresentation, fall utterly short of the real state of facts as they exist. I do not hesitate to say that of all the vast extent of Territory between the Missouri River and the Sierra Nevada or California Mountains, none of it will ever be settled by a permanent population of any importance. I except, of course, the land lying within 20 or 30 miles of the Missouri River, of which I have spoken formerly, and which is perhaps as fine land as any in the world. But I shall not speak of these things at present, but on some future occasion when we are again united, we will talk over all these matters in full.

I cannot say that we experienced any thing that can be called real hardships during our trip. After we left Fort Hall, however, the journey became excessively tedious. We were induced to believe, as was the case with all emigration, by the gross misrepresentations of writers, Fremont particularly, that on Humbodlt or Mary's River we would find any quantity of fine nutritious grasses for our animals — and the Cotton Wood and Willows spoken of, had in the distance an attraction to our imagination which only those who have travelled some fifteen hundred continuous miles, without scarcely once experiencing the luxury of reposing secure from the piercing rays of the sun, beneath the overhanging canopy or tree can appreciate.

After we reached this stream, however, and travelled on it some fifty or sixty miles, our pleasing anticipations were soon dispelled, for a more hideous and revolting desert, as totally devoid of every thing attractive, can scarcely be conceived. The

and sluggish course a single tree visible as thick as my arm — and notwithstanding it may continue to be an important feature in the future communication between the countries on the Pacific [and those] on the Atlantic, it will always be looked upon by emigrants as the most repulsive .... After we crossed the main chain of the Sierra Nevada, our descent into the valley of the Sacramento, a distance of more than one hundred miles, is by one of the worst and most precipitous roads, I venture to say, that ever wagon travelled over. No one could conceive it possible for a wagon ever to pass down many of the descents without being dashed to pieces, and yet hundreds did manage to get over safely, among the rest our own. They had a hard time after I left them, but have at length all arrived safely.

And now for a few words about the "Charlestown, Va. Mining Co." It at present exists, but in all human probability, even before this letter is mailed, will be among the things that were. Its materials are too discordant — and it is the case with every company of any size that has come out here — for it ever to remain together. There seems to be a general wish for a division of the spoils and a separation, when every man will be on his own hook, as they say, or will unite in small parties to suit themselves. I am satisfied from all I can learn and see that this is the best and only course for them to pursue. We are too large and cumbersome, as a company, ever to work to advantage, and besides, I do not believe we could find space enough on any [of] the streams, where the gold is worth digging, to allow us to operate together. Besides, there are a hundred other difficulties which I could readily suggest to you, did I imagine they would be interesting, in the way of our continued union. I am even now preparing to leave this place with Long and some men from Oregon — hardy sons of the forest — for the diggings on the head waters of the Sacramento, which are said to be the most productive in the country — and whether the company dissolve or not, my course is determined on. He not only furnished me a mule to ride — having brought several from Missouri with him — but also packs, provisions, &c. enough for both, which of course I have to pay for when I am able. Thus you see, my dear, that although penniless, I am not friendless, and although with the Apostle I can say "silver and gold I have none," yet I have a stout heart and an unfaltering courage, and doubt not I shall be able to make a raise before long. I think I am in luck thus far, and I know that it only requires industry, and a mind fixed to its purpose, to make Something out here, for I never thought for a moment that I was to pick up without labour a splendid competence in a few days or weeks. I expect to remain up on the Sacramento 3 or 4 months, by which time I expect to have gathered something quite handsome, or at least sufficient, perhaps, to enable me in the spring to return.

* * * * *

I cannot say that what I have seen of the country, prepossesses me strongly in its favor. Notwithstanding the proclamation of Mr. Benton, in the Senate, that the sooner the gold is exhausted in this country the better for it, I cannot help moderately insinuating that he lies — like a great many great men — under a huge mistake. The moment the gold, with which her soil teams, shall have been exhausted, or become so much diminished in quantity, as no longer to attract a large emigration here to work her mines, from that moment dates her decline in all the elements essential to an important state. I consider California, agriculturally, as nothing — commercially, as vastly overrated — for I look upon an overland communication by means of a Railroad — between her and this country as chimerical — and when these two great elements of her importance prove to be imaginary or in part so, her importance must vastly diminish. Yet great men say, she is to be our great Depot for the rich trade of Asia, and over those vast barren plains and rocky barriers, that interpose between the waters of the States and the Pacific, the rich treasures of China and adjacent countries — their fine silks and wares, and dye stuffs and what not — are to be borne on the swift and strong wings of steam, and then those distant countries be placed at our doors. It is well, I suppose, for men to conceive of great works, otherwise they would never be accomplished, but that this grand conception will prove an abortion I have no doubt.

But my dear, I fear these great matters will prove of little interest to you — but to carry out the ideas above expressed and farther to rebut the assumption that the gold of California is an injury rather than an element in her progress, a single remark and I dismiss this head. All over the country approximate, and every locality where gold has been discovered in abundance, cities and towns are springing into existence with an almost magical rapidity. Just here, now, about 3 miles from the umbrageous and veteran Oak, beneath whose shadow I have reposed for the last 3 weeks, doing nothing and waiting on the "Charlestown, Va. Mining Company," a city, within the last four months, has been laid off, called Sacramento — numbers already a population of from 5 to 6,000, and does a business five times as great as any town of the same size in Virginia. — The demands of trade have gone so far ahead of the means to accommodate it, that men live in tents, and hundreds of thousands of dollars worth of goods are sold weekly in frame houses covered and walled only with canvass.

This City is situated on the Map where Neuva Helvitia is placed at the junction of the American or Rio de los Americanos River with the Sacramento. A Steamer or two and very considerable sail vessels visit her daily. Now what is it that has thus planted in the wilderness the embryo of a great city? Nothing on earth but the rich golden treasures that lie embodied in the deep gorges and rocky streams and ravines of the Sierra Nevada Mountains. If the treasures continue as heretofore, Sacramento City becomes a place of importance. Should they cease however to hold out sufficient inducements to attract the emigration, her fall will be much more rapid than her rise. But enough of this.

* * * * *

The climate of California I believe to be as healthful as that of any other country in the world, and in the mountains and hills where I expect to spend most of my time more so than any other I know of. I have been here now upwards of 3 weeks, and this too is called the most sickly portion of the year, and yet I have enjoyed the most perfect and uninterrupted health. The sickness is principally confined to those who reach here by sea. They are turned loose from vessels, where in a crowded state they have, for five, six and seven months, been pent up together, having passed through every variety of climate, and their systems of course relaxed and enervated by such a course of life. In this condition they strike for the Mines, and it is not to be wondered that many should be sick from the sudden change of life, and many fall victims to disease.

Yet even among those I have heard of but little sickness and of course less mortality.

With us who have come across the Plains, the case is very different. We are trained and enured to exactly the mode of living the digger experiences. The ground his couch, the canopy of heaven his roof, pleasant thoughts of home, sweetened by the reflection that his labours are not in vain, his companions, and a plain but substantial diet, to recuperate the energies of nature. I feel now that I can live where any other man can live, and yet enjoy good health. What you would consider a hardship I can now regard as a comfort, and I would not exchange my couch here beneath these wide spreading Oaks where the wolves howl nightly almost over my head, for the downiest bed in California. As to Law and Order here, it is I can almost say, unexceptionable. There is, I suppose, less security given to man's movable estate here than in any Country in the world, and yet there are few infringements upon one's rights of property, far less than in Virginia. One half of the goods in Sacramento City are lying in the Street and the other half, not much less exposed, and yet a theft is rarely heard of. The letters in the Post Office there have nothing between them and the street but canvass, when a single rent with a knife would admit your hand to the whole of them, and yet no fear is felt for them. Whipping and death in some cases are the rogue's reward here. The miner leaves his tools in his hole, and they are as inviolable there as under guard of a Regiment. And as to acts of personal violence they are equally rare. But few persons carry arms, except for hunting, and pistols command little or no price. Every one seems to have come here to make money — they have gone to considerable expense, and undergone great hardships to accomplish this object, and each feels an interest in protecting the other in the enjoyment of his person and property. — Hence a thief or a cut throat stands no chance. — And as for the Banditti of whom you may have heard in the States, it is too absurd to think of. A man can ride through California, and particularly this portion of it, by night or day alone and without an arm for his defence, without a particle more to apprehend than when at home in the States.

* * * * *

A few words now as to the golden prospects here. As I have said before, there is plenty of gold throughout the whole mountainous regions of California, but it is not to be picked up without trouble, but requires, diligence, patience and the hardest kind of labor to get it and make it our own. There is, however, a certainty that he who will labour diligently will have his labours rewarded far more bountifully here than by any pursuit I know of in the states. Mining here is spoken of like farming in the states. It is regarded as the most independent pursuit a man can engage in. You are there your own master, can work where you like, and can rely confidently on a living when you do so. I have not heard of any extraordinary fortunes being picked up in a day, but it is not uncommon for men to make their thousand dollars and upwards in a week. — Of course, this does not happen with every one, and therefore must be looked upon as lucky hits. I expect to make from 30 to 50 dollars, and maybe more, where I am going, yet in this I may be disappointed. Of this I can give you more certain information when I shall have tried experimentally than at present.

Men, however, view the prospects here very differently. While some declare they are not at all disappointed, and every thing is equal to their anticipations, others are disheartened and lament the folly that induced them to abandon their homes for this wild and uninviting region. I learn that each homeward bound vessel carries back as large a number of passengers as the outward bound brings here, and that the passages are engaged.... is the number seeking to return up to the first of January. Many, with their outfit and all ready to go to work and disheartened at the process of gold getting, sell out and return without digging a lick. As for myself, things are about as I anticipated. I have no doubt the quantity of gold here will render it profitable to work the mines for the next fifty years and longer. If I succeed however in getting a reasonable pile in the next two or three years, I will give, as far as I am concerned, posterity a release of all farther interests in the premises.

* * * * *

Boarding cannot be had here for less than 20 dollars a week, and this includes simply your meals, while all kinds of labor commands the most extravagant prices. A physician will not make a pill or walk ten steps for less than an ounce of $16. — Wood is from $20 to 25 to 30 a cord, while other articles of household consumption command proportional prices. Potatoes are $2 per pound. Onions ditto. Beef 25 cts and Hams 60 cts.

* * * * *

And now as to my bodily comforts, about which you express such solicitude. I have said enough perhaps to convey the idea that in this respect I have nothing of which to complain. I am perfectly satisfied in this respect, and out here, desire no other mode of living than exactly as I now enjoy. — But to convey to your mind some idea of how I have adapted myself to circumstances, permit me to suppose the following case. Suppose that on the morning succeeding your marriage, when your heart was full of hope, and you entertained bright anticipations of the future, by some species of magical clairvoyance, unexplained by accompanying circumstances, you had seen your tidy and well dressed husband in the streets of a city, with an old weather-beaten slouched hat upon his head, his beard unshorn, his hair uncropt, and in his shirt sleeves, with a leather girdle about his waist. You watched him farther, and saw him pick up an old black bottle in the street, go to a well and wash it, thence to a store with it in his hand and get it full of molasses, and further continue his way in the same city, to a Bakery, buy a loaf of bread, and with it under his arm mount a mule and ride some four miles in the country, where beneath the shadows of the trees, with no human habitation near, he prepares his frugal meal and spreads his couch upon the ground. While he reposes beneath the moonlight, apparently as contented as lord of all around, the wolves are prowling about him, looking almost in his face to see if he is asleep, and finally steal the remains of his supper from his mess pan not far from his feet. What I say, my dear, would have been your feelings at beholding this picture? And yet the reality of it has occurred exactly as related. It is now nearly five months since I have slept upon a bed or beneath the shadow of a roof — and yet I have enjoyed as perfect health and sleep as soundly as ever before. Houses are useless appendages here. The climate is such as to do away with the necessity of them. There is no winter, no time for leaves to wither and fall, but here Nature wears her robe of green all year. Nine and often ten months of the year, no rains fall in the Valleys, and when they commence in December and January, it is the signal for the renewal of the vegetable kingdom. The rainy season then, is the only time a man needs any shelter from the elements, and this a good tent will afford him. It is said to be the best season of the year for mining operations. I expect to remain in the mines where I am going all winter. Bryarly, if the company dissolves, as doubtless it will, expects to join us in a week or two, so you see I shall not be without medical assistance if necessary.

* * * * *

The Company are generally well, with the exception of some diarrhoea, from overeating of fresh meat. The company held their meeting today (15th of September) and by a small majority, determined for the present, not to dissolve. I tendered my resignation, and I am no longer one of them. I expect to leave tomorrow for my expedition up the Sacramento.

* * * * *

Direct your letters to Sacramento City, California. [171]

By the end of the month, news from J.H. Kelly reached Charlestown. The rest of the Company had arrived in California!

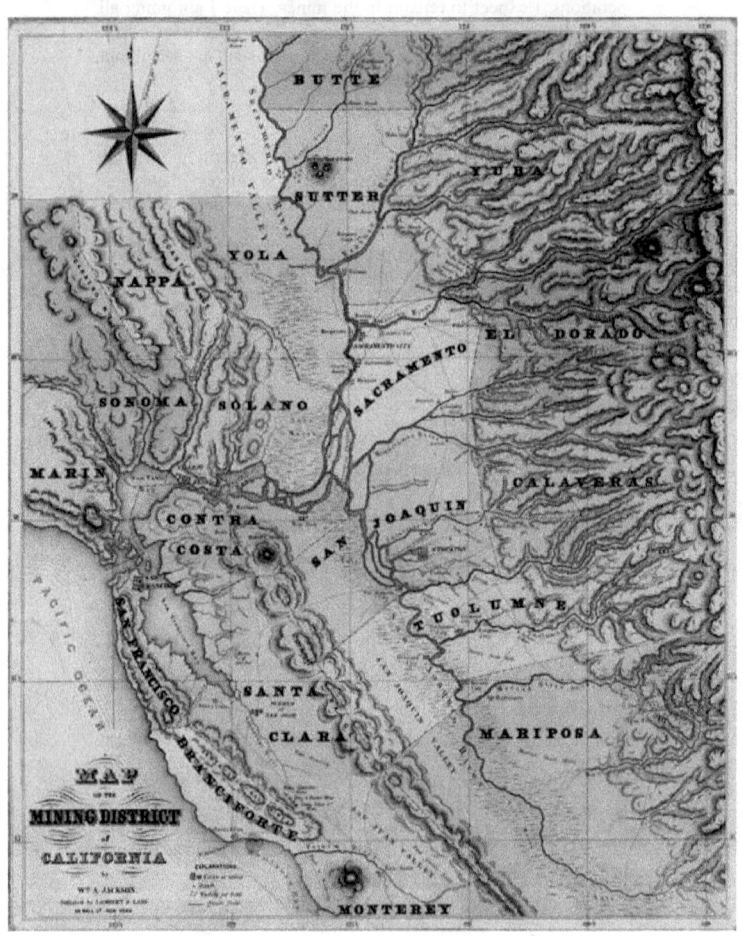

Figure 44. William A. Jackson, *Map of the Mining District of California*, New York: Lambert and Lane, 1851.

September 29, 1849, Sacramento, California

From J. Harrison Kelly.

The Charlestown Va. Mining Company have at last reached the desired El Dorado, which was to be rich in precious metals of every character. The Company reached Johnston's Settlement, which consists of one rough and woe begone looking tenement, on the 1st of September, where they remained some days in order that the poor mules might recruit.

Those having friends and relatives will be anxious first to learn something respecting them, and it is with deep feeling that I am compelled to announce that we have lost five members since we left the good old shores of Virginia. I wrote you some months since of the death of Messrs. Thos. W. Washington and Joseph C. Young. — Our next loss was that of Taliaferro Milton, who was drown in Thomas' Fork of Bear River, on the 9th of July. Our young friend had made him many esteemed friends by his activity and energy in matters relative to the Company. — The stream in which Mr. M. was drowned was about ten yards wide, and easily forded a mile or two above, but desirous to make a cut off, he in company with several others left the train and attempted to cross the Fork, when he was unfortunately drowned. The next was that of Mr. James Davidson, who accidentally shot himself in the abdomen, on the 8th of August, and died on the morning of the 9th. He died at what is known as the slough, 20 miles above the Sink of the Humboldt River. Newton Tavenner, of Frederick county, died near Johnson's settlement, on the 7th of September, of consumption.

The balance of the membership are generally enjoying good health. A description of the country through which we passed in reaching here might prove interesting, but it would be a work which could not be easily brought within the limits of a newspaper, and such as would make your readers startle. Hereafter, I may give you a sketch, but at present I cannot.

One thing I seek earnestly to impress on the mind of every friend of mine, and that is, never to cross the plains, in coming to California, unless they are prepared to meet scenes more appalling than ever entered into the mind of the wildest visionary. — When I wrote to you from the South Pass of the Rocky Mountains, we had seen nothing — no, nothing in the way of difficulty and danger. — When, however, we crossed the Green River, we began seeing sights, and after we left Fort Hall we had "nothing else" but the most stupendous difficulties to encounter.

We travelled down the Humboldt River about 300 miles — grass very good for 100, but an article very scarce the next hundred, and none at all the last hundred miles, except at the slough, twenty miles from the Sink. After leaving the Sink we had a desert of sixty-five miles to cross, (part of it a sandy waste,) and not one blade of grass on the route, and no water except at the Boiling Spring, which was not, of course, drinkable. The Boiling Springs consist of a dozen or more, which belches forth water a little hotter than a fire can produce! I threw in a spring a piece of meat and in the course of ten minutes it was sufficiently cooked to be eaten, as many of us can testify by the hearty repast we made. The suffering was very great, both to man and beast, in crossing the dreary waste, and at least five hundred dead and dying men and mules were strewed over the road. Many men became frantic for want of water, and several died because of excessive drinking, while warm, after reaching Salmon Trout River. We, however, were better provided than many others, having mown grass at the Slough for our stock, and filled kegs with water.

A most magnificent sight presented itself when within about a mile of the Salmon Trout River. Suddenly, on rising a hill, the River burst upon our view — a stream of pure, delicious water, and trees rich in their green foliage, a sight of surpassing beauty, as it was the first timber we had seen for many, many hundred miles. We were compelled to leave half of our train twelve miles off and drive the mules to grass — in a few days they had sufficiently recruited to return for the remaining wagons. At this point we found our provisions very scarce, having had no meat for more than a week, and on examination we found only enough of flour for three days, and we had yet a journey of three weeks before us! To many this might appear to be a critical situation, but the jest and joke went round as usual, and every face wore the most perfect unconcern. — We soon met a friend, Mr. Wm. McDaniel (formerly of Jefferson) who had more provisions than he wanted — particularly as his teams were weak. We obtained as much as we wanted, to be returned in California.

Salmon Trout or Tuckie river, is a beautiful stream — running between the tallest kinds of bluffs. We travelled up this river to its source, about 80 miles, and crossed it twenty seven times! The fording was extremely rough and the stream swift, as many of us can testify, for our Mules fell and we were a "beautiful" carrol to the river.

After leaving the river we commenced the first ascent of the Sierra Nevada, but we had to traverse many a weary mile before we reached the point known as the base of the mountain. The distance up the principal ascent is not more than five miles, but the road is rugged. Within a mile of the top we came to an ascent so steep that it was with the very greatest difficulty we could walk up it. By dint of perseverance, with double teaming, we gained the ascent, all safe and sound. — I observed a windless, to which horses and mules had formerly been attached, for the purpose of dragging wagons up the almost perpendicular elevation. After going down hill some three miles, over anything else but good road, we congratulated ourselves at having passed what we believed to be the worst part of the road. But look out, emigrant, breakers ahead, you are just into rough road. From that time onward, till we arrived at Johnson's, it was over roads on which rocks were piled high up — down the most steep and rocky roads you can imagine — and over hills you would decide were impassable for wagons. Some days we travelled five miles and then again ten, which was slow work, considering that we started at daybreak and kept on till sundown. The worst hill we descended was the Steep Hollow, 70 miles from here — half a mile down, and almost perpendicular. Ropes were fastened to the wagons and then tied across trees, and in this way many were carried down. — Whilst in other cases the largest oaks were cut and lashed behind the wagons, which answered a better purpose than ropes. There were several narrow escapes, but fortunately no accident occurred. Ropes and trees were frequently used before, but this last hill "capped the climax."

Thus hastily and imperfect I have brought you to our camp three miles from Sacramento City. The city is "tied up in a rag," as some one expressed himself, containing about 3,000 inhabitants, and situated in the Forks of the American and Sacramento Rivers, but fronting directly the latter river. There are quite a large number of vessels lying at anchor, and a vast deal of business is daily transacted. Lumber is very scarce, and three-quarter stuff is worth $65 per hundred feet. The Houses, for the most part, (indeed I may say with three or four exceptions,) consist of canvass thrown over a frame. The fronts of some are boarded, whilst the end and sides consist of muslin. Having dined the other day at the American, (price $ 1.50) we noticed a chap from the States take a chair and very deliberately attempt to lean back against the wall, but luckless wight, he had forgotten that he was in a paper house, and he came well nigh tearing out the whole side of the Hotel! Another old covy who was full "three sheets in the wind" was wending his way uptown, when he staggered and fell against a handsome house, which fell to the ground! The fact of it is, every thing seems to be erected temporarily.

Doubtless, the general anxiety you feel is in regard to our future prospects for acquiring gold. This I will answer briefly. There is gold in almost every tributary of the Sacramento and San Joaquin, but it is not to be found in the quantities many have imagined, nor is it to be obtained without the greatest labor and toil. I have no doubt but that some have made fortunes in a very short time, but it was one out of a thousand. I have seen many who have been in the mines who say they average from a half to an ounce per day. — That would do very well in the States, but it is not making money in California, where the commonest laborer can make one dollar per hour, either in chopping wood, unloading vessels, or any other kind of labor.

The question of dividing the Company was mooted for some time before our arrival. A meeting was held on the 13th, when the question was put, and decided by a vote of 41 to 32 to remain united. On the next day another meeting was held, when the question was reconsidered, and the following Resolution passed by a vote of ayes 50, nays 19.

"Resolved, That the Co-partnership existing between the members of the Charlestown Va. Mining Company be dissolved."

The principal reason of the dissolution was on account of the disability to procure a situation for so large a company to work together profitably. Mining, here, is different from that in the States. You follow up some small stream, through the mountain gorges, where wagons cannot penetrate, and almost impassable tor pack mules, and where you are compelled to change your location perhaps once or twice every week. Under this state of affairs the majority thought it practicable to dissolve, though they regretted the necessity of the measure. Companies here, generally consist of from three to ten members, but usually, the former number, and it is a matter worthy of note, that our's was the largest Company that ever crossed the plains, although many, when they started, were fully as large, but by reason of the difficulties of the trip, were induced to separate. One great bond of strength consisted in having for our guide and captain (S.F. SMITH) a man of the most indomitable energy and perseverance, united with a bland and courteous character.

The members of our company are generally forming themselves into messes of from five to ten members, who will go where they please and labor as suits themselves. We are disposing of our joint property at auction, and in the course of ten days will be scattered from the head waters of the Sacramento down to the lowest tributaries of the San Joaquin. The health of the country is good. Those who have travelled the overland route are now capable of standing any hardship and enduring the greatest fatigue, and the only sickness you hear of is among those who came across the Cape. If I had a choice, however, I would prefer doubling the Cape half a dozen times rather than encounter the desolate waste between this and St. Josephs, Missouri. If any of my friends have any idea of visiting California, I would recommend the Isthmus route, which is said to be a good one, and more comfortable than any other. An indolent man has no business here, where all is activity and enterprise.

Wages are high in this country for nearly every branch of mechanism — blacksmiths, tinners, carpenters, &c., are realizing fortunes by following their different pursuits.

Provisions are plenty, and are to be had at moderate prices in the city, though forty miles from here nothing in the eating line can be had for less than $1 per pound — beef, pork, flour, salt, coffee, &c. I have bought flour at $25 per bbl., and pork at $20 per cwt., in the city I could have bought the same for little over one half.

There will be a great deal of suffering and distress among those who are still in the mountains. A gentleman just told me that there were from four to six thousand teams — if so, I cannot imagine how they will ever reach this quarter, for there is no grass of any account on the whole road.

I have been informed that the Shepherdstown Company [172] are only two days back, so that they will get in, and that's all. Gov. Smith has sent men back to relieve the emigrants, but their service will be of little account, as they cannot cause one blade of grass to grow. $100,000 has been raised to send back relief, but money will be of little account except in the purchase of provisions to send them. I fear that we shall have more than one Donner affair to record by next spring.

None of the Company, except Mr. Blakemore, has had a letter from home since our departure from the States, but we all expect a rich repast in this way, in the course of the present week. To my friends I would say, let this letter answer for all, as it is out of the question to get time to write more before the steamer leaves for San Francisco. Let them direct to me at Sacramento City, California, until further notified.

J.H.K. [173]

Now comfortably settled in, William M. Gwin managed to get a seat at the California Constitutional Convention, but his attempt to be elected its president fell flat. He was defeated by Robert Semple 26 to 8. [174] Thanks to the huge influx of miners, El Dorado County had the largest population in California. Unfortunately, they had no delegates at the Convention.

Figure 45. *The Miners' Ten Commandments* (for those who had "seen the elephant") [175]

Part IV. Golden Shackles

> There is no part of the means placed in the hands of the Executive which might be used with greater effect for unhallowed purposes than the control of the public press. The maxim which our ancestors derived from the mother country that "the freedom of the press is the great bulwark of civil and religious liberty" is one of the most precious legacies which they have left us. We have learned, too, from our own as well as the experience of other countries, that golden shackles, by whomsoever or by whatever pretense imposed, are as fatal to it as the iron bonds of despotism. The presses in the necessary employment of the Government should never be used "to clear the guilty or to varnish crime." A decent and manly examination of the acts of the Government should be not only tolerated, but encouraged.

William Henry Harrison, *Inaugural Address,* March 4, 1841

October, 1849

Political debate at the national level had sunk to a new low. The Democrats claimed that their opponents were resorting to "proscription" (wholesale removal of political appointees) so that Whig supporters could have their turn at the trough. Whigs asserted that the Administration was only rooting out corruption, incompetence, and inefficiency. The Democrats, they said, were determined to block any Administration initiative. The tone of the national newspapers tended to reflect this animosity.

Charlestown, Virginia

Singling out the Washington *Union* and the *Heroic Age* as examples of the worst type of journalism, *Free Press* editor J.S. Gallaher reiterated the traditional rules of journalistic conflict:

> ... respect would ever be shown to those who advocated the doctrines of the opposite political faith. There was to be no bandying of epithets, no libations from the sewers of Billingsgate — if the people could not be convinced by a fair exposition of facts of the weakness and faithlessness of the powers that be, they could not be convinced by a resort to coarse, malicious and vindictive vituperation.

Not content with abusing the President in the public press, said Gallaher, these partisans had taken to attacking the President's family, sending them anonymous letters containing offensive and obscene language. "Such a mode of warfare may possibly seem justifiable to those whose moral sense is blunted by the determination to oppose the

Administration, whether right or wrong, 'till the bitter end,' but honest and well meaning men of all parties cannot but condemn a course of conduct so shocking to decency and morality." [176]

Rumors had been circulating for months that John S. Gallaher would receive a government position from the Tyler administration. Confirmation came in late October, when he was appointed Third Auditor of the U.S. Treasury, replacing Peter Hagner. The latter had been appointed a Treasury Clerk by George Washington in 1793 and had been serving as Third Auditor since the position was created in 1817.

Public reaction predictably split along party lines, although most Democrats grudgingly admitted that Gallaher was an acceptable choice. J.W. Beller echoed this opinion, noting that, as Hagner "was destined in all human possibility to walk the plank, we are pleased that one has been selected to take his place whom we believe is quite as acceptable to the Democratic party of the District as any Whig within its limits. [177]

In his parting words to his readers, Gallaher philosophized about his own connection to his paper,

> He has been 28 years in service as an editor, and is now the oldest but one in Virginia,... but in his case as in that of most others, fortune has not followed toil, and duty to his family has overruled inclination. It is painful to be separated, even temporarily, from the friends with whom he has been so long associated, but he will not be unmindful of the interests of the readers of the *Free Press* whenever opportunity is offered to serve them. The paper is a bantling that occupies a large space in his affections, and will be to him through life an object of deep solicitude. For a time he bids his friends an affectionate farewell.

California

J. H. Kelley began mining in early October, and throughout his residence in California remained close enough to Sacramento City to return periodically to deposit his gold, pick up supplies, and send and receive mail from home. Some of the Company would make Sacramento their permanent home, but most appeared periodically for similar reasons and passed their news to Kelly, who continued writing letters home throughout his stay. A few of these letters were written specifically for publication, but most of them, written to his brother-in-law or sisters, were heavily edited when published to exclude personal content.

October 4, 1849, Sacramento, California

From J. Harrison Kelly

To-day I go to the Diggings. Hamilton C. Harrison and D. Fagan had a streak of good luck this week, they made $200 in two days. There is gold here in nearly every stream, but the best has to be dug over and washed, so that we take the 'leavings' — whether they will be large or small will depend on our good luck. Different success attends those mining as might well be expected, — some make easily 50 to $100 per day, whilst others scarce make their board. We are here just at the most favorable time to commence operations, and in a few days every man will be in the mines up to his eyes. I am not so confident of realizing a 'pile' as when I left the States, but if perseverance, frugality and industry, can accomplish any thing, I shall most assuredly get something. What I say of myself, is equally applicable to every member of the Company, all of whom, with myself, may I hope have a streak of good luck.

Not more than two or three in the Company have received any letters, since leaving St. Josephs. The Mails are horribly managed out here. Direct letters and papers to me at Sacramento City, as I fear none will ever reach me that have been sent to San Francisco. In haste,

J.H.K. [178]

As the following letter to James W. Beller shows, Frank Washington's scouting expedition eventually changed his attitude about mining for gold. However, he stuck it out till November. The chances of striking it rich, he concluded, were not worth the effort. Instead, he joined the growing group of doctors and lawyers who settled in Sacramento or San Francisco to practice their own professions and keep their eyes open for other opportunities, such as real estate investment, or appointment or election to public office.

October 15, 1849, Upper Sacramento, 220 miles from Sacramento City

From B.F. Washington

My Dear Sir:

A little above where "Clear Creek" empties its waters into the Sacramento river, on the western side, beneath the overhanging branches of an old white oak, can be found at present my local habitation. Bryarly, in company with the Cunninghams [Charles, George, and James], Thomas, &c., reached here two days since.

* * * * *

Just before I left Sacramento City, I performed my last official act as President of the Charlestown (Va.) Mining Company by presiding over their deliberations, as to a dissolution and division of spoils. My functions, as I wrote to you from Fort Kearney, were, upon my own motion, suspended until our arrival in California, and the sole command given to F.S. Smith, of Missouri, our guide, who proved himself an efficient officer and guide. The result of the first day's deliberations was a bare majority in favor of adhering together. On the morrow another was held, and on motion the question was reconsidered, and by a majority of about three to one it was determined that the above named Company should no longer exist as such. It would have been madness to have remained together, as it would have been impossible for us to have found a place worth working, affording sufficient space for so large a Company.

Since I left, there has been a sale of all the property of the Company, and the result was a dividend of $129 to each member, exclusive of the provisions which were shipped around and which are not yet sold. These will increase it some $15 more, which amounts deducted from the $300 originally paid, will make our expenses from Charlestown here, a distance of upwards of 4,000 miles, $156. Each member, too, over and above this dividend, has a gun, a pair of woolen blankets, a gum blanket, and clothes bag, which, as these articles are selling here, would reduce our expenses $50 more. Thus far, this is pretty well.

I was induced to come up here from representations rife below that these were the richest mines in California, and being remote, were less crowded. I have found, however, the reverse to be the case, and I think I can say now from my own knowledge, gathered from observation mostly, as also from reliable sources, that the idea of making a fortune here by digging gold, in a week, a month, or a year, or, if you will, a half a dozen of them, is one magnificent humbug. The gold speculation has become to the eyes of many a poor deluded fellow, who has sacrificed his all to reach here, a splendid fraud, a most glittering cheat.

Of the thirty thousand individuals who have come here across the Plains, to say nothing of those who have come by water, there will not be two thousand who will ever make more than enough to carry them home again, much less pay them for the sacrifices made at home, the waste of time, and the labors and hardships of getting here.

I have been in the mines and mingled with the miners and seen them at work in a number of different mines, and while you will find here and there a few who are doing pretty well, making their $10 or $16 per day, or may be $20, you will find hundreds not making more than $2 or $3, and hundreds more discouraged, going some where else in the vain hope of doing better. Now, $16 or $20 a day, will doubtless sound really well at home, but you must look at the accompanying state of things, should you prove fortunate enough to fall upon such a "lead." In the first place, the days you are employed in finding this "lead," next the cost of provisions, in the next place that your "lead" is liable to run out any day, and then it may be a week or two before you find another — and, again, the liability to sickness, which in the form of fevers is very prevalent among the emigrants, and the Doctor's bills, which are bills indeed — throw all these into the opposite scale, to your $16 to $20 per day, and strike your average for the year, and you will find a result of a different tune.

The speculators and traders — and even this is becoming overdone — are managing to get possession of most of the gold here — and to carry out their schemes, a most splendid system of lying on a large scale is resorted to.

Upon nearly all the streams, on the head branches on which gold is found, there are one or more ranchos, which are converted into trading posts also. Now, it is the interest of each one of these ranch holders — in order to sell their provisions, including cattle for beef, of which they have an immense number — to induce by some means as many miners as possible to come up their respective streams.

To effect this they send out their runners and adherents, who put afloat in other mines and at the cities the most extravagant falsehoods about the mining prospects in their respective "diggings." The inexperienced in these matters catch at the gilder bait, and after traveling perhaps some two or three hundred miles, (which by the way affords him a fine opportunity of viewing the agricultural features of this great Eldorado, and if he be a Missouri or any other farmer from the States, they must seem to him about as attractive as the great Sahara, or some other desert,) and after working some week or so just to see if he has been fooled, for he is not willing to take the say so of others for it, equally unfortunate, he finds by the result of his labors, that there is no mistake whatever in the matter.

Then he must go back and go it blindfolded to some other mine. The idea of getting, through report of others, any satisfactory information relative to mining at particular "diggings" is an absurdity. If a miner, and especially an old one, is asked what he is making in this or that place, if it be little, and he thinks of leaving, he will tell you he is doing a first rate business—- if he be doing well he will swear he is not clearing expenses. One must get knowledge here, in these matters, not merely by seeking after it, but he must travel after it, and dig after it, and then ten to one if it is the knowledge he seeks after all.

Now for some facts connected with these mines bearing upon the prospects of these mines.

[Editor's Note: Portions below are illegible in the original source.]

[Some insist on looking] where gold has been found in sufficient quantities to justify the [effort], and upon those streams [where] it has [been] discovered — I will insist [on looking where it has not been found] before, for I'd rather [look where gold] has yet to be discovered where a pick has [not] been struck. [Otherwise,] you will find almost every [inch] turned up and every hole to have been scooped out and examined. Many of these, in fact in most of the old diggings, have been worked, and reworked, and are now being worked again. These mines are all so crowded, that if one is fortunate enough to strike a "lead," he will, as soon as it is found out, have perhaps [a] dozen neighbors disposed to be on very friendly terms. This is the state of things on the Feather River, Yuba, Bear, the tributaries of the American Fork, [and] the Stanislaus, and the further you go south the worse it becomes. [There] you had a mixed and heterogeneous representation of [men from] every [place] and clime, gathered together from every quarter of the globe, like vultures at their feast. In the dry diggings there is doubtless more remaining to be discovered, yet, even there I do not look upon it in the same favorable way as many do. While it is believed ... by many scientific men that there are certain places in the hills of large deposit for the precious ore, this kind of fountain head as it were, from whence have proceeded the large deposits found in the beds of streams, I am convinced that such is not the case. By some means to which I shall presently advert, large quantities of molten gold, varying from the dust up to pounds, has been scattered throughout and intermixed with the soil of extensive districts of country.

[In] the action of the great volumes of water, which in the spring of the year, when the snows in the vast regions of the California mountains begin to melt, some pouring down to the Plain, immense quantities of earth and loose rock have been removed from their original locality and carried off to the ... rivers, the soil passes..., while the rocks and gravel remain ...

In these ... deposits from time to time, the gold which was doubtless intermixed with the soil through which these washes have been made, was also carried down, and now finds its place, being the heaviest substance in motion.... the substratum of solid rock at the bottom of all of these river bars. Thus these gullies, ravines, and rivers may be regarded as great natural "rockers," and the gold found in them as the result of the washings....

Now the dry diggings only differ in their nature from that found in the wet or river diggings in this — they are the beds of streams which at certain portions of the year have no water in them, but which in the melting season send water in large quantities to the rivers.

These ravines, however, are generally right in among the hills, and as they are the medium through which the gold reaches the rivers, the larger pieces find resting places in them ..., while the smaller pieces are swept on by the force of the water until they find a resting place below.

In support, however, of the first theory, I had a conversation the other day with an old miner from Virginia who had worked in other mines for fifteen years, in which he informed me the best places for miners to explore for gold are right in along and on the tops of the mountains. Wherever you discover large quantities of white quartz or that intermixed with strata of ..., setting edgewise, there stick your pick, and although you may not be successful in the first or second attempt, yet persevere, and when you do find gold, as you doubtless will, you find it in considerable quantities. He is under the impression that if any of these ravine deposits proceed from such a place, it will turn out to be the case that a certain ... wide field open yet for operation ... here — but otherwise, as you perceive, I think there is ... show.

Now this gold has doubtless all been melted out in the ...sprinkled, as it were ,.. by the great volcanic forces that have thrown up these immense ranges, to the present .... elevation over the Plains. — As you approach the South Pass in the Rocky Mountains about where [lie] the head waters of the Sweetwater River, you can find innumerable pieces of molten flint of all shapes and sizes, and many of them very different in appearance, scattered all over the surface of the earth, and they resemble very much in form and [color] specimens of gold I have seen. That these have been thrown up to great distances in the air for miles around by volcanic explosions or earthquakes, in a partially liquid [form, produced] from heat and cooled before they reached the earth, is ... to admit of a doubt. It is the same case ... with the gold, and although ... have adhered to and remained with the white quartz, which I believe is always found with gold in its original deposits, I cannot but believe that such places are not from whence proceed the river and ravine deposits. This old miner further said there was gold enough in this immediate vicinity among the mountains to make all the [miners] rich. He had dug fifteen days and has $1,700 worth of gold.

I shall be here perhaps a month or more, yet, during which time it is my purpose to give the old miner's theory a fair trial, having already marked out several places during my solitary peregrinations over the hills, mule hunting, where I have come to the conclusion my fortune is hid.

Now, as many of my friends requested me to write to them, and advise them as to whether they should come here or not next spring, and as I find it impossible as yet to find the time to comply with their requests, you can say to them for me, if they have families and can get along at all at home, if their object in coming is to dig gold from the earth, I can see no inducements here that will be likely to repay them for the trouble. If he be a single man and desires to experience a little of the tough roll and tumble mode of living, let him come by all means. He can get along here certainly, if he tries, and he will have a fine chance of finding out what stuff he is made of. Tell him also, that rail-malling, ditch-digging and rock-blowing are all agreeable recreations compared with gold-digging.

Remembrances to all friends — to Beller my best regards and tell him he shall hear from me soon.

Yours truly,

B.F.W. [179]

November, 1849. Charlestown, Jefferson County, Virginia

By the time that the first monthly issue of the *Free Press* appeared, John S. Gallaher was already installed in his new job at Washington, D.C. By the end of the month, the newspaper's masthead had been changed to "H.N. Gallaher & Co." and Horatio Nelson Gallaher was the new senior editor.

Now age 41, 12 years younger than John, he had worked with his brother since 1820. For almost 20 years, he had overseen the operations of *the Free Press* while John served in the Virginia Legislature and helped run several Whig papers in Richmond.

Horatio had married widow Adeline Beeler Hayden, and the couple now had six children, the youngest being born last month. "H.N." owned eight slaves and was active member of the Odd Fellows, the Total Abstinence Society, and the Charlestown Presbyterian Church. He was one of the incorporators of the Charlestown Savings Bank and part owner of the Shannondale Springs resort. Like his brother, Horatio was an ardent Whig. [180]

The *Journal of the Times*, a fledgling Democratic newspaper at Harpers Ferry, folded after one year of operation. When owner George W. Chambers passed his subscription list to fellow Democrat J.W. Beller, the latter wasted no time making these subscribers his own. After Gallaher suggested that these orphaned readers might want to take the *Free Press*, Beller sniped that H.N. was "wanting in that spirit of liberality which should always characterize our profession." This brought a return salvo from H.N. Gallaher:

> It is doubtless very liberal in an editor, professing neutrality to transfer, like so many vassals, his subscribers to a Locofoco journal, but quite the reverse to speak of it. Our neighbor's ideas of "liberality" are certainly very peculiar, and we therefore, leave him to the enjoyment of them — hoping that his nerves may become steeled before the end of the year. [181]

If anyone thought Horatio could not handle a pen as well as brother John, they were in for a surprise.

California

J. Harrison Kelly and his partners were working a claim on Weber Creek, a tributary on the South Branch of the American River, about 200 miles east of Sacramento City. Kelly and many of his fellow miners were

Jefferson County's Fourth Estate, 1840-1850   139

living in El Dorado County, the most rapidly growing part of California. The cities of Sacramento and San Francisco were located in counties with corresponding names, and a few of Jefferson's County's '49ers had settled there.

November 13th was the date set for the popular election to determine the fate of the California Constitution and to provide residents with a Governor, State Legislature, and numerous minor officials. Elections for county and city offices were held separately. Thanks in part to the poor roads, rainy season, few newspapers, and a scattered population, campaigning was, at best, a haphazard process. In Kelly's letter, he provided his view of the event.

Figure 46. Weaverville, California, by James Hutchings, Shasta: A.R. Ross, 1855

November 1, 1849, Weaver Creek, California

From J. Harrison Kelly

Dear B[eller]

Knowing that a line from me will be acceptable, I commence thus early in the month a letter for the December mail.

* * * * *

November 5.

I have been here nearly five weeks, and have made but little progress in digging gold. We have been engaged for the most part in erecting our dwelling for the winter, and now have as comfortable a cabin as is to be met with in a twenty mile's ride.

Indeed, there is no one that I have seen which I would exchange for. The roof of our building is worth $600 — being made of inch plank which is worth $1 per foot, but as we had a whip saw of our own we erected a saw mill and got out our own lumber. — Our door is laid with the same material and we have a chimney that would take the shine off of some tenements of olden time, which I have seen. It would have been amusing to see me with an axe in hand, chopping down some of the majestic pines of the forest — but it was not much sport to me as my blistered hands fully attested. It took some time for us to build our house and haul three loads of provisions from Sacramento City, which retarded our mining operations greatly.

Two of us were engaged nearly two weeks in throwing up the dirt from a dry ravine in order to wash it when the rain should fall. I suppose we threw up two hundred bushels which will average us about 75 cents per bushel. One of the greatest difficulties with us was the scarcity of water, for although quartered along a creek, we found it to be so only in name and not in reality. The bed of the creek is the best point for digging but for miles up and down it has been dug up and washed. I suppose, however, that we have gathered nearly, (in the aggregate,) two hundred dollars. Two persons generally work together, and we worked regularly for five days at mining (six of us). All told, we made only a little over $100, and mighty hard work at that. On the first day, two of the mess made $32 — two made $8 — and two $4. — Second day they ranged $32 — $8 — $1.50. So you perceive that it is all luck, chance, or something of that sort. The remaining three days we worked, no two made over $8 per day. The flying clouds induced us to quit mining and go to our house, and we did so just in the nick of time, for it commenced raining of Hollow Eve night, and has continued with slight intermissions up to this time. I think, however, that we shall have a few more weeks of sunshine before the rainy season comes in earnest — but this is mere conjecture. One thing is certain, we shall live comfortably this winter, and make enough to pay expenses, between rains, which we can do, and then start out early in the spring for some spot more richly studded with the precious metal. There is gold to be had in California, but I may be like the fellow in Irving's *Alhambra* who, all his life lived next door to fortune, but never chanced to get under the same roof.

We live about one and a half miles from Wevertown, and the same distance from Gallows or Hangtown, having some four or five thousand inhabitants. The last town derives its name from three executions which took place in January last. Two Frenchmen and a Spaniard resolved to rob an Italian. They entered his habitation at midnight, and whilst the Frenchmen searched for gold, the Spaniard stood over the Italian's bed ready to inflict the fatal blow, should the sleeping victim awake. The Italian, however, was too wary and though wide awake, was to all appearances dumb and motionless as a statue. After the booty had been secured, the trio departed, but the Italian had an armed party on their track, and they were taken, tried, found guilty and executed. The Frenchmen confessed to a number of piracies in which they had been engaged, but the Spaniard was morose and dull, true to the instincts of his nature. But it wont do for me to indulge in yarns of this sort. It had, however, a most beneficial effect, for no country can boast of a better community, so far as externals are concerned, than

California. Theft is unknown, and I have not heard of a single murder.

I visited Hangtown a few Sundays since to hear a sermon — (there is preaching in each town every Sabbath) — the first house I came to was an Auction establishment, and the loud and quick voice of the youth who officiated, evidenced that he was up to his eyes in his trade. Passing along down the street, I found a respectable crowd at the other end of the town engaged in religious exercises. All was quiet and order beneath the shades of a stately oak, although at least a dozen nations — Chilean, Sandwich Islander, Mexican, Irishman, German, Frenchman, Chinese, &c. A Methodist officiated, and his remarks were listened to with respect and attention. Truly, here was an offering up to the Throne of Grace, to the one great IAM.

As I returned, I involuntarily exclaimed, an Auction at one end of the town, for the gay and thoughtless — a large gambling house in the centre — though I did not see any gambling going on — and religious worship at the other end! Strange medley.

You are no doubt aware that we have a Constitution to be voted on Tuesday next, which makes California a free State. There is no doubt but that it will be adopted. The election will be a perfect humbug, as there are not twenty men in this whole region of the country who are acquainted with either of the candidates for Governor, Lieut. Governor, Congress, &c., or know their politics. Had I seen the Constitution two weeks ago, I would have been a candidate for the Legislature and stumped the district. Indeed, some of my friends wanted me to run at any rate, but I don't think one week sufficient for electioneering purposes.

The California Constitution proposed several measures that were controversial in "The States" back East: Slavery and dueling were outlawed; both married and unmarried women were able to own and control their own property; and "Every citizen of California, declared a legal voter by this Constitution, and every citizen of the United States, a resident of this State on the day of election, shall be entitled to vote at the first general election under this Constitution, and on the question of the adoption thereof."

November 11.

You perceive that I take my letter by "fits and starts," but you know that miners haven't time, in clear weather, to convey their ideas on paper. Yesterday, Elisha Lock started for home, which I suppose he has reached by this time, unless his illness terminated fatally, whilst on the route via the Isthmus. Elisha has been in bad health for a month past, and doubtless would have died had he remained, particularly as he was low in spirits. There is no prevailing disease, unless it is diarrhoea, and I have not suffered one day, nor lost one by sickness since I have been in California. We have had only one or two days sunshine since Hollow Eve, so that I am half inclined to believe that the rainy season has set in, though this morning the sun is out in all its brilliancy and dazzling splendor, and the air is as warn and refreshing as a Spring morning in the States. Vegetation seems to be starting up, as tiny blades of grass are peeping up, on the parched hills and in the deep ravines. There seems to be no fall here — that is a season out of season in California, for the trees still retain their fresh green foliage, so pleasing to the eye and refreshing to the senses. Yesterday I met an old gentleman who has only been in two weeks — he reports that there was deep snow on the Sierra when he crossed. I believe that all who left the States in the spring are now safely in.

On Friday, two of us went to work, and after toiling all day, we only made about $1. On Saturday, three of us started to go to a point I had before been to, about six miles off. The day was cloudy, and after going three or four miles in the right direction, as we thought, we halted at a ravine, where we worked for three hours and made some $50. — The sun came out and we found that we had lost our course, so we started for camp, and never were three persons more completely bewildered. First, we traversed one course and then another, until, finally, instead of finding ourselves several miles below camp, we came out above Wevertown, two miles above our camp. The difficulty originated in our crossing the Sacramento City road, which we took for a small byroad as the rain had altered its appearance vastly. That was, however, the best day's work I have made here, being a little over $16. The largest piece we picked up was worth $4.

There are many stories told about large pieces of gold, &c., which appear incredible to those in the States, but they are nevertheless true. The public should remember, however, that where five thousand people are at work, as is the case in Hangtown, it would be singular indeed if some one did not make a lucky strike each day. For instance, I know a man who took out, one day last week, a pound and a half and then on another day $196. Well, a fellow not ten feet off did not make enough the whole week to pay his board. I have seen some beautiful lumps of gold, but then it is only some few who are lucky enough to gather them. I have seen some half dozen men who have made $2,000 apiece, and not been here any longer than myself, and I have seen five hundred who have not made expenses. The rush of water, produced by the heavy rains has compelled those who have been doing well in the beds of creeks to abandon their holes, and seek for gold in the deep ravines — many of those are good, and I have no doubt living wages will be made by all this winter.

You can have but a faint idea of the cost of living out here. It costs each of us $2 per day, if we count the rations allowed to soldiers. Flour is worth 50 cts. per pound and will bring $1 by spring. Pork and beef the same. Onions $1.50 per pound. Potatoes $1 per pound, and all vegetables that can be had, in like proportion. Dried fruit is $1 per pound. I think, however, that we shall be able to kill enough fresh meat this winter, to serve us, as there is an abundance of elk and deer.

With regard to other members of our Company, all I know is this: John, James, and Henry Moore, together with Smith Crane, Bradley, Manning, and Garnhart are in Wevertown. Jim [Mc Curdy?] and Crane have been sick, but are up and about. Aisquith, Harrison, Murphy, Boley, Burwell, Marmaduke, McCarn, Barley, B.F. Seevers and Fagan in one mess, together with Jesse and Keyes Strider, Davis, Stonebraker, Showman, Rohrer, Duke, Cockrell, T. Moore, Joseph and Jacob Engle, in another mess, are ten miles above Weverton, on Wever Creek. Kelly, Purcell, Clevinger, Bowers, Smith, Ferrill and S. Davison, in one mess, together with Lupton are 1 1/2 miles below Wevertown. Geiger, Showers, Krebs, Keeling, Slagle and Gallaher, in one mess, together with James, Charles and George Cunningham. Dr. Bryarly, Hayden, Blakemore, Bender, Thomas Gittings, McIlhany, Herbert and Lewis, in one mess, are 150 miles above Sacramento City, on

Sacramento River. Rissler, McCurdy, Hoffman, Comegys, Wagner and Walpert, in one mess, started for the Mokulmne River. Allen, Dr. and John Humphreys, Daugherty and Mc Coy [McKay?], started for the Stanislaus. N. Seevers went to the Middle Fork of the America River, as did also Morgan and A.R. Miller. B.F. Washington, with Long, formerly of Berkeley, is up the Sacramento River, some 150 miles. L. B. Washington started for Monterey on the .... Hooper and Donnelly, probably went South, Conway was in Sacramento City when last heard from, as also Riley. Roland and Simpson are on the Yuba River. The first named mess and fourth [?] have been engaged up to this time pretty much in building, and have made but little money by mining. The second and third messes were doing ... well at the last accounts, and I have not heard from either of the other messes since we parted.

You are no doubt aware that we have a Constitution to be voted on Tuesday next, which makes California a free State. There is no doubt but that it will be adopted. The election will be a perfect humbug, as there are not twenty men in this whole region of the country who are acquainted with either of the candidates for Governor, Lieut. Governor, Congress, &c., or know their politics. Had I seen the Constitution two weeks ago, I would have been a candidate for the Legislature and stumped the district. Indeed, some of my friends wanted me to run at any rate, but I don't think one week sufficient for electioneering purposes.

I will endeavor to send you a letter monthly, but may not be able to do so on account of the inconveniences of getting a letter to Sacramento City. I have only received one letter from you since I have been in California.

I have good quarters for the winter, if we are to have any winter, as the weather is so fine that I am half inclined to believe that we could have remained in our tents. There is no family in California better fixed than we are. One is delegated as cook, and during rainy weather we have nothing to do.

Trusting to be with you all in good time, I remain your affectionate brother.

J.H.K. [182]

Figure 47. **Jacob Engle**. Charlestown, (Va.) Mining Co.

Figure 48. <u>Edward W. McIlhany,</u> Charlestown (Va.) Mining Co., 1849.

November 13th, 1849

Election day in California was accompanied by heavy rains, transforming what passed for roads and streets into rivers of mud. Although voter turnout had been forecast to be about 5,000, less than 3,200 persons cast their ballots.

Democrat Peter H. Burnett won the governorship, beating opponent John A. Sutter by a mudslide. John McDougal was elected Lieutenant Governor. Although the regular Democratic ticket for State Senators and Assemblymen had been elected by a large majority, the party was sharply divided. The Northern part of the State contained Democrats chiefly of the

Jefferson County's Fourth Estate, 1840-1850   145

antislavery persuasion, while the proslavery, pro-Southern residents were concentrated in the less populous Southern part. [183]

December, 1849

The *Shepherdstown Register* made its debut on December 4th, published by Henry Hardy and H.W. McAnly. The owners declared that,

> First and foremost, ... it is a Shepherdstown paper, the advocate, organ, and exponent of all the interests of this community.... neither partizan nor neutral, but really independent, generally inclining nevertheless, to those principles and sentiments which are understood to distinguish the Whig party, and the admin-istration now in power....

Greeting his new competitor, *Free Press* editor Horatio Gallaher announced "we extend the hand of fellowship and bid them God speed." [184]

Jefferson County residents learned of California's adoption of a constitution about the middle of the month. The clause outlawing slavery in the new State was a disappointment to some — others asserted that California, and residents of other future states, had every right to determine the slavery issue for themselves — and still others hoped that southern California could be severed from the rest and transformed into a haven for slave owners. There was no guarantee that the U.S. Congress would accept California's constitution and her statehood without modification. The devil would be in the details

William Gwin, hoping to gain a seat in the U.S. Senate, had not objected to the antislavery clause and had convinced the Chivalry Democrat majority to follow suit. He reasoned that delivering a complete, approved constitution with an anti-slavery clause would improve California's chances of achieving statehood. [185]

On December 20th, the California Legislature elected John C. Fremont (pro-abolition) and William M. Gwin (proslavery) as their State Senators. The men then drew straws to see which one would get the short term, which ended in March 1851, or the six-year term. Gwin won the draw and became the longer serving Senator. Charlestown Mining Company member, Vincent Geiger, who had sought a lower office, was not elected. [186]

Lumber was expensive in Sacramento and San Francisco, and most buildings were cobbled together from scraps of wood or were merely wood frames covered with canvass. So when a fire started at a San Francisco gambling house early on the morning of December 24th, there was little the citizens could do to keep it under control. It spread quickly, devouring city blocks. Desperate citizens (for there was no fire department) finally contained the inferno by dynamiting buildings to create a fire break. They called it the "Great Fire," but it was the first of many.

Thanks to the poorly functioning mail system, most of the Charlestown miners had received few or no letters since they arrived. Had their own letters reached home? They learned the hard way that mail addressed to San Francisco was rarely forwarded to Sacramento. Kelly's letters to Beller expressed the frustration felt by many.

December 30, 1849. Weaver Creek (California)

From J. Harrison Kelly

Dear Friend:

I have deferred writing to you this month until this late period in confident hope that I should previously receive some tidings from the States. But I find now that unless I write to you at once it will be too late for the January mail. I regret exceedingly that I have been so unfortunate as only to hear from you the once since I left St. Joseph. It is now nine months since I left home, and I find that all our Company are about on a par with me in regard to letters. I have understood that there were wagon loads of letters lying at Panama and no means of keep them from exposure to the weather.

I have seen members of the Aisquith and Strider messes within a few weeks and they are all reported as being well. I have seen Moore's mess frequently of late and they are all well, though Garnhart had been complaining. The mess I am with are all well. Edwin A. Riley died in Sacramento City on the 6th of November. That is the only death I know of since the division of our company. In regard to the other messes I know nothing. Those I have referred to are doing tolerably well in the way of "making gold." None but will make expenses this winter, and that is as much as we can expect. — All that we want is a good outfit in the spring and then we will make an effort to do something in the way of accumulating the "glittering dust." Although I never did credit the many tales about gold in California, still, I believed that what there might be, would be more easily procured.

Suppose I give you a description of our operations: Imagine that you are on the top of a hill overlooking a deep ravine. In that ravine you will see men of all nations, in all costumes, with picks, shovels, crowbars, and pans or washers. After digging a little, and throwing away the top dirt, the balance is generally put in a washer or pan and by the free use of water the dirt is washed off, and if there be any gold it will collect in the bottom of the pan. The richest earth is generally found in the crevices of the rocks in the bottoms of the ravines. Others are to be found digging along the different water courses, and in low flats — indeed, you can see persons digging where no one would have any idea of finding gold, except those engaged. Some of those mining average an ounce per day, and a few will do even better for a few days, but as a general thing you might put down from four to six dollars as the average during working days. The past week, for example, there has been but two working days, so that it is hard scratching to make both ends meet. Indeed, unless we had laid in our stock of provisions at low prices, it would be impossible to live at present prices. Boarding in Hangtown and Wevertown is worth six dollars per day! and that is not dear when we take into consideration the price of provision. — flour $4 per pound — mess pork $1 per pound — potatoes $1 per pound — onions $1.50 per pound, and so on to the end of the chapter. In Sacramento City boarding is $25 per week.

I have not seen much of California, but such as I have, has not impressed me favorably. The land along the rivers is of a most excellent quality, but it is covered by Spanish or Mexican grants, so that it is almost out of the question to locate a farm except on some other man's possessions!

The streams in this country rise with a rapidity unknown in the States, and fall again as quietly. The creek near which we are camped was swimming high one hour and easily forded the next. The cause of this is, the very steep and rugged nature of the country. In an hour after the rain ceased, nearly all is found in the rivers and creeks, running off rapidly. The roaring of the creek serves as a lullaby to sleep and to awaken the sluggard in the morning — but as to indolent men here, there are but few, for it is either work hard or no grub when the cravings of the stomach are experienced.

I suppose our good friend, Elisha Lock, told a rather dolorous tale of California. Well, I don't wonder much, for he had poor health and not that degree of spirit necessary to keep a man alive where he is forced to combat so hard with fortune. When I look around and compare my situation with that of many others I cannot but congratulate myself, as I have a fine house, plenty to eat, and a prospect of being quite as well off by spring as I was when I came here. Probably I shall have some $250, which will satisfy me, and whatever I shall make next summer over $2,000 or $3,000 will be over and above my calculations. It is hard for me to say where I shall locate in the spring. I think it will be either on the Middle Fork of the American River, (known as the Rio de la Americanos) or else on the Yuba River, the former 70 miles and the latter some 150 to 200 miles from Sacramento City. In either case that City will be my Post Office.

I have a great desire to eat my Christmas dinner in 1850 with you, and I trust that my desire will be realized.

* * * * *

On Sunday we had H. Moore, Jas. Moore, and Smith Crane to dinner. We gave them three courses of dinner, the best bean soup that ever met an epicure's palate — next, roasted pork, delicious — and to cap the climax, the best peach pies, made of stewed fruit, spiced with a mixture of Old Port and a little Cognac.

The climate thus far has been warm and far more pleasant and agreeable than in Virginia at this season. The live oak and tall pines are as fresh, green and vigorous as though it were the month of May, and indeed November resembles that month very much. Although it is now bleak and stormy December with you, and all housed and ensconced around the social hearth or "piping hot" stove, yet we have our door open nearly all the day, and feel quite comfortable — but probably our door would be closed a little more were it not that our cabin is devoid of a single pane of glass, and our only skylight coming in at the door. — The roads here now are almost impassable. — Frequently teams pass with from twelve to twenty oxen attached, and they even have difficulty in dragging a wagon with 1500 [pounds] upon it. Hauling has been (for sixty miles,) as high as fifty and sixty dollars per hundred, which makes every article vastly dear. I have understood that a good article of boots was worth $75 per pair in Sacramento City, but this is by no means the average. There are many who are just landing in California, and they have arrived at the very worst period. No comfortable houses to receive them, no season to work, and every article in the eating line to be had only at exorbitant price.

I saw Frank Clark the other day — Harry and Billy Clark are well, they live twelve miles from this. Fig Hunter is next door neighbor, now, and is in excellent health. Jim and Tom Perry live near Weaverton — Jim has made about $1,000.

I send you a list of the weather in California: Commenced snowing in the Sierra Oct. 10 — first rain — Oct. 30, continued two days — Nov. 3 clear — Nov. 4, 5, 6, 7, 8, rain moderate — Nov. 9, 10, 11, 12, 13, rain, — 14 clear — 15 cloudy — 16, 17 rain — 18 clear and warm — 19 rain in the forenoon and clear and warm P.M. — 20 clear and pleasant, evening cloudy — 21 rained hard all day, cleared off at night — 22 clear and pleasant, frost at night — 23, 24, 25, 26, warm and pleasant, frosty nights — 27 moderate rain morning, hard in the afternoon — 28, 29, 30, clear and warm, heavy frosts at night — Dec. 1 quite warm — Dec. 2, variable, cloudy and sunshine, at night a large fall of snow — 3 sun rose clear, clouded at 10 A.M., no rain — 4 clear and warm — 5, 6, 7, 8, 9, 10, 11, clear and warm, with heavy frosts at night — 12 rained all day and night — 13 rained hard — 14 rain, hail, wind, and snow 2 inches deep — 15 clear and cold, P.M. cloudy — 16 blustery and cold, with rain, hail, wind, and snow — 17, 18, rained all day and night, but not cold. — By this it will be seen that our climate is not quite so bad as has been represented, though I believe we shall have pretty constant rain for a few weeks at this time.

Yours, truly,

J.H.K. [187]

Part V. Conflict and Compromise.

Figure 49. President Zachary Taylor`

No civil government having been provided by Congress for California, the people of that Territory, impelled by the necessities of their political condition, recently met in convention for the purpose of forming a constitution and State government, which the latest advices give me reason to suppose has been accomplished — and it is believed they will shortly apply for the admission of California into the Union as a sovereign State. Should such be the case, and should their constitution be conformable to the requisitions of the Constitution of the United States, I recommend their application to the favorable consideration of Congress. The people of New Mexico will also, it is believed, at no very distant period present themselves for admission into the Union. Preparatory to the admission of California and New Mexico the people of each will have instituted for themselves a republican form of government, "laying its foundation in such principles and organizing its powers in such form as to them shall seem most likely to effect their safety and happiness." By awaiting their action all causes of uneasiness may be avoided and confidence and kind feeling preserved. With a view of maintaining the harmony and tranquility so dear to all, we should abstain from the introduction of those exciting topics of a sectional character which have hitherto produced painful apprehensions in the public mind — and I repeat the solemn warning of the first and most illustrious of my predecessors against furnishing "any ground for characterizing parties by geographical discriminations."

Zachary Taylor, *Message of the President of the United States to Both Houses of the Thirty-First Congress*, December, 1849.

January 1850, Washington, D.C.

The President's message failed to break the Congressional stalemate over California's admission to the Union or on the status of slavery in the District of Columbia and future states. Rather, State legislatures, such as Vermont, passed resolutions on these issues and forwarded them to their national counterparts, who presented them to Congress for passage. This disorderly approach generated much heat and little light during the Congressional debates. [188]

Feeling the pressure of Northern abolitionist resolutions, Southerners pushed back. Senator John C. Calhoun called for representatives from the Southern states to meet at Nashville in June to discuss the future of the Union — an ominous sign, considering the Senator supported Southern secession.

Trying to sidestep some of the general causes of the Congressional deadlock, President Taylor issued a special message to Congress on January 23rd that focused on statehood for California and New Mexico. He explained that,

> In advising an early application by the people of these Territories for admission as States I was actuated principally by an earnest desire to afford to the wisdom and patriotism of Congress the opportunity of avoiding occasions of bitter and angry dissensions among the people of the United States.... [189]

Taylor's efforts did little to clear the log jam. Then, near the end of the month, Senator Henry Clay rose to address the Senate. It was, he said, "desirable, for the peace, concord, and harmony of the Union of these States, to settle and adjust amicably all existing questions of controversy between them arising out of the institution of slavery upon a fair, equitable and just basis...." What followed was a version of "The Compromise of 1850." Several congressmen rejected it immediately, but it contained elements that appealed to both proslavery and free soil advocates. Perhaps it could survive the negations that would follow. [190]

Jefferson County, Virginia

County residents responded predictably to the perennial Whig and Democratic issues such as tariffs, banks, internal improvements, political appointments, and the President's ability to govern. However, issues such as states' rights, loyalty to the Union, and preservation of slavery where it currently existed were producing political realignments that would eventually fracture the Democratic party and morph the Whigs into several factions.

Jefferson County's Fourth Estate, 1840-1850

All three local editors, both Democrat and Whig, were opposed to dissolution of the Union. All three maintained that the Constitution guaranteed Southern states the right to maintain slavery within their own boundaries. And all three viewed the Congressional struggle over slavery as a Northern plot to weaken and dominate the South. Remarking on the "Vermont Resolutions," *Spirit* editor Beeler noted,

> We cannot believe that the action of the North upon this subject in the respect now under consideration, will be at all controlled by the course that Southern members may pursue in either house of Congress. We have long since been convinced that the North is lost to all sense of courtesy to the South which any question involving slavery is concerned. But there is something due to ourselves, as well as to the Senate of the U. States. Because others adopt the tone and style of blackguards, is no reason why we should be wanting in those qualities which would enable us to be respectful and courteous. [191]

When Henry Wise supported John C. Calhoun's anti-Union sentiments in the Virginia General Assembly, *Shepherdstown Register* editors warned readers of a more sinister plot:

> There are men in both sections of the Union who are tired of the Union — it is too regular, systematic and orderly — does not offer their vaulting ambition speed and scope enough, and they are burning to gratify the passion for novelty raging in their breasts. For a time this passion measurably spent itself in playing out the Texas game, in maintaining the Oregon flurry, and in prosecuting the Mexican War, now it seeks gratification in gnawing upon the vitals of the Union itself.
>
> Is evidence demanded of the secret unanimity subsisting between the Extremists of the North and South? It can be found in the sameness of the note they both sing, when the fit is upon them — it is the destruction of the Union, the poor Union, that makes the burden of their identical cry. The Union is the common cage against whose bars they chafe and beat, in their relentless struggle for change. [192]

News about California's struggle for statehood and from Jefferson County's '49ers could now reach home in about two weeks. If it were not lost or destroyed on its trip from the mines to the local post office, the mail was carried on a steamer from San Francisco, toted overland across the Isthmus of Panama, placed on another steamer, and transported to New Orleans. From there, the more urgent information could be telegraphed up the east coast in a matter of hours. Letters continued on their way by boat.

By midmonth, Jefferson Countians learned that fifteen thousand votes had been cast in the California election. Peter H. Burnett was elected Governor, and John McDougle, Lieutenant Governor. George W. Wright and Edward Gilbert had been elected to the House of Representatives. Senators John C. Fremont and William L. Gwin had been elected by the state legislature and embarked from San Francisco to Washington, D.C., on January 1st.

Readers familiar with the style and tone of *Free Press* editor H.N. Gallaher probably detected a note of tiredness and resignation in the early January issues of his paper. He praised the content of President Taylor's first message to Congress, asserting that, "although the carping presses of the opposition find fault and indulge in idle criticism, the great body of right judging men will give it their unqualified approbation." [193]

Many Northerners, he believed, supported abolition in the abstract but were quick to set aside their scruples if they had a chance to make a buck. As for the institution of slavery,

> Our opinion ... has been frequently expressed, and we do not hesitate to say that nine tenths of our African population are happier in every respect than the same proportion of whites. We do not include free negroes, for it is known and admitted that they are the most indolent, indigent and worthless portion of the community. [194]

He would favor a resolution before the General Assembly that banned free negros not sponsored by whites from residing in the state.

For those editors wishing to express critical, independent opinions, he warned: "In this country a fate almost as severe [as beheading] awaits the man who attempts to allay "party spirit" for there are so many newspapers that exist solely by political fermentation, and it has become so much a TRADE to keep up a pother that he who rebukes the authors of it, is directly denounced." [195]

In the last issue of the month, Horatio N. Gallaher put his own stamp on the *Free Press* by adding the words "and Farmers' Repository" to its name. The editor explained that the change was, in part, a tribute to Richard Williams, the original publisher of the *Farmers' Repository*, which the Gallaher brothers had purchased in 1828 and transformed into the *Free Press*. However, the change also signaled a change in attitude:

> We have long believed, although we have not devoted as much space to farming subjects as we think would be proper and useful, that the *Free Press* has always been an agreeable Farmers' Repository. We are under this impression, from the hearty welcome the paper always meets in the household of the intelligent Farmer.
>
> ... Whatever is to be found in a newspaper, worthy the approbation of a sensible farmer, is very likely to present some [of the same] attraction to the general reader. A Farmers' Repository may well excite in the mind a sense of abundance and variety. In the natural world, it awakens a thought of all that is substantial and nourishing, and all that is ornamental and pleasing to the eye. In the intellectual creation, it presents images of fruits and flowers to enrich and adorn the mind, and it carries the heart up in gratitude to the Giver of every good and perfect gift. As the Spring opens with its buds and blossoms, every one thinks of the country and its teeming fields, and the old and young exhibit a desire to traverse the ... fields and flowery paths over which they have

[trod] the year before. We therefore fall back upon the old title and greet our readers with the wish that each and all of them may be spared to read this paper 41 years more! [196]

Was Gallaher's change in tone a sign that he lacked the political energy to battle the Democrats, or was it an indication that his view of the North-South conflict was evolving?

California

Carrying copies of their new constitution, California's Senators Fremont and Gwin set sail on January 1 to make their case to the U.S. Senate for admission as a free state. Convinced that the U.S. Senate would reject California's application for statehood unless it prohibited slavery within its boundaries, Gwin had been instrumental in convincing his pro-South cronies to support this measure. As for Fremont the abolitionist, Gwin planned to distract him from interfering in important business.

On January 8th, a violent northeaster slammed Sacramento City, dumping torrents of rain and causing the Sacramento River to overflow its banks and rise into the city. The City Hotel had two feet of water on the dining room floor, and the old site of the *Placer Times* office disappeared under the water. Citizens were frantically building dams to stop the water from entering their buildings. The rainwater deposited in the mountains was rushing into the rivers, tearing out the old sand bars and depositing new ones - a dream come true for some miners and a nightmare to others.

During the following weeks, water levels receded in Sacramento City, leaving small flakes of gold in the streets. Being so far from the mountains, the amount found was generally too small to bother with, but it did not stop large numbers of would be miners from panning for gold within city limits.

Governor Peter Burnett's first Annual Message to the California Legislature dealt mostly with the nuts and bolts of assembling a new State — budgets, taxation, appointments, and so forth. The issue of slavery had been resolved in the constitution (it was banned), but the status of free persons of color had not. This group had no right of suffrage and was prohibited from holding offices of honor or profit within the state. Slave states, Burnett continued, might free their negroes and try to hire them out as low wage workers in California. Furthermore, he warned,

> If we permit them to settle in our state, under existing circumstances, we consign them, by our own institutions, and the usages of our own society, to a subordinate and degraded position — which is in itself, but a species of slavery. They would be placed in a situation where they would have no efficient motives for moral or intellectual improvement, but must remain in our midst, sensible of their degradation, unhappy themselves, enemies to the institutions, and the

society whose usages have placed them there, and forever fit teachers in all the schools of ignorance, vice, and idleness.

The best approach, he felt, was to ban all free blacks from the state, now, while their numbers were small. The new legislature would have to grapple with this topic.

Near the end of the month, the newly elected California legislature met at San Jose and passed bills dividing the State into counties and incorporating Sacramento City. (San Francisco would not incorporate until April 15th.) The topic on everyone's lips was the mail service — or lack of it. Letters were lost by the barrelful, prompting some correspondents, like J. Harrison Kelly, to send their materials overland to St. Louis. [197]

Frank Washington had picked up an appointment as postmaster in Sacramento, which lasted just a few months. He was on the lookout for other political appointments, possibly from the Democratic Governor Burnett. [198]

January 20, 1850, Webon Creek, California

From J. Harrison Kelly

MR. BELLER:

As I have a private opportunity of dispatching a letter to St. Louis, I employ it, for I fear very much that most of my letters from this point have been miscarried. The arrangements are very imperfect, for I have not received a single letter since the first from September last. I was, however, very much gratified a few weeks since, at receiving copies of the *Spirit*, with as late dates as 9th ....

How they reached Sacramento City, without my letters is a deep mystery to me, for I know that some friends have written long ere this. — The gratification of perusing these papers was greater than you can have any idea of — old familiar names were brought up, and deep ... are experienced by noticing the ways of the .... I was gratified to find you had received ... letter from the Rocky Mountains, for I feared [it] would never reach you.

[Hemmed] up as I am, in the mountains, I have nothing of interest to state. In fact I do not [know] of anything that is of moment. There [have] been some two or three white men killed by [Indians] within the last two or three weeks, some [about ten] or twenty miles from here, but it is rather [attributable] to imprudence on the part of the [white men] than the ferocity of the Indians. Indeed, I [have heard] of parties of whites who have formed themselves into a company with the purpose of [hunting] the Indians. When such a feeling [exists] of course retaliation must be the order of the day. The majority of the miners are peaceful and inoffensive — rather disposed to live on [friendly] than hostile terms.

[Since] December the weather has generally [been] of the rainy character, though the air is not as keen and chilly as in the Old Dominion at this season of the year. Singular as it may appear, I have not had my coat on more than three times this winter. Sacramento City has been [inundated] several times, and a great deal of [property] lost. The place must have large levys, somewhat after the order of New Orleans, if it [is to be] of any note. Indeed, so much has already been expended in erecting ... that ... them will make vigorous efforts in [building] a levy.

With regard to the mines there is but little [activity] at this time — the high waters ... preventing all work. There are thousands returning ... heartily sick of mining, tired and disappointed. I have determined to remain until the ... I first fixed upon next fall, and will then [decide if I should] leave off seeking a [fortune] in California. Indeed [if I had] lost my health I should make some effort to take my leave earlier, but as the country ... I shall remain.

I understand that our friend John Allen has left the country, having become disgusted with the picking and grubbing at the mines. Dr. Humphreys died at Sutters Fort, a mile from Sacramento City, about the [first] of December. His brother John, is clerking at a store on the Middle Fork, and E. Daugherty [has relied on] the compassion of those around him, being so much afflicted with the rheumatism that [he has been] unable to work. Richard Barley has had a [severe] attack of the scurvy but is getting better. Joseph Engle has been sick for some time, he has ... the dropsy, I believe. With these [exceptions the] company are well, [of whom] I have any tidings. Ned Aisquith got some letters a few weeks since which were the [first] since he has been in California. I presume that several members of our company will be for leaving this country by the next rainy season.

Two weeks ago I started, in company with ... others to the Georgetown mines, upwards of twenty miles off. I packed my bed together with pick, shovel and pan. We had to cross the South Fork, which we did in a frail canoe. The [cliffs] were at least a mile high on the ... side of the river and almost perpendicular. [Loaded] as I was, I found the fatigue to be very [great] — at one part I had to climb up a perpendicular [wall] of five hundred feet height, and had I [fallen] would have been dashed to pieces. After ... to the Oregon canon at Georgetown, we [found the] water too high to work, so that I had to shoulder my pack again and trudge homeward. I returned by another route some four or five miles further, but decidedly preferable. — I visited Sutter's mill, and saw the point where the first gold discovery was made — that is on the South Fork. On our route to Georgetown we [proceeded] haphazardly through an untravelled country with no road to guide us. We passed through an Indian camp at even tide, but they proved peaceable. During my trip we slept out in the open air for three nights, building large fires to keep us warm, as well as to keep the wolves at a respectable distance. Their piteous howls and barking could be heard all the night. — For a common sized ginger cake I paid $1.50 at Georgetown, and for half a pound of mess pork which we bought in order to have grease to fry other meat, we paid $1. Bread, a mighty poor article, we paid $1.50 per pound.

January 22, 1850

Snow is now three feet deep at Georgetown and three or four inches here, having been coming down pretty constantly for some hours. We have had several fine chases after a species of rabbit, called the Canadian hare — they have ears as large as any mule, and in speed are almost equal to a streak of lightning. We go it mighty strong in the meat line — eight of us can knock a hind quarter of beef "crazy" in less than a week, and we ate a deer weighing 150 lbs in about a week.

J.H.K [199]

Figure 50. Sutter's Fort, ca. 1850.

February 1850, Washington, D.C.

Henry Clay's Compromise resolutions captured much of Congress' attention from the time he first presented them to the Senate in late January, through February, and beyond. He also electrified the public, some for the content of his speeches but many for his reputation as a great orator. Learning that Clay would discuss his resolutions on the 5th, Washington women flocked to the capitol, occupying the floor of the Senate chamber and part of the reporters' gallery. "If these ladies could only vote," said the correspondent of the *Baltimore Sun*, "Mr. Clay would long ago have occupied the white house." [200]

California's Congressional delegation arrived about a week later, causing another stir, for it seemed like they might have to wait a while until the Senate granted them statehood. (Everyone knew that they had outlawed slavery and prohibited free blacks from remaining within their borders.)

Clay's oratory and the arrival of the California delegation, complete with an approved constitution, raised the hackles of the Southern Congressmen. Some presented a resolution to dissolve the Union. Others vowed to boycott the manufactures of any state that criticized their right to hold slaves. And many renewed their efforts to hold a Southern Convention at Nashville in early May. Democrats also heaped abuse on President Taylor, whom they accused of sending an emissary to California to dictate the contents of its constitution. [201]

Jefferson County, Virginia

Virginia's Democratic General Assembly tended to support the positions held by their colleagues in the U.S. Congress. The Assembly passed a resolution supporting the Southern Convention, declaring that "the most effective means of doing this are to be found in the cordial union of the whole South for the maintenance of the Constitution, and the preservation of the Union if it can be preserved, and for their own preservation, if it cannot..." Jefferson County and other local governments would soon need to select their own convention delegates. [202]

At the county level, all three newspaper editors opposed the dissolution of the Union and supported California's admission as a new state. However, they differed markedly on the way to achieve these goals.

Democratic editor James W. Beller was skeptical about President Taylor's assurances of noninterference in the drafting of California's constitution. Clay's resolutions, he said, would never work — California must follow Senate procedures when applying for statehood, procedures which allowed them to resolve the question of slavery at the national level. 203

Whig editor Horatio Gallaher supported Clay's resolution calling for a fugitive slave act. The Constitution, he pointed out, guaranteed that fugitives from service are to be secured and returned. Clay's measure provides the means to carry out the provision. As for the call for a Southern Convention or possible disunion:

> The people at large have a veneration for the Union, which should in no wise be impaired by discussions upon propositions from madmen or knaves... [W]e are opposed to sending delegates to the proposed Southern Convention. There is no necessity for it, and it will be a very useless waste of money to send men to Nashville to join in high-swelling resolves. If the people of the South mean to fight, they had better be preparing bullets instead of resolutions. Gen. Taylor will keep the fanatics in order. 204

The Whig editors of the *Shepherdstown Register* came out strongly against the decision to hold a Southern convention. Its goal, they argued, was agitation. Its purpose was faction. And talk of disunion was treason. Favoring the pen over the sword, the editors of the *Register* argued that the Southern states have a right to be upset about Northerners' refusal to return fugitive slaves, but the remedy should be through persuasion and legislation, not by violence:

> The only legitimate course, then, for the North is an amendment to the Constitution. If it can succeed in procuring this, all sections of the Union must abide by it, but until that can be done, the subject of slavery in U.S. Territory belongs as much to the Norwegian Storthing as to Congress. 205

Both parties were making plans for the State and local elections (April 28th), the Whigs having scheduled a precinct meeting for March 15th and 16th and the convention at the Court House on March 18th. 206

News from the Charlestown Mining Company was scarce, the accounts of San Francisco's Great Fire putting everyone on edge. In mid-February, the *Register* received a letter from Dr. Richard Parran, president of the Shepherdstown's Mining Company. He had new information about the Charlestown Company, and his description of life in the mines was not encouraging. "It takes the strongest, the hardiest, and most athletic men to work in the mines," he said, "and they often lose their health." If they could stay healthy and active, they might make $4,000 or $5,000 in a year. Sacramento, now a city of 5,000, had 20 to 30 deaths a day:

> You can scarcely meet a man without a cough. Most deaths occur in great measure from inflammation of the lungs and bowels. — I think that is owing, in great measure, to their manner of living, scarcely ever having on any clothes, or a dry and comfortable bed to sleep on. A

house weather proof will rent for 4 or 5 hundred dollars a month, no matter how small.... [207]

Despite the hardship, the Doctor vowed to stick it out till he made a pile. However, he would earn his money by selling merchandise to miners and practicing medicine.

California

About the time that the Washington ladies were swooning over Henry Clay, J. Harrison Kelly was poking his head out of his cabin at the end of California's rainy season. Although he had not travelled as extensively through the mining areas as Frank Washington, Kelly was keeping tabs on the men with whom he had crossed the plains. Like Washington, he could piece together disparate information from the people he met and form a broader picture of California than could most individual miners. He knew that you must maintain strong relationships to survive, and diversify your holdings while you had money and health. And he realized, that no matter how hard you work or how savvy your investments, luck could make or break you. It was luck that you staked a lucrative claim and your neighbor did not, that you remained healthy while others sickened and died, and that you knew to quit when you were ahead.

For Kelly, it was time to decide what came after mining for gold. "I have been considering the practicality of establishing a paper at this point," he said, "and after mature reflection have determined to engage therein. Its title to be "Sacramento Express."

For Frank Washington, his future was not in mining, or commerce, or even the law, but in politics. By grabbing a place in California's Democratic party, he could gain an elected office or political appointment and fight for the principles of Southern Democracy.

February 16, 1850, Webon Creek, California

From J. Harrison Kelly

As one of our mess starts for Sacramento City tomorrow, I thought it a favorable moment to send a letter to that point. There is nothing stirring, however, of sufficient importance to write you, and I write only to say that I am in the enjoyment of good health, and have been ever since my arrival. Those who were stoutest & most athletic in the States, seem to fare the hardest here. — Many who never knew a day's sickness are contained to their beds by some of the diseases of this climate. Those most prevalent are the typhoid fever, scurvy and diarrhoea.

Since my last letter Joseph Engle, of Strider's mess [Isaac?], has died. He died about the 20th of January, of typhoid fever, having also an attack of scurvy and diarrhoea. A very large portion of those who crossed the plains have more or less of scurvy. I have but little if anything of it, but have been using spruce pine tea, which is an excellent antidote. I believe that I have sent you regularly the deaths that have taken place among our number. Burwell, Frank Seevers, and several of that mess had the scurvy but are entirely well at this time. Aisquith is as fat as a Grizley bear. Clem Davis and all of his mess are in good health at this time. John Moore's mess are all stirring about in the mines.

There is but little doing in the mines at this time. No one is making any thing like good wages. The rainy season I believe is now over, as we have not had any for two weeks. The fact of it is, there is not half as much rain here as there is in the States. We had three months, November, Dec. and Jan., in which but little was done in the mines. For the last two weeks I have worked hard and have not averaged over $5 per day. The place I have been working is nearly worked out, so that I shall stop soon. Gold digging is a perfect lottery, some make lucky strikes, and others make scarcely enough to pay their grub.

As an instance of the price of eating here, I bought six lbs. of Potatoes today for which I paid $6. Mess Pork has been selling at $1 per lb., and until within a few weeks past, flour commanded the same price. Onions are scarce at $1.50 per lb. I suppose that we shall leave our comfortable cabin in the course of 10 days. Probably we shall go to the Middle Fork of the American River, not more than 30 or 40 miles from here. I was within 4 or 5 miles of that point during Christmas week, and was almost fatigued to death.

The hills are so high, and the ravines of canons (pronounced Kanyon) are so deep that they are only accessible with pack Mules. We shall be compelled to pack, if, indeed, we ever obtain our stock. We placed them at a ranche last Fall and have since learned that the Chap who had them in charge had left without notice, so that we greatly fear losing our mules. Mules are worth from 250 to $300 in Sacramento City. The great increase in price is owing to the fact that a great deal of stock was drowned during the recent stormy season. Out of 600 head of Oxen, only 16 were saved. This took place at a ranche on the Sacramento River. The corporate authorities are about taking measures for levying Sacramento City. If they succeed that City will soon be the largest in California. Last year the first building was erected, and now it has a population of at least 20,000. In a few months it will double that.

I understand that not less than 60,000 persons are on their way to this land of gold. The largest portion of them will rue the day when they forsook good homes and severed fond ties to come in search of an Aladdin's Lamp in California. But in most cases they will find themselves severely "bit." The fact of it is but few of those who come out have any idea of the labor required to procure gold. Those who generally come out are not stout and athletic, not those who are used to ditching and breaking stone, but those who have stood behind the counter, or served their apprenticeships in a Law Office or Doctor's Study. Such characters are sure to suffer from the fatigue incident to mining, even though they pass free of disease.

Leander Luther Rye, of the Shepherdstown Company died of typhoid fever, on the 5th of the month. He was formerly of Sharpsburg, Md. — He was aged about 21 years. Robert Anderson, formerly of Shenandoah, died early in the month of February. There were seven deaths in Hangtown on the 5th of typhoid fever. The sickly season may now be considered over, and I trust that we all may have good health during the summer. Five of the Fredericksburg Company, out of a mess of fifteen, died on the Yuba River last fall.

As an instance of digging, I give you this: One of our mess set in digging at a point where I had ditched a stream, and in one day took out $60. The next day I worked at the same point, and have done so for a week, and scarcely averaged $5. There have been several large hauls within a few weeks — one fellow at Georgetown (25 miles from here) took out eight pounds in one day! There are thousands engaged and it is not at all strange that one should be this fortunate. I know of instances where men have been engaged, making at least from one to two hundred dollars per day, and within two yards, others have not been able to make their board.

The mails are abused by all hands engaged in the mines, and Mr. Postmaster General Collamer must do a little better for the Californians, if the Administration ever retains what friends it once had in California. There is gross mismanagement in some quarter, and those in office are alone responsible. I have not had a single word of intelligence, since the first month of my arrival, and there are hundreds and thousands who have never heard at all. You would be amused to see with what interest I peruse a paper two or three months old. The last I saw was a *Picayune* of the 15th Dec. No election had taken place for a Speaker, and of course no message published. I believe I read every article in that paper, for reading matter is as scarce as hen's teeth here. Newspapers are worth $1 per copy in the mines!

I find that most of the emigration of last year intend returning to the States during the present year — but few, very few have accumulated anything, but all hope and expect to realize something during the present summer.

I hope you receive my letters regularly, but you must not be disappointed, if, during the summer, you hear from me but seldom. I may be so high up in the mountain as to find it impossible to send a letter to the city. I will have no fixed habitation during the summer, but will go wherever I think may be the best location. The

Middle Fork will be the principal point of my range, and I trust I may be able to make a few of the "shiners" before the next rainy season.

Send me the "Spirit" and write as often as you can find it convenient. I do not wish to press you on this point, for I know your duties are arduous enough in the way of writing. I find that the "Spirit" is known beyond the confines of Virginia, and it has an enviable reputation. I trust that you and the paper may continue prosperous, for I find a feeling of interest in my breast far deeper than I had supposed, when I was with you.

Frank Washington is still in the city, though I cannot tell you anything about the extent of his practise. I suppose he was compelled to shift his quarters during the high water in the city.

J.H.K. [208]

Feb. 27, 1850, Sacramento City

From J. Harrison Kelly

Dear Beller:

I received your letter of the 12th December, two weeks since, which were the only communications I have received, except those of September last. On yesterday morning I started from my cabin on Webon Creek, some 55 miles from here, and arrived at this city at noon. It was a most disagreeable trip, raining for half the day, and at night sixteen poor fellows were compiled in a space of less than ten feet square. We were as completely packed as any pork that was ever barreled. Sleeping on the ground and about half a blanket for covering — price 50 cents. I was taken rather sick last night when I was in the packing business, but it was owing to the good treatment rather than to anything else. This morning, however, I got up "right side," except that I felt as if I had been in a row and received a drubbing or severe beating, as my limbs were exceedingly sore from walking.

I have been considering the practicality of establishing a paper at this point, and after mature reflection have determined to engage therein. Its title to be "Sacramento Express."

James McCurdy died at the Volcanic Mines early in the month of February, of typhoid fever. I was shocked at the intelligence, as he was one of the heartiest members of our company.

When I shall be in the States is now uncertain, possibly next spring, but not to remain.

J.H.K. [209]

Figure 51. Senator Henry Clay, 1777 – 1852

Figure 52. Senator Daniel Webster, 1782 – 1852

Figure 53. Senator John C. Calhoun, 1782 – 1850

Figure 54. Disunion over slavery. From *Punch,* November 8, 1856

March 1850

In the history of our country, it is unlikely that three speeches given by three men so electrified public opinion in such a short period of time:

On January 29th, Henry Clay proposed a series of resolutions intended to provide both North and South with a basis by which they could compromise on extending slavery into new territories and states. It prompted both sides to dig in their heels, but it helped move the conflict from legislative delaying tactics to the discussion of critical issues.

On March 4th, John C. Calhoun aired the South's grievances against a powerful federal government determined to eliminate their constitutional right to own slaves anywhere in the country:

> Now I ask, Senators, ... what is to stop this agitation, before the great and final object at which it aims — the abolition of slavery in the States — is consummated; Is it, then, not certain, that if something is not done to arrest it, the South will be forced to choose between abolition and secession? ... [210]

On March 7th, Daniel Webster dismissed "peaceable secession" as impossible, criticized both the North and South for their inflexibility, and urged that

> ... instead of speaking of the possibility or utility of secession, ... let us devote ourselves to those great objects that are fit for our consideration and action; let us raise our conceptions to the magnitude and the importance of the duties that devolve upon us; let our

> comprehension be as broad as the country for which we act, our aspirations as high as its certain destiny; let us not be pigmies in a case that calls for men.... Let us make our generation one of the strongest and brightest links in that golden chain which is destined, I fondly believe, to grapple the people of all the States to this Constitution for ages to come. ... [211]

Calhoun would die before the end of the month. Webster's criticism of the North would cost him re-election. But the deadlock had been broken, and Congress slowly moved toward implementing Henry Clay's compromise.

Jefferson County, Virginia

Jefferson County's weather had been as stormy as the political discourse raging in Washington. Wind, rain, snow, sleet, and low temperatures attacked the population, prostrating many, and prompting others to huddle around the wood stove with their newspaper. Heated political discourse, accompanied by a hot toddy, helped cut the chill.

The county's editors reacted swiftly to the verbal duel between these Congressional leaders.

The *Shepherdstown Register* concluded that "... Mr. Calhoun is disposed to make his continuance in the Union as difficult as possible, by the exhibition of a perfectly ultra spirit, and the demand of conditions which he knows to be utterly unattainable."

The *Virginia Free Press* added:

> We may expect dissenters from some of the positions of Mr. Webster in the South, and perhaps opposition and abuse from the fanatical portion of the North but we believe the great conservative masses will respond to Mr. W.'s former noble sentiment, so happily enforced, and join with renowned fervour in the cry, "Liberty and Union, one and Inseparable, now and forever!"

Editor Beller, who might become the Democratic nominee for the Virginia Legislature, was more muted in his criticism of Calhoun and his praise of Webster. However, he basically shared the feelings of his fellow journalists. Calhoun's address, though an able and clear exposition of the conflict, did nothing to diminish the animosity between North and South. The Constitutional amendment he advocated to create an equilibrium between the two factions was premature. Nevertheless, Beller agreed that

> ... the course of the South alone can save the Union. The chief causes of the decline and fall of all governments, have been a disregard of fundamental laws, and encroachments upon the rights of a portion of

its inhabitants. — And these will be the causes of the disunion of our government.

As for Daniel Webster, Beller concluded that

> ... his speech seems to be universally regarded as one among the ablest and most patriotic of his life. We hope that it may put a check to that spirit of fanaticism at the North, which seems to be pre-determined to wrest from the Southern States of the Confederacy every principle that is held sacred, or to sever the Union in twain. [212]

At the local level, Jefferson County Democrats' morale was low. They were outnumbered and had little chance of defeating the Whigs' candidates for the Virginia Legislature. Nevertheless, Beller attempted to rally the faithful to action:

> It is true that we are almost hopelessly borne down by the influence of numbers, and he who enters the contest has a reasonable prospect of defeat. Yet this is no reason for yielding the day, without at least breaking a lance. [213]

They must, at least, make an effort to keep the party alive, and they must send legislators to Richmond who will work to approve a much needed Constitutional convention. The Democratic Mass Meeting scheduled for March 18th would determine if they would nominate candidates. When they met, they chose T.A. Harrington and James W. Beller as their candidates.

Jefferson County Whigs met at the Court House on March 18th and nominated Talbot S. Duke and John M. Jewett on the first ballot. Democratic nominee Beller had received much of the credit for defeating John S. Gallaher for re-election. Anyone voting for Beller, warned H.N. Gallaher, "will sustain the man of all others, who for six years has made it his business to heap abuse on Whig men and measures." Reminding his readers that those elected to the Virginia Legislature would participate in selecting a U.S. Senator, the editor warned:

> REMEMBER that you have an enemy in the field, who, although often repulsed, boasts that this Spring he will take the "Whig Castle" by storm. If you bear these things in remembrance and do your duty, your whole duty, and nothing but your duty, all will be well. [214]

April, 1850

Daniel Webster's 7th of March speech was still resonating throughout the country. The optimism it generated was probably prolonged by Calhoun's death, which silenced the South's strongest advocate of secession. Recalling the recent fear of disunion, *Free Press* editor H.N. Gallaher asserted, "Certainly nothing more fearful may be dreaded now — for Reason has asserted her empire, and Passion is cured by its own violence."

However, California's admission to the Union was not imminent. Senators agreed that legislation dealing with the Territories took precedence over her statehood. The South would not risk having California's votes cast on issues related to slavery in the territories. [215]

Jefferson County

Electioneering in the county was off to a slow start. Editor Beller droned on about the Whig administration's removal of qualified Democratic appointees from office. Editor Gallaher grumbled about rumored plans of vote swapping and warned Whigs not to be lazy and complacent in the upcoming election.

He prodded his competitor several times to stir up some excitement, but Beller only responded that he was too busy campaigning at the moment – he had a long reckoning to bring forward when he had time. "We already tremble at the very idea of it," said Gallaher, "particularly if he should be elected to stay at home. We will endeavor, however, to bear the chastisement with christian resignation — hoping that in his wrath he will be merciful. [216]

Sacramento City, California

Sacramento held elections for city and county officers on the first day of the month. Frank Washington, who had been campaigning hard on the "Rancho" ticket, won the seat of Recorder for the City. The *Sacramento and Placer Intelligencer* had called him "one of the clearest headed men elected on the 1st inst." J.H. Kelly enthusiastically agreed, noting, "[a]lthough he came here a comparative stranger, forced to build his own fortune, yet he now possesses a popularity equaled by few in the city." Washington had also garnered the support of Democratic Governor Peter H. Burnett, for he was appointed a Notary. Back in Jefferson County, *Free Press* editor H.N. Gallaher calculated that Washington would probably collect an annual income of about $15,000. With these impressive victories, he had decided to bring his wife and children West. [217]

When back copies of the *Spirit* and *Free Press* did reach the miners in California, Kelly and Washington discovered that the editors at home had been publishing letters intended for friends and family. Beller and Gallaher had removed some of the more personal sections, but probably not as much as they should.

April 12, 1850, Sacramento City, California

From J. Harrison Kelly

Dear Beller:

Unless you cease publishing my letters pretty soon, you will lose me all the credit I ever possessed for scribbling — if I had any to lose. All my late letters have been designed for your perusal, little dreaming of seeing them paraded before the public. They were written so hastily, and were generally of such a desultory character, that I fear they were rather a burden than of interest to your readers.

At this season most of the members of our old company are changing quarters, as no one will be long satisfied with any particular location. — [I learn] that my letter was received containing ... will soon proceed to that point — that they are expecting to stay more than a month. Clevenger, Farrell and Purcell are engaged in the grocery business and butchering in Placerville (Hangtown). Aisquith's and Strider's messes are both at the same town, and will remove to the Middle Fork as soon as practicable. Walper, and I think, Geiger, have gone to the latter quarter. Rissler, Hoffman, Wagner and Comegys will remain for the present at the southern mines, where they now are, and all well, as Mr. R. told me yesterday. Conway has entirely recovered, and leaves for there today.

Cunningham's mess [Charles, George, and James] and the one to which J.W. Gallaher was attached, are on the Yuba River. Messrs. N. and B.F. Seevers are on the North Fork of the American river.

I have heard from all within a week, except the two last messes, at which time all were in good health. Probably, the Yuba river affords the sweet reward of labor in California, but no money could induce me to remain along it later than the month of July. Sickness, disease, and death thinned the ranks of those who were there before the rainy season set in last fall.

First, let me correct some information I sent you in my last letter. I wrote you that Mr. Walper had made $2,600, and Messrs. Comegys and Wagner $1,000 each. Mr. W. told me all this himself, but I have since been informed that it is not correct, as he did not clear the one with that amount, not $500, nor the story correct as far as concerns these three gentleman. That being the case, I find that the average amount by each of our company to be a little over $150! — Rather a slow way to make a fortune. Some of your readers will say, why fortunes are made there, because I see names and places published. I agree that fortunes are made, but very few in the mines, and to illustrate how they are made I will give you an instance or two.

The gentleman who was elected Sheriff of Sacramento county (two weeks ago) came from the States via Texas and Mexico to Mazatlan, where he took passage for San Francisco. On arriving there he hadn't money enough to get off the ship. One of his companions got ashore and succeeded in raising enough of the "needful" to get Kinney off. [218] K. went ashore, entered into a game of monte, (a game at cards, or rather betting on particular cards,) and came out of the establishment $15,000 winner, a pretty snug sum, when he "jumped the game," and engaged in business. He is now worth $250,000! made by "many a twist and turn."

Today, at noon, two gentlemen were pointed out to me whilst dining, a former steamboat captain and his mate. The latter possessing no tact or ability, but fortune threw him into a fortune, by speculating in lots — the captain has also made a fortune, all by speculating in town lots. But to show still further some of the freaks of fortune, I will note one of the most worthy firms that has been in the city, Priest, Lee & Co. The Co. consisted of two or three gentlemen. One of the firm went out a month after engaging, and drew about $600 — another, shortly withdrew, drawing $1,000 — Mr. Priest withdrew six weeks ago, receiving $125,000 — and last, Mr. Cornwall sold out to Mr. Lee, the remaining partner, last week, for $132,000 — retaining some $1,000 worth of property on city lots. How did they make their money? Why, a great deal of it by merchandising and trading, but the vast bulk by speculating in city lots — Mr. Lee left Oregon a year ago, I am told "worser than broke," but now he wakes up, and finds himself a millionaire! This is the way fortunes are made, and those who leave the States this spring for the mines will find fortunes as scarce as "hen's teeth."

There is more gambling carried on here than in any State in the Union. Three men sat down at a faro bank at the Sutter House, Tuesday evening, at 5 o'clock, and remained there the whole night. The lowest bet was $500 on the turn of a card, and frequently thousands were depending. A friend of mine who happened to be present, told me he saw $27,000 down on a card, and that $10,000 bets were frequently made that night. $10,000,000 it is estimated were lost and won that night, but I think he estimated too high.

An election for city and county officers took place throughout the State on the first Monday in this month. Edward J. Willis, Esq., of Charlottesville, Va., was triumphantly elected County Judge, receiving three fourths of all the votes cast! He is a noble hearted fellow, and well known throughout Virginia as formerly being Grand Worthy Patriarch of the Sons of Temperance. On arriving yesterday, I learned he was very ill. The city being again partially inundated, I procured a boat and was ferried to his office. Judge Willis has quite a severe attack of dysentery, but I entertain great hopes of his recovery. Although we were previously acquainted by character, our first meeting was at the Western base of the Rocky Mountains. A slight acquaintance has ripened into a warm friendship, and, I, with the community in general, would greatly deplore his loss.

Our mutual friend, B.F. Washington, Esq., was a candidate for City Recorder, an office of honor, trust and profit. He had some half a dozen of competitors, but completely distanced them all. Although he came here a comparative stranger, forced to build his own fortune, yet he now possesses a popularity equaled by few in the city. The urbanity of his character and gentlemanly deportment have won him the high regards of the most distinguished in the city. I sincerely rejoice at his election, and his friends at home have reason to be proud of the position he now occupies and gratified at his growing popularity. Mr. W. looks better than I ever before saw him, and designs sending for his family.

I have just learned that Mr. W. has just received another appointment of a highly honorable character from Gov. Peter H. Burnett. I furnish you a Transcript of his commission:

"THE PEOPLE OF THE STATE OF CALIFORNIA:

"To all who these Presents shall come — Greeting

"KNOW YE, That reposing special confidence and trust in the learning, integrity and industry of Benjamin F. Washington, I, Peter H. Burnett, Governor of the State of California, in the name and by the authority of the people of said State do, by these presents, appoint him, the said Benj. F. Washington, a Notary Public, for the County of Sacramento. In testimony whereof, I have caused the Great Seal of said State to be hereunto affixed.

"Given under my hand at the Pueblo de San Jose the 1st day of April, in the year of our Lord 1850, and of the United States the seventy fourth. [219]

While California's statehood bill crawled through the U.S. legislature, slowed by the section outlawing slavery, its territorial government was busy enacting laws to control interaction among the races. It passed bills for the "government and protection of Indians" and "to prevent the immigration of free negroes and persons of color into this State." The latter legislation mimicked the efforts of Southern Slave States to restrict or remove free blacks before they caused trouble.

The notorious act to govern and protect Indians put most of the enforcement power at the local level (sheriff and justice of the peace), where it was frequently abused, keeping many Native Americans in virtual slavery for decades. Although some whites found it a useful tool for keeping Indians in line, it also provoked hatred and violence from both races. [220]

May 1850

Washington, D.C.

After Senator Henry Clay proposed his compromise resolutions to Congress, they formed a Select Committee of Thirteen (seven Northerners and six Southerners) to draft legislation based on Clay's proposals. Critics derisively called it the "Omnibus Bill" because of the number of persons who were "on board." The Committees' Report appeared on May 8th. It revised Clay's language to placate opponents looking for loopholes or hidden agendas, and it recommended how legislation should be organized and brought forward. Senator Stephen Douglas would be responsible for shepherding his colleagues through what promised to be a long, disputatious process.

Californians could rest assured that they would be admitted to the Union with their Constitution intact, but their concerns would not head the agenda. [221]

Jefferson County, Virginia

The county's fourth estate pounced on the Compromise Bill and worried it for several weeks. *Spirit* editor Beller took issue with the clause forbidding territorial legislatures from passing laws affecting slavery – wouldn't this allow the territories to deal with slaves under laws designed for free men? Henry Clay's motives for the language bothered him:

> We cannot rid ourselves of the idea that Mr. Clay is always more willing and ready to minister to Northern prejudices and fanaticism than to put forth one single effort to protect Southern rights. [222]

Gallaher echoed the warning of the Richmond *Times* that Virginia Senators Mason and Hunter appeared to have taken up the secessionist mantle from John C. Calhoun. They may be plotting to derail the Compromise effort,

> But if they have any regard for the sentiments of the people of Virginia, they will hesitate much before they take upon themselves the awful responsibility of the loss of this compromise. Were the question put to-day to all the voters of the commonwealth, whether it should be acceded to by her representatives, we believe the response would be almost unanimous in the affirmative. [223]

Jefferson County's gold rush fever began to decline as the mails brought news of miners' deaths. Those who had remained at home had accepted the risks faced by loved ones travelling the Oregon Trail – Joseph C. Young had died of typhoid, Thomas W. Washington of cholera, T. Milton drowned, James Davidson accidentally shot himself, and Newton Tavenner died of consumption. [224]

Now they learned that James McCurdy and Joseph Engle had died of typhoid at the mines, E.A. Riley had met the same fate in Sacramento. Dr. Humphreys succumbed at Sutter's fort, and E.A. Dougherty died at Panama on his return voyage home. Returning miners John Allen and John T. Humphreys brought back little or no gold and tales of hardship that could dampen the spirits of most men still itching to go west. [225]

Results of the statewide April 25th election were now in. Turnout had been low. Democrats Beller and Harrington had lost to Whigs Duke and Jewett, but not by much. Shepherdstown, the "Unterrified Precinct," had saved the day, since both Smithfield and Harpers Ferry had gone to the Democrats. Both parties strongly supported the measure to hold a State Constitutional Convention, which passed by an overwhelming 927 to 47.

Reviewing the lackluster contest with the *Spirit of Jefferson*, H.N. Gallaher mused:

> Our neighbor bears his defeat with so much fortitude, that he has really won our admiration. We almost regret having opposed him politically to the "bitter end," but the rules of war would not allow us to make an exception even in his case. We thought his silence for many weeks before the election was indicative, that he was "nursing his wrath to keep it warm," and that in the event of a defeat we would be in danger of our life. But we are agreeably disappointed, and therefore prepared to measure as many "sharp sticks" with him in the future as we have done in the past. [226]

On May 28th, Mr. Hardy, editor and part owner of the *Shepherdstown Register* left his position, selling his portion to Joseph Entler, Sr. The new proprietors changed the political stance of the paper from favoring the Whigs and the Taylor administration to neutral and from covering a broad spectrum of issues to focusing on Shepherdstown and its vicinity. [227]

Sacramento, California

Although not yet admitted to statehood, Sacramento had held elections for city and county officers on the first day of April. Voters selected the following:

* Mayor — Hardin Bigelow;
* Recorder — B. Franklin Washington;
* City Attorney — J. Neely Johnson;
* Marshal — N. C. Cunningham;
* Assessor. — J. W. Woodland;
* Council — Jesse Moore, Volney Spaulding, C. A. Tweed, J. R. Hardenburg, C. H. Miller, J. M. McKenzie, Demas Strong, A. P. Petit.

The *Sacramento and Placer Intelligencer* had called Frank Washington, who had been campaigning hard on the "Rancho" ticket, "one of the clearest headed men elected on the 1st inst." J.H. Kelly enthusiastically agreed, noting, "[a]lthough he came here a comparative stranger, forced to build his own fortune, yet he now possesses a popularity equaled by few in the city." Washington had also garnered the support of Democratic Governor Peter H. Burnett, receiving an appointment as Notary Public.

Washington's duties included trying all persons arrested for a breach of the peace or violation of city ordinances. Thus most of his business was likely to involve shootings, stabbings, barroom brawls, and other nefarious activities fueled by gambling, liquor, fast women, and miners with more gold dust than good sense. And since the titles to lands in and around the City of Sacramento were often ambiguous, he was likely to become involved in disputes over who owned what. To round things out, he was also the police superintendent and tax collector. [228]

June 1850

Washington, DC

In mid-June, Louisiana Senator Pierre Soule proposed an amendment to the Compromise Bill, allowing new territories to tolerate or exclude slavery as they may think best. The measure passed, securing the vote of several reluctant legislators in both Houses of Congress (including Mason and Hunter of Virginia), and taking some of the wind out of the Nashville Convention. However, the pro-slavery faction still had a few tricks up their sleeves – Senators Soule and Stephen Douglas wanted to divide California into two or three parts, hoping that the population would approve at least one slave state. *Free Press* editor, H.N. Gallaher, noted that, "This is providing for the future largely in advance of the progress of things." [229]

Despite the hopeful news of compromise coming from Congress, Southerners attending the Convention in Nashville, resolved to institute an economic blockade of the North if the Compromise Bill didn't go their way. Still optimistic of their chances, they resolved,

> That California is peculiarly well adapted to slave labor, and if tenure of slave property were by recognition of this kind secured in that part south of 36 30, the south part would in a short time open into one or more slaveholding States, to swell the number and power of those already in existence. [230]

As passage of the Compromise Bill became more likely, Southerners rightly feared that opportunities would diminish for moving their slaves West, or of ridding their own states of free blacks. Virginia was one of the states attempting to deal with the increasing number of free negroes within her borders.

Southerners often characterized free negroes as lazy, insolent, a burden on society, and a poor example to slaves. On March 13th, the Virginia Legislature had passed an act appropriating $30,000 per annum for five years, for colonizing the free colored people of the state in Liberia. The sum was insufficient to achieve the goal, prompting the American Colonization Society and other private groups to seek public donations. As one financial appeal in the *Shepherdstown Register* pleaded, "Politicians, Patriots, Philanthropists, and Christians would be well to consider if there is any other way they can do so much immediate practical good in the cause of patriotism, humanity, and religion." [231]

Figure 55. James Rumsey House, Shepherdstown, Virginia, from a drawing by Henry Howe, 1843.

Jefferson County, Virginia

The heated debate in Congress over the Compromise Bill prompted James Beller to publish in the *Spirit* an extensive explication of Southerners' Constitutional right to take their property (i.e., slaves) where they wished. Only two Virginians had attended the Nashville Convention, and Beller viewed the generally poor turnout as a lost opportunity for the South. They could have, he believed, gained some bargaining power to take their slaves West and to recover runaways in the North. Now, he concluded, "We should take our stand upon the Constitution, and then calmly, consistently and fully maintain our rights, and in doing so we contribute as much to the preservation of the Union [as] to the protection of Southern rights." [232]

Amidst the debate generated by the threats to the South's "peculiar institution," the *Shepherdstown Register* noted the passing of another landmark commemorating the county's heritage:

> We have observed that the tenement known as the "Rumsey House" has been razed to the ground, and a Brick house commenced on its site. Pleased as we are to see improvements of this kind going on, we cannot say that our pleasure was very great in this case…. We admire the reverence for such relics as this, which we find evinced in some portions of our country." [233]

As the summer wore on, Virginians began to divide their attention between the Compromise debate and the upcoming constitutional convention. Scheduled for October, it would discuss a variety of issues, such as extending the right of suffrage, direct election of all officers of the state, revising the system of county government, and whether slaves would be included when the population was calculated. Those competing to

Jefferson County's Fourth Estate, 1840-1850   179

attend the Convention were a political who's who of Jefferson, Berkeley, and Clarke counties. [234]

The news from the Pacific Eldorado brought Californians' grumblings over their slow progress toward statehood. Fed up with the excruciating delays in Congress, some threatened to set up their own independent government. Worried about a Western bid for independence, the *Shepherdstown Register* editor warned,

> We can without much difficulty appreciate the inconvenience in a hundred ways that the better classes in California must experience in the present state of their affairs, but we hope nevertheless, that they will use forbearance, and commit no rash or hasty step which might become the source of bitter repentance and regret. Undoubtedly the present anomalous state of things in that distant territory should be terminated at the earliest moment, and not wantonly indulged in to gratify a spirit of uncompliance or downright obstinacy. [235]

As residents received more news about life in California, some attitudes changed.

California

Many of the letters written home by the ex-members of the Charlestown Company were not published at the time. Considering that the Company contained approximately 80 men, it is surprising that more of letters have not come to light. Communications from California that appeared in the local Jefferson County newspapers were often heavily edited, sometimes to remove personal information. They were probably censored as well to excise internal conflicts that appeared along the journey West or because some of the sights were too horrific to tell the folks back home. Even before leaving St. Josephs, Missouri, Kelly had written that "I have already witnessed scenes that would make your blood run cold..."

For many of the Charlestown Company, the trip had been a manly adventure, a journey that tested their resourcefulness and courage, and helped them build relationships that kept them safe and partly relieved their homesickness. They had "seen the elephant," and they were better men for it.

However, making a living in California was another test of strength and character. By the summer of 1850, the huge influx of immigrants had transformed the area and the residents. A letter from a businessman recently returned from the West painted a bleak picture:

> It is a singular fact that men who now go to California lose all compassion for one another. Even those who have been friends and companions all the way from the States — friends for life — even

brothers, have been known to desert one another when in the very jaws of death....

Let a man in the United States picture to himself being sick in a foreign land, perched on a wet and muddy soil, with no floor but the damp ground, with no fire in the tent to dry it, or to dispel the gloom within; no feeling friend to bathe his burning forehead, or moisten his parched lips; no sympathetic sign from those he called his friends.... and many has been the instance that the patient died without the presence of a friend to close his eyes; and if the dead man has left money enough to buy him a coffin, he is placed in it without ceremony, and hurried away to a shallow grave prepared for him. If the patient has left no money, his remains will be wrapped in his own bed sheets and placed in his grave with as little ceremony as possible. It is, indeed, heart rending to see the depravity of the public mind in relation to the burial of the dead. In San Francisco the suburbs are one vast burying ground,.... You can frequently see graves not three feet deep, with coffins, and sometimes the corpses exposed, and not one grave in one hundred has an epitaph, or even the name of the occupant. [236]

Having some spare time, J.H. Kelly drafted a long letter to his friends back home, outlining the hardships faced by the immigrants and putting a humorous spin on events where possible.

June 20, 1850, Weber Creek, California

From J. Harrison Kelly

Presuming that you will be expecting a line from me by the next mail, I shall not disappoint you. Since my last, nothing of much importance has taken place. A party of whites had a battle with a large party of Indians on the north Fork of the American River, in which fifteen Indians were killed, and several white men wounded. Those in the fight believe that the Indians were led on by a white man.

You would be astounded to know the extent of the emigration to this country. Thousands are landing almost daily at San Francisco, all bound for the mines. The larger number of them will find mining any thing else than what they anticipated. There are comforts, however, here at this time, which were not attainable last fall. — The roads to the mines are thickly settled, and the traveler will not be compelled to go "from early morn to dewey eve" without a drop of cool water or refreshment. The sun is so hot already, that no one can endure its piercing rays at noon.

The small streams along the ravines are generally drying up, and in two weeks more, labor on them will be suspended. Then will come daming rivers and creeks, and to give you an idea of the chance "young 'uns" will have here, I give you briefly the result of my own investigations or those of friends: The Upper Sacramento is being rapidly occupied — the Feather River taken at every advantageous point — Yuba jammed with emigrants to its sources. On the three Forks of the American River: the north Fork pretty well taken — the Middle Fork not room enough for a stranger to sink his spade in, every lead being taken months ago — the South Fork probably less occupied than any other in California, for which no good reason can be given. Bear River is thickly settled — Deer Creek and Gold Run are completely dug up and washed out — the Marcossamy and Weber Creeks are already damed off, and the miners busy — The Dry Diggings at Webertown, Hangtown, Georgetown and Kelsey's are pretty well exhausted. so that it will be no easy matter to find good diggings, unless some further discoveries should be made this summer, which will probably be the case, although they can by no means be sufficient to yield a very large share to the five hundred thousand miners who will be here by the 1st of September next.

A law has been recently established requiring unnaturalized foreigners to pay $20 per month for the privilege of mining. This is most onerous and unjust in many respects, and yet salutary in one view. It is entirely too much, which will render it inoperative, and it is oppressive on those who have left their papers in the States — had it been $5 it would have been better. But few miners have much over $20 per month, after defraying all the expenses necessary to a decent living here. When I speak of decent living, I mean no better than is enjoyed by most of the slave population in the South — about which so many rampant philanthropists have raved for a few years past.

I have been somewhat surprised at the absence of fruit of any kinds here — not having seen apple, peach or plumb. Last fall I saw some miserable choke pears, as large as a walnut, selling for two bits apiece, but I wouldn't have eaten one for four bits!

The Southern part of California is reputed to be the most lovely in the world — fruits are said to abound, particularly the grape, the vintage affording a fine drink. The land is doubtless more fertile and much more of it susceptible to cultivation, But in this region, a farm must be located close to the river, or you find yourself "dry as a whistle" for five months in the year.

I am strongly inclined to believe that the great influx of population will have a material effect on the climate — that instead of such protracted deluges, we shall have an occasional shower during the spring and summer months. This course is strengthened when we compare the last three with three former springs — the rains formerly started in the month of January or early in February, whilst, this year, rain fell in the month of April. Whenever there is any thing approximating an equilibrium between the seasons, any land which is now deemed unproductive will be taken up and cultivated. That portion of the land suitable for farming is sadly defective in most cases for summer, but there is a superabundance of that substance thirty five or forty miles from the Sacramento River.

The forests here are generally composed of pines and oaks, the trees being somewhat scarce, but as you approach the Sacramento, the pine gives way to the oak. The fir tree is the noblest specimen of the forest I ever beheld — tall, straight, and like the pine, wears a perpetual livery of green. When crossing the Sierra I saw thousands, and was forcibly reminded of the references to them by Solomon.

An examination of the country, the abundance of gold at that time, and fir trees, together with many other matters, might reasonably point this out as the renewed land of Ophir from whence King Solomon obtained his treasure to decorate the temple. But be that as it may, it is quite certain that Solomon's servants were expert in mining and must have "lit down" on the richest diggings when they arrived, to return in the time specified, laden with so much of the "dust."

You have had so many descriptions of the country, its climate, productions, &c., that I shall desist a further in that direction at this time, as it must sound to your ear with all the familiarity of a juvenile story.

There are some productions here, however, which I doubt very much their being noted, viz: snakes, lizards, toads, horned frogs, mice, ants, and every other pest of the kind ever known to mortal man. I have seen but one reptile verging to the centipede order and not one tarantula, which I do not much regret. We have several species of snake: the rattle, spotted, and striped — neither of them appear vicious, and I doubt very much whether either are very venomous — although some Spaniards say the spotted are incurable.

Whilst writing in the cabin, an hour since, my attention was attracted by an unusual scampering of the mice, and on looking up, I saw a large spotted snake making his way up the logs for an evening's repast among the mice. Although no friend to the latter, I immediately snatched this snake up and found him to be some 3 feet in length. He was a beautiful specimen, and seemed to take the blow so good naturedly, that I almost pitied him in his dying moments! As to lizards they are so plenty that no one who has been here long, pays any attention to them — although it is quite interesting to see the live Yankee just set down from his ship when he finds himself surrounded by these "terrible creetur's."

Last fall, I recollect being vastly amused at the expense of some of the "live lumber" from the Eastern States. A company had just arrived, and were pitching their tents below us, when suddenly, some one of the party observed lizards running about, almost "thick as hail." A deputation immediately posted off to our camp to learn the nature, character, and qualifications of the lizard kingdom. Having seen millions, in crossing the plains, we assured them of entire safety, and were willing to issue policies of insurance for a nominal sum! I have never had any exactly in bed, that I am aware of, though there is not a night that they do not have races over it after mice.

We "did" one of our mess a few nights ago in an amusing style. Two of them grew tired of the cabin and the pests around, and resolved to rear the tent and take the fresh air. The day after, one of them killed a snake, unknown to the other, and placed it in an interesting coil under the head of the partner's bed, on the ground, resolving to have some "rare sport" in the course of the evening. Accordingly, about nine o'clock, after we had been telling snake stories in the cabin, and had our friend's mind well charged, ready for an explosion, the "knowing one" and his "victim" proceeded to the tent with a candle. The tent strings were tied inside, and all means of escape cut off. The "knowing one" had the candle where he could tip it over on the first discovery. The "victim" sat down to examine his bed, and on lifting up the pillows (overcoat) there lay a snake coiled, just ready to spring.

With sudden terror and a shriek of "a snake!" and out went the light! What a situation! in close proximity with a poisonous monster and surrounded by Egyptian darkness! The other, insisted with mock earnestness, that it was no snake — that his terror had got the better of his judgment — to all to no purpose. Matches being at hand, a light was soon struck, and the poor "victim" was found "roosting," very uncomfortably, half up the tent pole! A club was at hand, and after a most unmerciful drubbing — even for a living reptile — his snakeship was pronounced beyond recovery, and the trophy forthwith brought to the cabin, although I had witnessed all as it took place and had hastily retreated, expecting a visit from the "victim." It was amusing to see with what right hearty good will the blows were inflicted by the "victim" of the joke, and it is interesting now to hear him tell of his snake adventure, to those who pass, as he does not doubt the snake's being alive, when he first discovered it, and we have never informed him any better.

In justice to a gentleman and mechanic of your town, Mr. GERVIS S. GARDNER, I must say, that the picks he manufactured for the Charlestown Mining Company were, and are, the best I have seen in California. They are not quite the "bend" for mining, but the steel and material of which they are composed, show, conclusively, the honesty of his heart and good intentions. An "honest man is the noblest work of God," and those who possess his friendship have that which they should esteem highly.

The various messes of the old company are so divided and subdivided, that I can no longer speak of them in general terms. Those whom I have lately seen or heard from were generally in good spirits, viz: Messrs. John and Henry Moore, Bradley, Crane, Manning, Lupton, Bowers, Ferrill, Parcell, Clevinger, Smith, Aisquith, Harrison, Burwell, Boley, Murphy, Fagan, Barley, Walpert, Jesse and Keys Strider, Showman, Rohrer, Davis, T.C. Moore, Cockrell, Engle, Stonebraker, Duke, Mackaran, Marmaduke, Rissler, Hoffman, and Wagner. I have not seen those who went to the Yuba and Southern diggings, since we separated at the city last fall. There have been no deaths, I presume, save those I have already forwarded

Knowing the gallantry of the Editor of the "Free Press," I would not recommend him to visit this country until ladies become less of a rarity. Just think of the accommodating lassie who was married one hundred and thirteen times, and nine hundred more claimants for her hand!

There was a tall wedding at Weber the other day. It was done up State fashion — with full as much silk, satin and broadcloths. Wishing you, and all my friends, health and happiness, I am your friend,

J.H.K. [237]

Figure 56. Washington Monument, Washington, D.C., ca. 1850

July 4th, 1850
Washington, D.C.

Citizens celebrated the 74th anniversary of their Independence in various ways throughout the city, but the festivities held at the Washington Monument were the center of attraction. Partially complete, the structure was slowly rising skyward, propelled by private donations. The day was hot and humid, but about two thousand persons attended the event, including President Zachary Taylor, part of his Cabinet, and many Senators and members of Congress.

The Rev. Dr. Butler gave the opening prayer. He was followed by patriotic music, after which Walter Lenox, Esq., Mayor of the City, read the Declaration of Independence. Senator Henry S. Foote of Mississippi then rose and delivered the oration. After presenting admonitions taken from Washington's *Farewell Address*, he made a sweeping gesture that encompassed the impressive surroundings, and urged,

> ... here, in the midst of the assembled wisdom of the nation, and in presence of this vast multitude of my patriotic countrymen, I urge you, and all of you — I entreat you, I beseech you, at this moment of awful peril to the republic — that ye do your duty, and nothing but your duty, to the constitution, to the Union, and to the sacred cause of liberty itself! [238]

During the celebration, the President ate some raw fruit and iced milk as an antidote against the heat. That evening, he developed indigestion.

Jefferson County, Virginia

In his first issue of the month, James Beller shared his satisfaction that his *Spirit of Jefferson* has survived its sixth year. Thanks to his patrons, his paper was now the largest county journal in the State. He also reminded the public that persons who did not read newspapers could not intelligently perform their civic duties. Those who did read the *Spirit*, but whose subscriptions were in arrears, were warned to pay up, "make amends for the past, and sin no more." Perhaps residents were just tired of Congress' excruciating inaction, or the interminable invective hurled by one party against the other. [239]

Early in June, Martinsburg and Winchester were already at work, planning their own Independence Day celebrations. Jefferson County lagged behind. Noting the plans of his neighbors, editor Beller remarked, "it would be gratifying on all hands if arrangements were made in our midst for this purpose." As the day approached, he explained that farmers were in the middle of their harvest and the weather was unusually warm — the county would not hold a public celebration this year. Shops would be closed; there would probably be some festivities at Shannondale Springs; but the public was pretty much on its own.

Editor Hardy of the *Shepherdstown Register* had departed on June 4th, taking his Whig principles and literary agility with him. His position as co-publisher was taken by Joseph Entler, Sr. Entler and McAnly announced that the paper would henceforth be politically neutral, focusing on the more edifying interests of local readers. (The paper would fold before the end of the year.) As the 4th approached, they published an article, extolling the accomplishments of the country since its inception, barely mentioning the crisis that threatened to fracture the Union. [240]

In her *Domestic Manners of the Americans* (1832) Frances Trollope had remarked that, on the Fourth of July, every American aroused as from a three hundred and sixty-four days' sleep. In 1850, it appears that most Jefferson County residents did not.

John H. Kloth, a member of the Shepherdstown Mining Company, managed to reach home in time to enjoy the subdued festivities. He returned, he said, "with a fortune — a fortune in being once more in the bosom of his family and in the enjoyment of good health, and the comforts of his home." He reckoned that he had more "dust" thrown in his eyes before he left home, than he brought back with him from the land of "dust." [241]

Sacramento, California

At Sacramento, waters were still receding from the recent flood, and citizens traversed the city in boats, making it the reluctant Venice of the West. The Independence Day celebration began at noon on higher ground at Brighton Pavilion on the western outskirts of the city. Attendees included the Governor, Lieutenant Governor, Col. Sutter, and other local officials. The toasts were briefly interrupted when a participant was slightly injured by a canon discharge. Festivities resumed with an oration by Frank Washington. An impressive series of official and volunteer toasts followed including:

> The Union: He that would sever it should have his head severed from his body.
>
> California: She is ready to be embraced when her sisters are to embrace her.
>
> The Ladies: If Congress would comply with their wishes our admission would no longer be procrastinated — for they, as Californians, are in favor of Union.

The evening concluded with fireworks and a *Ball Soiree*, with former Charlestown Company surgeon, Dr. Wake Bryarly, serving as one of the managers.

The Sons of Temperance held their own "dry" celebration in town at Queen's Hall. Their toasts, drunk with water, not spirits, included:

> G. B. Stevens: Ladies and gentlemen, let us drink of the waters of the Sacramento, ever pure, sparkling and bright.
>
> Rev. J. A. Benton: [Holding up a tumbler of water.] — The pure water of the Sacramento — who fears another overflow?

San Francisco's celebration was almost as impressive as Sacramento's, and throughout the would-be state smaller communities demonstrated their enthusiasm, using firearms instead of fireworks, hollowed logs instead of canons. Many conducted their orations and toasts in both English and Spanish. [242]

July 9, 1850, Washington, D.C.

On the days following the July 4th celebration, President Taylor complained of digestive problems. His physician diagnosed the malady as "cholera morbus," a catchall phrase that included a variety of intestinal ailments. He developed a fever and failed to respond to treatment, dying on the evening of July 9th. Millard Fillmore took the Presidential oath of office the following day.

The funeral was held on July 13th, with about 100,000 mourners lining the funeral route. The funeral hearse was drawn by eight white horses, led by negro grooms dressed in white and wearing white turbans. Members of Congress, military units, Masons, Odd Fellows, and other fraternal orders followed, the procession extending nearly two miles.

By mid-July, speculation was rampant about the composition of President Fillmore's Cabinet. Horatio Gallaher, joked that "Every man who has ever 'set a squadron in the field,' thinks himself fit for Minister of War." When the positions were finally filled, Daniel Webster was heading the State Department and solid Whigs filled the ranks. Gallaher challenged,

> Now let the Democrats open their batteries and do their worst.
> "We have a strong team," able to resist successfully all assaults. [243]

Jefferson County, Virginia

The local papers were bursting with articles from candidates wanting to attend the Virginia Constitutional Convention. At one point, there were as many as 27, even though only 4 could be chosen. They held numerous meetings, explicating their positions, trying to join with other like-minded candidates to strengthen their influence at the Convention. All of the editors urged the candidates to speak out, providing the voters with the information they needed to make intelligent choices. Few issues within the past decade had generated such public interest. [244]

Even before Zachary Taylor's funeral had taken place, Jefferson Countians were planning their own event to honor him. Led by H.N. Gallaher, a bipartisan Committee of Arrangements set August 3rd as the day for a funeral procession and oration. [245]

With all the convention electioneering and funeral planning, most citizens had paid little attention to Henry Clay's Compromise. Editor Gallaher noted that the people were tired of the protracted debate and wanted Congress to vote. At this point many citizens preferred to see Congress pass the Bounty Land Bill and the Appropriation Bill. "California will doubtless be admitted," he said, "but not until every parliamentary expedient shall have been exhausted." [246]

California

By the end of the month, Kelly had returned to Sacramento, where some of the more successful members of the Charlestown Company had congregated.

News of President Taylor's death reached California on August 23rd. Penned just two days after the President's death, letters from the *Daily Alta California's* Washington correspondent brought discordant rumors about the fate of California's statehood – Fillmore would push through the Compromise; OR Congress, would focus on Appropriations and the Texas – New Mexico border dispute and then adjourn (i.e. no Compromise or statehood this session). [247]

July 27th, 1850, Sacramento City, California

From J. Harrison Kelly

There are quite a number of the old Virginia Company in this city at present. Dr. Bryarly, B.F. Washington, Esq., S. Davison, V.E. Geiger, John Moore, Jas. Moore, Henry Moore, J.M. Lupton, T.C. Bradley, E.M. Aisquith, John S. Showers, and J.H. Kelly, all of whom are well and either engaged or about to be engaged in business. I saw J.W. Gallaher a week since, he was quite well and reported favorably of the county he is in. He is keeping store at Nevada City. Cockrell's old mess are, I believe, on Feather river, and are reported to be in good diggings. Clevenger's old mess are pretty much separated, but all well at last accounts. You would be astonished to know what a city we have here. It beats all creation! and it will not be long before we have a city of some note in the Utah country, or between the Great Basin and California, on the Eastern slope of the Sierra.

Remember me kindly to all friends,

J.H.K. [248]

> ... we dissent from this bill, and solemnly protest against its passage, ... as it is destructive of the safety and liberties of those whose rights have been committed to our care — fatal to the peace and equality of the States which we represent — if persisted in, to the dissolution of that Confederacy in which the slaveholding States have never sought more than equality, and in which they will not be content to remain with less.
>
> *The Protest of Southern Senators to the Admission of California, August 13, 1850.*

August 1850

Washington, D.C.

Daniel Webster had resigned from the Senate and joined President Fillmore's Cabinet as Secretary of State. Without his presence on the Hill, the Compromise sputtered and stalled, its fate rising or falling with almost every session of Congress. By the end of the month, members had passed the Texas Boundary Bill and Appropriations Bill, and the Fugitive Slave Bill was on the verge of being approved.

Seeing the handwriting on the wall, Southern Senators (including Virginia's Mason and Hunter) had gone on record as opposing California's admission to the Union. It's passage, they believed, would set a precedent preventing Southerners from bringing their "property" (i.e., slaves) into the territories. [249]

Jefferson County, Virginia

The funeral ceremonies honoring President Zachary Taylor began at dawn with bells tolled and canon fired. At 11 AM, Capt. John W. Rowan formed up the procession in front of the Court House in Charlestown. The Martinsburg Band and the Masonic Order were in the lead, followed by a hearse with six dun horses, led by six negro men, clad in white gowns and turbans. Next was a riderless horse, appropriately caparisoned, and led by a negro man clad in white. Then came the militia, local officials, fraternal organizations, and members of the public. The procession moved to the Presbyterian Church, which was filled to capacity. [250]

The solemnity of the occasion was compounded by the gloom spread by news that cholera was at their doorstep. Physicians and veterans of earlier epidemics warned the public to abstain from eating vegetables, lime their cellars, and remove trash from the streets. But they didn't know that cholera was spread by a bacterium in water – that good sanitation and basic hygiene were worth more than all the patent medicines they could buy.

By the end of the month the disease had spread from Harpers Ferry to the rest of the county, producing about a dozen fatalities. Reprinting an article from the Washington *News*, H.N. Gallaher urged the Virginia Legislature to incorporate Harpers Ferry so that that could get the municipal authority and resources to fight this scourge before it infected other parts of the State. [251]

Campaigning for representatives to the Constitution Convention continued hot and heavy throughout the month. When ballots were counted, William Lucas, C.J. Faulkner, Dennis Murphy, and Andrew Hunter, all local men and all in favor of using the "white basis" had been selected to represent the district. [252]

California

Since his arrival in California, Captain John Sutter had accumulated hundreds of acres near his settlement, including substantial holdings in what became Sacramento County. He had sold some of it but had not been diligent in keeping track of what was, or was not, his property. As the population increased, some conmen tried to claim property they did not own. Other immigrants, with no resources and no place to live, "squatted" around Sacramento, assuming that the unoccupied land was in the public domain. If it was "public," they reasoned, they had as much right to it as someone else.

As expected, an alleged land owner eventually filed a suit to remove a squatter from his land. Then dissatisfied residents formed a squatters' association and lawsuits on both sides of the issue proliferated.

The dispute came to a head on August 10th, when John P. Rodgers and De Witt J. Burnett sued John F. Madden, in the recorder's court, B. F. Washington presiding, under the statutes concerning "unlawful entry and detainer." F.W. Thayer, lawyer for the defendant, first plead that the court had no jurisdiction over the land – Washington overruled him. Thayer then plead that, if the land were public property, his client owned it because he had made improvements – Washington overruled him again. Finally, Thayer asked for a change of venue because Washington was biased against him – no again. Washington returned a judgment against the defendant, fining him $300 and court costs.

The defendant appealed the decision to the county court on August 8th, where a different judged affirmed Washington's ruling and overruled the plaintiff's request for an appeal to the Supreme Court of California. Throughout the litigation, angry squatters and anti-squatters had met regularly, and when the judge's verdict was announced, the organized squatters vowed to "appeal to arms, if necessary, to protect their sacred rights with their lives."

J. Harrison Kelley noted that he

> ... attended a meeting of Squatters last evening [August 13th] on the Levee, which overtopped all meetings I ever witnessed, in the wave of "noise and confusion." The speakers were annoyed incessantly, and sharp words spoken. The squatters resolved to defend their property to the last extremity and at all hazards. What the end will be I shall not attempt to prophecy.

On the afternoon of August 14th, a group of squatters, led by Maurice Maloney, a former Lieutenant in the Mexican War, protested in Sacramento City after one of their associates was evicted. Mayor Bigelow, leading law enforcement and government officials to quell the demonstration, was shot four times by the protesters. Assessor J.W. Woodland, standing beside the mayor, was killed on the spot. When Maloney could no longer rally the squatters, he spurred his horse into the men defending Bigelow. He was shot and killed by Frank Washington. [253]

Shortly thereafter, Brigadier-General A. M. Winn of the militia declared the city under martial law and restored the peace. The city council appointed Frank Washington Marshal. Remarking on his heroic actions, one reporter noted that,

> Mr. Washington has charge of all the arrangements for preserving the peace of the city, and is a most gallant gentleman. His life would not be worth much if a Squatter could get a fair shot at him; and yet, I met him this morning, at two o'clock, perambulating the streets, with his rifle at his shoulder, as cool as a snow flake. [254]

The next day, Sheriff Joseph McKinney took a posse in pursuit of some squatters who had fled the city. McKinney was killed by a man named Allen in the confrontation that followed. Allen was wounded and captured by Dr. Wake Bryarly, who had accompanied the posse.

When the smoke had cleared, the blood scrubbed away, and the peace restored, just about every Sacramento resident knew who Frank Washington was and what he could do. Mayor Bigelow survived the encounter but died of cholera several weeks later.

Despite the heat and confusion in Sacramento, the emigrants kept arriving, by boat or over land. The latter route was particularly dangerous this year due to lack of water and forage. Even worse, some outfitters skimped on the supplies needed to complete the last leg of the trip. As J.H. Kelly noted below, many pioneers would not live to see the West Coast without resupply.

Figure 57. Daniel Jenks, Humbolt River Valley, 1859 [255]

August 14, 1850, Sacramento City, California

From J. Harrison Kelly

DEAR BELLER:

As several steamers leave on the 15th, I concluded to drop you a line, although but an hour elapsed before the closing of the mail. The overland emigration is still coming in slowly. — You are probably aware, the first of the emigration arrived more than a month ago. Those who got in thus early were generally packers, or those having mules and horses. Those having oxen seem to be in the rear this season. There is a great deal of distress reported along the waters of the Humboldt or Mary's River. The emigrant travels along this stream for three hundred miles. On either side of this river is a barren and desolate waste of country principally of a sandy character where there is no vegetation. The emigrant, heretofore, always found nutriment for their stock along the flats of the river, and between the high bluffs. This year, however, these flats are reported to be almost inundated, and when spots are found, stock are only gotten to them with very great difficulty. — Last year we had only two streams to ferry, the North Platte and Green River, whilst this year, a gentleman informs me, he was compelled to ferry his property over fourteen streams — some of them being only a few yards wide!

It appears that all the emigration intended to be among the first into California, and that to effect this they loaded lightly, taking only some sixty days provision. Under any circumstances, rations for sixty days will catch the emigrant many miles on the eastern slope of the Sierra, and those who have their stock stolen by the Indians — or lose it by reason of the alkali waters, or from any other cause, will soon discover to their sorrow, that they have either been improvident in the use or lacked judgment in the purchase of their outfit.

Accounts reach us almost daily of trains far off as yet who subsist on mule or horse meat! The mule or horse is killed and the emigrant slices off the delicious steaks — leaving the forequarters at the mercy of the "Digger Indians," who infest the Humboldt country.

The eastern slope of the Sierra is somewhat settled at this time, and doubtless before many years there will be quite a respectable inland city along Carson River. The bottoms along the river are large, and susceptible of being rendered quite productive. We have many reports of the existence of gold along the eastern side of the mountain, and should the anticipations of many "knowing ones" be realized, a large population will locate in that region of country.

The small towns near the mountains in mining districts, are rapidly filling up, and considerable trade is carried on between them and those along Carson river. the greatest disadvantages a settlement on the eastern side would be subjected to the everlasting big snows which fall in that region. American genius can do almost any thing — overcome any thing, and probably some live Yankee might invent a plan for turning the congealed mass which falls into lucid [?], limpid water.

The timber on the Sierra is the noblest in the world, consisting almost exclusively of the pine and fir tree. I have seen many out of whose base a comfortable room might be "dug," sufficient in dimensions for a young and growing family. It would be quite interesting to live in one of these natural shelters, and as the family increased all that would be necessary would be to add another story, not by building, but by "digging out."

The mining country does not hold out as strong inducements this season as last, and it must naturally lessen in value, unless discoveries are made. I have never had reason to change my opinion of this country — either as regards its mines or the adaptation of the soil for culture.

As for the mines, I have written that a few realized fortunes, whilst the vast majority made but little more than their boarding. By this I mean that they make on an average from $4 to $8 and pay from $1 to $3 per day for board. Most of the miners do their own cooking and washing, and as the mines yield so do they live. If they make half an ounce per day they live high, that is indulge in vegetables. Every article of food is sold by the pound, and can be had in this city at reasonable rates. Cucumbers and Tomatoes are worth about a bit apiece, water melons have been sold at 85 — but now can be had for $3; potatoes can be had in the city for 10 cts. a pound, I have paid one dollar per pound on many an occasion. The fact of it is, as the mines give way, every thing else must decline. The supply of gold must regulate the market.

Most of our old Company are interested in river claims — that is, draining the river, and draining its bottom by means of races. Last fall this kind of work was found to be the most profitable, and I hope that success may attend those now engaged.

[Some of the emigrants have arrived here about] the middle of June, which is somewhat early. Those who have established themselves in a ranch — that is taken up land and built a house on it — have made money in selling vegetables. Yesterday I visited a ranch a mile and a half below the city, and found the rancho largely engaged in raising fowls. I presume there could not have been less than three hundred little chicks running about. I got a bowl of milk which cost three bits (37 1/2 cts.)

The land is generally taken up at this time, that is, so much as can be turned to profitable account. The Spanish grants take up so much that it is difficult to locate a farm without trespassing upon those boundaries. Considerable excitement prevails here in regard to the Sutter claim of land. The land contained within the limits of the city was laid off into lots which were bought up in large parcels by speculators. A large number of these lots have been seized upon and taken possession of by settlers, or squatters as they are termed, who contend that the Sutter title is not perfect, and that this land was not embraced in the grant made him by Gov. Alvarado, who possessed certain authority under the Mexican Government. I attended a meeting of Squatters last evening on the Levee, which overtopped all meetings I ever witnessed, in the wave of "noise and confusion." The speakers were annoyed incessantly, and sharp words spoken. The squatters resolved to defend their property to the last extremity and at all hazards. What the end will be I shall not attempt to prophecy.

I have been informed that James M. Manning, died on Feather River a few weeks since, whilst afflicted with one of those spasms to which he was subject. His death is a matter of the deepest regret, as Mr. M. was highly esteemed.

The members of the Old Virginia Company are so much separated at present that it is impossible to give you items in regard to all of them. As far as I can learn, they are well. Within a week I have heard of the majority. Friends in the Old Dominion are doubtless waiting anxiously for the return of the California wanderers — they will find but few returning this fall. A few of those having families will return and they will be perfectly right. Those having wives should not hesitate, even though their bright prospects have not been realized. — no one should disappoint the partner of his bosom, for doubtless many an anxious night has been passed in caring for the welfare of the absent one. The rainy season commenced last November and I presume will be of the same date this year. For a month or two after the rain sets in, the dry diggings can be worked most profitably, so that the majority will defer returning before January or next spring.

On August 24th, the steamer California brought news of President Taylor's death. By this time, of course, the country had a new Chief Executive and the battle for the passage of the Compromise Bill had resumed. Funeral obsequies were quickly arranged at several locations, the most prominent being those at San Francisco, which were held on August 29th. Correspondents from Washington, D.C., believed that California's chances for statehood had improved. The arrival of more emigrants is accompanied by even more stories of hunger, sickness, and death on the trail. Asa Clevenger, one of the Charlestown Virginia Company, died at the mines. But the rest are still trying to make their "pile." [256]

August 31, 1850, Sacramento City, California

From J. Harrison Kelly

There is and has been great, awful suffering, on the part of many who crossed the plains this season. Three-fourths of the emigration calculated to make the trip in sixty days, and laid in provision lightly; they have been much nearer one hundred days in making the trip. Supplies of course gave out hundreds of miles from here, and many were glad to have a piece of horse or mule flesh with which to satisfy the gnawings of hunger. — Those who could do no better, were compelled to kill their stock and pack off, on foot, whilst yet the Sierra Nevada was between them and this highly favored city. One gentleman informed me that he passed on the desert, six dead bodies which had never received the rights of sepulture — each emigrant anxiously pressing on to avert a similar fate. Another told me that he had fed on the desert another, father and two children with several tablespoonsful of flour and water. A generous nature, a philanthropic heart is shocked at the recital of such tales of woe. Relief has promptly been sent out from this city.

Intelligence from the mines, I presume, has lost some of its wonted charms by this time — if it has not, it is time it should. There are thousands in the mines who are cast down and sorrowful — who lament their ever coming to California, whilst there are others who "bless their stars" that they are here. I have seen a few, and very few indeed, who have realized over $5,000 after having been here more than a year — but I might say I have seen five hundred who have not cleared that sum — or the half of it either — after a year's hard labor. For the "big stories" I refer you to the papers I send. The publications are true, most of them — some to my own knowledge. Remember that it is only the big stories which ever find their way into the columns of our papers.

Mr. Asa Clevinger, of Frederick county, died in Placerville on Wednesday the 19th inst. His death will be a severe stroke to a fond wife and affectionate daughter. Mr. C. was respected and highly esteemed by every member of his old company.

All of my acquaintances here, are well, as far as I can learn. Seventeen members of the old company were in the city the other day, including those who reside here — Messrs. Washington, Bryarly, John Moore, James Moore, Henry Moore, Bradley, Davison, Lupton, Harrison, Mackaran, Boley, Geiger, Rissler, Gallaher, Showers and this "hombre." I received a letter from J.C. Davis a few days since. He writes me that he has a claim which he can sell at $2,000 at any time, but as he feels satisfied that there is more ore than that in it, he means to work it himself. Were it my case, I would sell. He is in company with T.C. Moore, Rohr and Showman — all of whom are well. I have no late intelligence from others of our company, but I would have heard if they were ill.

Kindly,

J.H.K. [257]

September 1850, Washington, DC

By the end of the first week, Congress had passed the Texan Boundary Bill, the bill establishing a territorial government for New Mexico, the bill admitting California into the Union, and the bill establishing a territorial government for Utah. President Fillmore signed them into law. Details on the Fugitive Slave Bill were still being hammered out.

A hundred guns were fired in honor of the majority that passed these important Bills — the National Hotel was brilliantly illuminated, and Secretary Webster, Senators Clay, Foote, Cass, Dickinson, and others were serenaded by the Marine Band, all of whom responded in speeches replete with sentiments of devotion to the Union. By mid-month, the Fugitive Slave Bill was also law. Only the bill to abolish slavery in the District of Columbia had not yet been passed.

On the 10th, California Senators Gwin and Fremont and Representatives Wright and Gilbert entered Congress to take their seats. Several members objected, claiming the men were not legally elected. They were overruled. [258]

Jefferson County, Virginia

The Whig editors of Jefferson County received the news of Compromise passage with elation. Horatio Gallaher crowed:

> The great body of the people of the Union are gratified with the adoption by Congress, and approval by the President, of the measures of peace so long discussed by our loquacious representatives. It is true, the Abolitionists of the North are weeping, and declaiming that the "Banner of Freedom trails in the dust," and the Disunionists of the South swear "every thing has been sacrificed to the fell spirit of Abolitionism," yet the masses of the people are gratified, and all works well.... But as all is now safe under Whig auspices, we will not indulge in boasting at the expense of our opponents' feelings. We are all brothers now. — Let's be merry, and happy.

Equally ecstatic, the *Shepherdstown Register's* editor shared his visionary expectations for California's statehood:

> The passage of the Bill admitting California into the Union ... we regard as one of the most important which has marked our progress as a nation.... when we consider that the settlement of California and its union with the Atlantic sea-board by railway will produce a revolution in the commercial world, the event becomes invested with ten-fold interest.... many of us will live to see the Western prairies and the passes of the Rocky mountains threaded by a Rail Road, which will become the great thoroughfare of the world, and the line of inter-communication for Europe and Asia. Then the riches of the world will pass through our country, from the Pacific to the Atlantic.... [259]

Despite Gallaher's optimism, neither the Abolitionists nor the pro-slavery Southerners had given up the fight. The "Harrisburg Outrage" gave people a glimpse of the trouble yet to come.

Early in the month, before the Fugitive Slave Bill had passed the House, two slaves escaped from Clarke County, Virginia, stealing horses from their masters, and making their way North. Their owners caught up with them at Harrisburg, Pennsylvania (about 90 miles from Harpers Ferry) and prepared to return home with their property. The authorities, instead of assisting the owners, placed them in jail and released the negroes.

The *Shepherdstown Register* editor railed against Pennsylvania authorities, from the State to the local level, whose actions could ignite another powder keg of hatred and violence. Exasperated that factions would sully the spirit of compromise that had taken so long to establish, he asked:

> ... is this the Union of our forefathers? Is it the Union, the offspring of the combined efforts of Northern and Southern men, who fought side by side, and shoulder by shoulder through the dark days of the revolution, and whose commingled blood flowed in one stream at

Bunker's Hill and the Place of York Town? Is it the Union of the Constitution? We fear not. We fear that the fraternal feelings which should animate the different members of a confederacy of sister States, and which alone can preserve it in it's original features, no longer exist. The Union in name exists, but unless the patriotic men of all sections unite in some strong effort, its spirit will soon have fled; the substance will have wasted away, the shadow alone remaining; the constitution will not then be worth the parchment upon which it is written, and the Union will be but as the whitened sepulcher, beautiful only in its fair proportions. [260]

Figure 58. Servility of the Northern States in arresting and returning fugitive slaves.

Preparations for Virginia's Constitutional Convention were progressing with much less friction. Overall, the delegates selected to attend favored the Mixed Basis over the White Basis by a small margin. Gallaher noted, "We have a hope, however, that moderate counsels will eventually prevail — and that after a few of the gaseous members shall have been relieved of their flatulency that has so long troubled them, there will be something like reason left to control the deliberations of the Convention."

On a brighter note, the county's cholera epidemic seemed to be subsiding. And then there was the bridge. About the time that Henry Clay had offered his resolutions to a dysfunctional Congress, Engineer Fiske had begun building a bridge spanning the Potomac River at Shepherdstown. It was now finished, and if the roads leading west to the Winchester and Romney Turnpike could be graded, the bridge was on a direct route from the Western Counties to Baltimore and other Eastern markets. Not exactly a transcontinental railroad to California, but it was a start. [261]

California

> "... shuttlecock's a wery good game, vhen you ain't the shuttlecock ...."
>
> Charles Dickens, *Pickwick Papers*

Since Henry Clay introduced his Compromise resolutions in February, Congressional factions had insisted on packaging California statehood with the other parts of the proposal. Senator Gwin and California's other would-be legislators watched helplessly as negotiations went back and forth. Through it all, many Washington legislators assumed that Californians could fend for themselves. They could wait until other bills were passed, even if it meant being postponed until the next session.

In fact, the fires, floods, and riots in the newly incorporated cities of Sacramento and San Francisco were draining their resources. They heavily taxed their citizens to pay for needed improvements (such as levees) and elected public officials that expected to be paid. Fluctuations in property values destroyed the confidence of investors in Sacramento and bankruptcies began to skyrocket. Yes. California could use any help it could get from statehood. [262]

Sept. 12, 1850, Sacramento City

> From J. Harrison Kelly
>
> John Moore, Aisquith and Rissler have gone to Carson Valley to purchase stock from the emigrants.
>
> As far as I am aware, all our Virginia boys are well.
>
> I met Mr. Fouke, formerly of Shepherdstown, three days since — he has been in a week or two, having stopped at Nevada city, dry diggings.
>
> About two weeks ago I met Mr. Cleveland, formerly merchant in Charlestown.
>
> About a month since, Mr. Whiting, of Clarke county, arrived.
>
> Bradley has been working in town six or eight weeks but left yesterday. Some of the boys talk of leaving during October and November.
>
> Yours,
>
> J.H.K. [263]

November 1850, California

During the summer and fall, Indian raids in California had increased, jeopardizing the lives of settlers, miners, and small towns beyond military protection. The man charged with handling the problem was Albert M. Winn, Brigadier General of the California Militia.

Shortly after arriving in Sacramento, this native Virginian organized the first Odd Fellows Lodge in Sacramento, a deed which brought him into contact with J. Harrison Kelly, former Grand Master of the Virginia Lodge. Although Kelly had no military experience, Winn appointed him a Major in the California Militia, ordering Kelly to gather information on the state of affairs in El Dorado County, the site of Indian hostilities. [264]

Kelly's first dispatch was sent from Johnson's Ranch, a trading post on Bear Creek at the end of the California Trail:

Head Quarters, (Johnson's Ranch,) November 14, 1850.

Gen. A. M. Winn:

Sir:

In obedience to your order, I repaired to this point — Head Quarters of Col. Rodgers — and finding that officer absent, reported myself to Lieut. Col. Boone, in command of the post.

The troops have been in a state of inactivity for some days past, owing to the absence of Col. Rodgers, who it is understood left this point for the purpose of receiving further instructions from the Executive of the State.

The impression seems to be somewhat general that the first movement of the army will be southeast of this place, along the tributaries of the Cosumnes — particularly the south fork of that stream, where it is reported the Indians are gathered in large warlike parties. The Indians have large rancheries along the Cosumnes, and it is said that one division numbers some five hundred warriors, who have at least two thousand head of stock, which they have stolen from immigrants and ranches. It is a matter of entire certainty, that the Indians have been concentrating their forces for the last two months, and equally true that they have been the first to make an attack, and consequently are the aggressive party.

It seems to me that sufficient importance has not been attached to the warlike character and ability of the Indians with which the soldiery have been recently engaged. They have by some means received a misnomer in being called Digger Indians; for it is entirely certain that the Indians quartered along the Cosumnes subsist, not upon roots and acorns, as is the case with the tribe referred to, but upon meats, both wild and tame. They are possessed of all those powers of endurance peculiar to the red man, and when aroused have lost none of that natural vindictiveness which forms a striking trait of Indian character.

It may be proper to remark upon the situation of this section of country three weeks since as compared with the present. At that time within a circuit of three miles of this point, there were from five to six hundred persons engaged in mining; at this moment, from the most authentic evidence before me, there appears to be only one company, twenty in number, thus engaged, within the prescribed limits. On the breaking out of the Indian disturbances, the miners deserted their claims — their cabins — thousands of bushels of thrown up earth — their all — seeking personal safety at the sacrifice of much, in a pecuniary point of view.

It is an established axiom that every Government is bound to protect her people and cherish her peculiar institutions. The peculiar institution of this country is the mining interest, and Government should afford all possible aid to those engaged in this highly laudable pursuit. The mines around which the largest part of our population have gathered, although not entirely exhausted, do not afford such yields as are expected by the hardy pioneers of this country. The old mining range has been so thickly settled that the more enterprising are not content to remain within their confines, but are desirous of prosecuting where white men have never trod before; but in the present unsettled condition of the country, it would be madness to engage in such a project.

Should the State Government deem it proper to establish posts for the purpose of keeping the Indians in a state of subordination, it seems to me that the head of Pleasant Valley, about ten miles east of Weberville, would be the most central location for Head Quarters. Provision depots might also be established at Johnson's Ranch, (El Dorado county,) on the north, and some point south of the Cosumnes. The troops might then move with great facility from one point to the other, and a large body of Indians, comprising several tribes, be kept in a constant state of awe. This would entirely obviate the transportation of military stores, an item of no ordinary expense. The additional expense of maintaining the two additional posts referred to, would not be more than the cost of a sergeant and file of men. Thus then that whole mining region, extending from the South Fork of the American River on the north, to the South Fork of the Cosumnes on the Mokulme on the south, would be amply guarded and protected, and thousands of waiting miners would quickly avail themselves of the protection thus afforded, and engage in the further development of the rich mineral resources of the State.

Should Government fail to provide a military post for this section of country, and should the troops in service be disbanded without an exhibition of their power, many of the miners will be compelled to remain in a state of inactivity (in the more thickly settled villages,) during that season of the year which is most propitious for mining in what are termed gulch or dry diggings. Those occupying the eastern frontier will be kept in a constant state of alarm and fear from the hostile demonstrations of the Indians; and the rainy season will be the signal for general depredations, during which period many valuable lives will be lost.

The troops assembled at this point constitute an efficient force, and are composed of the material best adapted for Indian warfare — they hail principally from the extreme west and north-western States.

> Within the last week preparations have been made for the erection of a blockhouse at this point — timber has been felled, and all the preliminary arrangements made.
>
> I have the honor to be,
>
> Your obedient servant,
>
> J. H. KELLY,
>
> Maj. 2d Brig. 1st Div. Cal. Mi [265]

Published in several Sacramento papers, Kelly's report helped quell Winn's critics, who had dismissed the reports of Indian hostilities as exaggerations and efforts to fortify the area as an expensive boondoggle. [266]

The Indians reacted to the new show of force by retreating into more remote valleys with their plunder. Col. Rodgers and his battalion pursued them, hoping to dislodge them before the rainy season made roads impassable.

Kelly sent another dispatch from Mud Springs in Calaveras County, where he had accompanied Col. Rodgers on his search and destroy mission.

November 22, 1850, Headquarters, Grass Valley, Calaveras Co.

> Gen. A.M. Winn:
>
> In report No. 2, from Mud Springs, I stated that the volunteer force under Col. Rodgers, was en route southwardly. Leaving Mud Springs, the line of march extended along the North Fork of the Cosumnes, until the confluence of the Middle and South Forks — thence along Indian Creek and other tributaries — Dry Creek and its numerous branches — Rancherie Creek, &c. At Lower Rancherie the mounted men under Capt. Graham were detailed to scour the country between that point and Volcano; and rejoin the main division at this point. By the direction of Col. Rodgers I accompanied Capt. G.'s command, which composed some twenty mounted men. In the course of the march the command discovered a number of Indian rancheries, some of them consisting of half a dozen tenements, but in every case the Indians had decamped, or were in the act, before our arrival. In some instances we were so close upon them that we found meat broiling on the coals, and bread of peculiar composition, in a state for baking; but all efforts to capture them in a body, proved fruitless. An Indian chief named Soleto was taken, but upon examination he proved to be friendly, and was subsequently discharged.
>
> The Infantry captured a few Indians on their route, who were brought into camp. Two of the number were chiefs, Dari and Pelouti. It was ascertained that the first named chief had been in the first skirmish near Johnson's Ranch, (South Fork); and from

other information it appeared that he had been harboring a number of hostile Indians. He was instructed by Col. Rodgers to dispatch three of his tribe to bring in the hostile Indians. He accordingly gave directions in Indian dialect to three of his men, the substance of which we learned the next morning to be, that they should gather all the warriors they could arm — repair to within a short distance of his camp, and secrete themselves in a canon — send in three of their number as though friendly, and, as is now presumed, make an attack, when we least expected it.

The rain on the night of the 19th injured the fire arms of the soldiers very materially, and the next morning an order was issued to discharge all the pieces. A large number were discharged, which the prisoners took advantage of, broke the guard and decamped. Two of the three, however, who attempted the escape, were pursued and shot a short distance from the main camp. The chief Dan escaped, possibly wounded. Firing was heard in a southwestern direction the next morning, and a body of troops dispatched, but the Indians fled before the arrival of the soldiers.

The heavy and constant fall of rain during nearly the entire period from our arrival here up to this lime, has prevented any general demonstration on our part — altho', each day, from three to five scouting parties have been dispatched in various directions. Some of these parties came suddenly upon rancheries of Indians, who decamped at once, taking to the heights, where they snapped a few caps, which proved that their fire arms were in a bad condition.

Scouting parties have been along the Mokulumne and its tributaries, but they report that the Indians have generally left their rancheries and gone farther east into the canons and valleys of the Sierra Nevada. Col. Rodgers despatched a messenger yesterday for Casuse, the most noted chief in this region, but it is very doubtful whether he will leave his mountain home. If he comes in, it is contemplated to enter into a treaty with him.

Should the rain cease, and it be considered at all practicable, Col. Rodgers meditates a direct march from this point, over the mountains, to the emigrant road on the Carson route — intending to strike the head of Pleasant Valley. The route will be a most toilsome one — over craggy heights and descending into canons of great depth, lined with chapparel and dense undergrowth. It is reported that the Indians have repaired to these spots with large herds of stock, and deem themselves safe in these almost impregnable mountain fastnesses. From these points it is contemplated they will make incursions on the mining districts during the rainy season. Col. R., intends, if possible, to rout them, but I fear greatly that the season is too far advanced to accomplish much.

Considerable excitement and trepidation is felt in this entire region of country, lest after the withdrawal of the troops, the Indians will make fresh attacks on the miners, committing murders, stealing stock, &c. A large number of citizens at the Volcano, two miles distant, and in this neighborhood, have a petition they contemplate sending the Governor, asking, for the establishment of a small garrison in this section.

Allow me to remark, that a more resolute and efficient officer could not have been obtained than Col Rodgers — he is the soul of honor — in judgment strong — his probity and honesty unquestionable.

I have the honor to be,

Your obedient servant,

J. H. KELLY,

Maj. 2d Brig. 1st Div. Cal. Mil. [267]

Despite Kelly's published reports and Col. Rodger's efforts to pacify the Indians and protect the miners, the conflict was not solved to anyone's satisfaction. Public attention turned to the upcoming political conflicts in Sacramento, San Francisco, and other cities and counties throughout the state. Both Whigs and Democrats were forming their own political parties. Existing newspapers were choosing sides and new sheets were born to support candidates and enunciate party platforms.

California's Fourth Estate was on the rise. [268]

Figure 59. Peter H. Burnett, 1807 – 1895

December 1850, California

> The two races are kept asunder by so many causes, and having no ties of marriage or consanguinity to unite them, they must ever remain at enmity. That a war of extermination will continue to be waged between the races until the Indian race becomes extinct must be expected. While we cannot anticipate this result but with painful regret, the inevitable destiny of the race is beyond the power or wisdom of man to avert. Situated as California is, we must expect a long continued and harassing irregular warfare with the Indians upon our borders and along the immigrant routes leading to the States.

Governor Peter H. Burnett, *Annual Message to the California Legislature,* January 1, 1851

Epilogue

> The past is never dead. It's not even past.
>
> William Faulkner, *Requiem for a Nun*

For Jefferson County residents, the decade of the 1840's must have thundered past them like a freight train, hurling into the future, leaving scraps of the past in its wake. Remnants lay beneath the tombstones in local cemeteries, in unmarked graves along the Oregon Trail, and beneath the backlots of California's boomtowns. In yellowing newspapers, tied with twine. In well-worn letters tied with ribbons, entombed in perfumed tins and tobacco-scented cigar boxes. Fused into the memories of those who had "seen the elephant" and those who had only heard of it.

Some folks celebrated and sighed with relief that the Union had been saved. Others waited for the other shoe to drop. Ideologues and malcontents, both North and South, were planning their next moves. In Jefferson County, many issues still kept the Whigs and Democrats apart, but they shared a distrust of Northern politicians and newspapers. Both believed that slave ownership was a Constitutional right which they carried with them wherever they went within the Union. And the "Harrisburg Outrage" had been a warning that the Fugitive Slave Act would not stop Northern abolitionists from interfering with their sacred institution.

But the struggle was now more than an effort to balance Northern and Southern interests. California and other parts of the West could now emerge as political powers of their own. They would weigh in on the subdivision of the territories, on issues of residence and suffrage for Indians and Chinese, and on other issues that affected national policy. From statehood would emerge political parties, patronage, and newspapers to promote them. Within the decade, scores of Jefferson County residents had emigrated to California. Some were still mining. Others had found more reliable ways to make a living. A few were ready to use their journalistic and political talents to promote their ideals or line their pockets.

Meanwhile, alarmed that slavecatchers would descend on free negroes in the North, a wool grower in Springfield, Massachusetts, began drafting "Words of Advice," a defense manual for active resistance. Soon John Brown and the League of Gileadites would put a face on the Northern threat. [269]

Thus far, the power of the pen had out matched that of the sword. Legislators, with the help of the Fourth Estate, had managed to avoid disunion and civil war. How would they meet the challenges of the next decade?

Notes

[1] To view the sources cited in thse notes, use this link to the *West Virginia GeoExplorer Project*:
   http://www.wvgeohistory.org/Search.aspx#v=69841.
[2] Thomas Jefferson, Letter to Edward Carrington, January 16, 1787.
[3] "The Presidential Contest," *Virginia Free Press*, 11/5/1840, p. 2, c. 1.
[4] Charles James Faulkner, "John S. Gallaher," *Aler's History of Martinsburg and Berkeley County, West Virginia*, Hagerstown, MD, 1888, pp. 116-123.
[5] Horatio Nelson Gallaher (1/16/1808 - 11/3/1883). NSDAR. Bee Line Chapter. *Tombstone Inscriptions and Burial Lots [in Jefferson County, West Virginia]*. Charles Town, WV: Walsworth Publishing Company, 1981.
[6] Jonathan Daniel Wells, *Women Writers and Journalists in the Nineteenth-Century South*. Cambridge University Press, 2011.
[7] Faulkner, "John S. Gallaher."
[8] "The Presidential Contest," *Virginia Free Press*, 11/5/1840, p. 2, c. 1.
[9] John Tyler, "Address of President Tyler to the People of the United States," *Virginia Free Press*, 4/15/1841, p. 2, c. 4-5.
[10] J.E. Norris, "Zion Episcopal Church," *History of the Lower Shenandoah Valley*. Chicago: A. Warner & Co., 1890, p. 360.
[11] John S. Gallaher, "Tribute to the Memory of the late President," *Virginia Free Press*, 4/15/1841, p. 2, c. 2.
[12] Moler, Captain John, 12/5/1791 - 2/3/1871. Kennedy, Andrew, 7/27/1797 - 2/27/1858, NSDAR. Bee Line Chapter.
[13] John S. Gallaher, "Veto on the Bank Bill," *Virginia Free Press*, 8/12/1841, p. 2, c. 2.
[14] John Tyler, "Veto Message," *Virginia Free Press*, 8/19/1841, p. 2, c. 5-7.
[15] John S. Gallaher, "The Veto Power," *Virginia Free Press*, 8/19/1841, p. 3, c. 1.
[16] John Tyler, "Veto Message," *Virginia Free Press*, 9/10/1841, p. 2.
[17] Oliver P. Chitwood, John Tyler, *Champion of the Old South*. Russell & Russell, 1964, pp. 249-251.
[18] John S. Gallaher, "President Tyler ... has vetoed the second Bank Bill....," *Virginia Free Press*, 9/16/1841, p. 2, c. 1.
[19] William D. Theriault, "Washington, Benjamin Franklin. Profile," *West Virginia GeoExplorer Project*. Accessed 2/26/2016.
[20] John S. Gallaher, "The Exposition of Jonathan Roberts," *Virginia Free Press*, 9/22/1842, p. 2, c. 5; see Jonathan Roberts.
[21] "Whig Defeats," *Virginia Free Press*, 10/27/1842, p. 2, c. 5.
[22] "The 4th of July," *Virginia Free Press*, 7/13/1843, p. 2, c. 3-7; p. 3, c. 7.
[23] Theriault, "J. Harrison Kelly, Profile," *West Virginia GeoExplorer Project*. Accessed 1/26/2016.
[24] Theriault, "James W. Beller, Profile," *West Virginia GeoExplorer Project*. Accessed 1/26/2016.
[25] John S. Gallaher, "The Fourth," *Virginia Free Press*, 7/11/1844, p. 2, c. 5.
[26] "Clay Club," *Virginia Free Press*, 6/20/1844, p. 2, c. 5.
[27] From Findagrave.com, accessed 12/14/2016.
[28] From Findagrave.com, accessed 12/14/2016.
[29] "Democratic Meeting," *Virginia Free Press, 7/17/1844*, p. 2, c. 4.
[30] "Democratic Meeting," *Virginia Free Press*, 7/17/1844, p. 2, c. 4.
[31] The first article, a biography of James K. Polk, was written by Beller's friend, Benjamin Franklin Washington.
[32] John S. Gallaher, "A Broken 'Constitution,' " *Virginia Free Press*, 9/5/1839, p. 2, c. 1.
[33] "The Jefferson Banner," *Virginia Free Press*, 5/6/1841, p. 3, c. 3.
[34] James W. Beller, "To the Patrons of the Spirit of Jefferson," *Spirit of Jefferson*, 7/17/1844, p. 2, c. 1-2.
[35] John S. Gallaher, "Spirit of Jefferson," *Virginia Free Press*, 7/25/1844, p. 2, c. 2.
[36] "Democratic Meeting," *Spirit of Jefferson*, 7/17/1844, p. 2, c. 4; "LAWRENCE B. WASHINGTON, attorney and Counsellor at Law," *Spirit of Jefferson*,

7/26/1844, p. 3, c. 4 ; "The Meeting at Smithfield," *Spirit of Jefferson*, 8/9/1844, p. 2, c. 2; "Jefferson Mass Meeting*,"* *Spirit of Jefferson*, 7/25/1844, p. 2, c. 1.
37 "Jefferson Meeting. A General Invitation," *Virginia Free Press*, 8/8/1844, p. 1, c. 1.
38 "Temperance Delegates," *Virginia Free Press*, 7/18/1844, p. 2, c. 4.
39 "Temperance Delegates," *Virginia Free Press*, 7/18/1844, p. 2, c. 4.
40 "The Celebration," *Spirit of Jefferson*, 7/4/1845, p. 2, c. 4; "The Fourth at Shannondale," *Spirit of Jefferson*, 7/11/1845, p. 2, c. 4; "Fourth of July Celebration," *Virginia Free Press*, 7/10/1845, p. 2, c. 1
41 Theriault, W. "Washington, Benjamin Franklin. Profile," *West Virginia GeoExplorer Project*. Accessed 2/21/2016.
42 "The Glorious Fourth," *Spirit of Jefferson*, 7/11/1845, p. 2, c. 6.
43 John S. Gallaher, "The Fourth," *Virginia Free Press*, 7/11/1844, p. 2, c. 5.
44 James W. Beller, "Close of the Volume," *Spirit of Jefferson*, 7/11/1845, p. 2, c. 1.
45 Theriault, W. "J. Harrison Kelly, Profile," *West Virginia GeoExplorer Project*.
46 James K. Polk, "Message of the President of the United States, December 2, 1845," *Virginia Free Press*, 12/4/1845, p. 2, c. 6 - p. 3, c. 5. In April 1845, Thomas Ritchie and John Heiss acquired the *Washington Globe*, changed its name to the *Washington Union*, and established it as the official organ of President Polk's administration. See Mark E. Byrnes, *James K. Polk: A Biographical Companion,* Barns & Nobel, 2001, pp. 143-144.
47 James McDowell, "Annual Message of the Governor of Virginia, December 2, 1845," *Virginia Free Press*, 12/11/1845, p. 1, c. 5-7.
48 John S. Gallaher, "Meeting of Congress," *Virginia Free Press,* 11/27/1845, p. 2, c. 1.
49 "Education Meeting," *Spirit of Jefferson*, 11/21/1845, p. 3, c. 1.
50 John S. Gallaher, "Education Convention," *Virginia Free Press*, 12/18/1845, p. 2, c. 1-2.
51 "Education Meeting," *Spirit of Jefferson*, 11/21/1845, p. 3, c. 1.
52 James W. Beller, "The Education Convention," *Spirit of Jefferson*, 12/26/1845, p. 3, c. 1; "Dedication of Odd Fellows Lodge, Shepherdstown," *Virginia Free Press*, 11/6/1845, p. 1, c. 6.
53 James W. Beller, "The War With Mexico: Mexico and the U.S.," *Spirit of Jefferson*, 6/5/1846, p. 2, c. 1.
54 "Course of the Whigs," *Virginia Free Press*, 6/4/1846, p. 2, c. 3.
55 "California," *Spirit of Jefferson*, 12/19/1845, p. 1, c. 2.
56 "Odd Fellows Dedication at Harper's-Ferry," *Virginia Free Press*, 7/30/1846, p. 2, c. 2.
57 "Education Meeting," *Spirit of Jefferson*, 7/24/1846, p. 2, c. 3.
58 James W. Beller, "Close of This Volume*,"* *Spirit of Jefferson*, 7/10/1846, p. 2, c. 1.
59 Lee A. Wallace, Jr., "The First Regiment of Virginia Volunteers, 1846-1848"; *Virginia Magazine of History and Biography*, vol. 77, no. 1, Part One (Jan., 1969), pp. 47-50.
60 "Public Meeting," *Spirit of Jefferson*, 12/18/1846, p. 3, c. 2.
61 "Meeting on Monday," *Spirit of Jefferson*, 12/25/1846, p. 2, c. 2.
62 "Meeting on Monday," *Spirit of Jefferson*, 12/25/1846, p. 2, c. 2.
63 "The Meeting on Monday," *Virginia Free Press*, 12/24/1846, p. 2, c. 5.
64 "An Affecting Scene," *Spirit of Jefferson*, 1/8/1847, p. 2, c. 3.
65 "Capt. Sappington's Address," *Spirit of Jefferson*, 1/15/1847, p. 3, c. 3.
66 "Jefferson Volunteers," *Virginia Free Press*, 1/14/1847, p. 3, c. 2.
67 "Our Volunteers," *Spirit of Jefferson*, 1/8/1847, p. 2, c. 1-2.
68 "The Jefferson Volunteers," *Spirit of Jefferson*, 1/15/1847, p. 2, c. 2.
69 "Jefferson Volunteers," *Spirit of Jefferson*, 2/5/1847, p. 2, c. 3. "Seeing the elephant" meant having a major, life changing experience. In the context of the War with Mexico, it meant someone had seen combat.
70 "Odd Fellows Lodges," *Virginia Free Press*, 1/14/1847, p. 2, c. 5.
71 "Whig Meeting," *Spirit of Jefferson*, 2/26/1847, p. 1, c. 3.
72 "Disingenuousness," *Virginia Free Press,* 2/11/1847, p. 2, c. 1.
73 "The District School Bill," *Spirit of Jefferson*, 5/28/1847, p. 2, c. 1; "The School Bill," *Spirit of Jefferson*, 6/18/1847, p. 2, c. 7.

[74] "Fourth of July," *Spirit of Jefferson*, 6/18/1847, p. 2, c. 7"; "Celebration at Shannondale," *Spirit of Jefferson*, 7/9/1847, p. 2, c. 3; "Fourth of July," *Virginia Free Press*, 6/24/1847, p. 2, c. 2.

[75] "Celebration," *Virginia Free Press*, 8/12/1847, p. 2, c. 5.

[76] "Our Enlargement," *Spirit of Jefferson*, 7/16/1847, p. 2, c. 1.

[77] "The Spirit of Jefferson," *Virginia Free Press*, 7/22/1847, p. 2, c. 3.

[78] "Democratic Meeting," *Spirit of Jefferson*," 1/18/1848, p. 2, c. 5-7.

[79] "Whig Meeting," *Virginia Free Press*, 1/22/1848, p. 2, c. 4-5.

[80] Virginia's 10th Congressional District was composed of the counties of Jefferson, Frederick, Clarke, Berkeley, and Loudoun.

[81] "Doings at Richmond," *Richmond Enquirer*, 2/22/1848, p. 2, c. 5; "Married," *Spirit of Jefferson*, 2/22/1848, p. 2, c. 4.

[82] "Whig Senatorial Convention," *Virginia Free Press*, 2/12/1848, p. 2, c. 2.

[83] "Mr. Gallaher's Letter," *Spirit of Jefferson*, 2/22/1848, p. 2, c. 2.

[84] "Election Day," *Virginia Free Press*, 4/27/1848, p. 2, c. 3.

[85] "Used Up – Laid Out," *Virginia Free Press*, 5/5/1848, p. 2, c. 3.

[86] "Virginia Elections Jefferson County," *Spirit of Jefferson*, 5/2/1848, p. 2, c. 1.

[87] "Our Anniversary," *Spirit of Jefferson*, 7/4/1848, p. 2, c. 1.

[88] "Fourth of July," 7/6/1848, *Virginia Free Press*, p. 3, c. 1.

[89] "Fourth of July," 7/6/1848, *Virginia Free Press*, p. 3, c. 1.

[90] "A Welcome To Volunteers," *Spirit of Jefferson*, 7/4/1848, p. 2, c. 7.

[91] "Welcoming the Volunteers," *Virginia Free Press*, 8/17/1848, p. 1, c. 3.

[92] "Col. J.F. Hamtramck," *Virginia Free Press*, 9/7/1848, p. 2, c. 6.

[93] "The Great Flash of the Season! The Bubble Exploded!" *Virginia Free Press*, 8/24/1848, p. 2, c. 4-7.

[94] On Saturday August 8, 1846, David Wilmot, a Democratic congressman from Pennsylvania, offered an amendment to President Polk's request for $2,000,000 to bring about the final settlement of the war. The proviso, which has since borne his name, reads as follows:

> Provided, That, as an express and fundamental condition to the acquisition of any territory from the Republic of Mexico by the United States, by virtue of any treaty which may be negotiated between them, and to the use by the Executive of the moneys herein appropriated, neither slavery nor involuntary servitude shall ever exist in any part of said territory, except for crime, whereof the party shall first be duly convicted.

> Summing up the consequences of the Wilmot Proviso, historian Allan Nevins noted: "Thus the contest was joined on the central issue which was to dominate all American history for the next dozen years, the disposition of the Territories. Two sets of extremists had arisen: Northerners who demanded no new slave territories under any circumstances, and Southerners who demanded free entry for slavery into all territories, the penalty for denial to be secession. For the time being, moderates who hoped to find a way of compromise and to repress the underlying issue of slavery itself — its toleration or non-toleration by a great free Christian state – were overwhelmingly in the majority. But history showed that in crises of this sort the two sets of extremists were almost certain to grow in power, swallowing up more and more members of the conciliatory center. See Alan Nevins, *Ordeal of the Union: Fruits of Manifest Destiny 1847-1852*, 1947, pp. 12-13.

[95] "Election on Tuesday, 7th of November. TO THE VOTERS OF JEFFERSON COUNTY," *Spirit of Jefferson*, 11/7/1848, p. 1, c. 2-4; "Committee Men, to Your Post! Democratic Meeting," *Spirit of Jefferson*, 11/7/1848, p. 4, c. 3; "The Taylor Platform," *Virginia Free Press*, 11/2/1848, p. 2, c. 1-2.

[96] "The Result," *Spirit of Jefferson*, 11/14/1848, p. 2, c. 1.

[97] "The Glorious Triumph," *Virginia Free Press*, 11/16/1848, p. 2, c. 2.

[98] "Illumination in Charlestown," *Virginia Free Press*, 11/23/1848, p. 2. c. 5; "[ROUGH AND READY CLUB... Congratulatory Meeting.]" *Virginia Free Press*, 11/23/1848, p. 2, c. 7.

[99] "Illumination," *Spirit of Jefferson*, 11/21/1848, p. 2, c. 2.
[100] "A Word to Our Readers," *Spirit of Jefferson*, 11/21/1848, p. 2, c. 1.
[101] "The Land of Gold," *Virginia Free Press*," 9/28/1848, p. 4, c. 1.
[102] Polk, James K. Fourth Annual Message, December 5, 1848. See "President's Message," *Virginia Free Press*, 12/7/1848, p. 2; cols. 1-7, p. 3, cols. 1-6.
[103] *James K. Polk: A Biographical Companion*, By Mark Eaton Byrnes. Barnes & Nobel, 2001, pp. 143-144.
[104] Walther, Eric H., *William Loundes Yancy: The Coming of the Civil War*, pp. 118-122.
[105] John S. Gallaher, "Slavery in the District," *Virginia Free Press*, 12/28/1848, p. 2, c. 2.
[106] John S. Gallaher, "To the Public," *Virginia Free Press*, 12/14/1848, p. 2, c. 3.
[107] "The Olden Time," *Virginia Free Press*, 5/10/1849, p. 2, c. 3.
[108] "In adverting to the California organization," *Virginia Free Press*, 1/25/1849, p. 2, c. 2.
[109] "Ho! For California," *Virginia Free Press*, 12/281848, p. 1, c.6..
[110] "The California Expedition," *Virginia Free Press*, 1/1/1849, p. 2, c. 2; "California Enterprise," *Virginia Free Press*, 1/11/1849, p. 2, c. 2.
[111] "The Virginia Pioneers," *Virginia Free Press*, 1/18/1849, p. 2, c. 1.
[112] "Expedition to California," *Virginia Free Press*, 1/25/1849, p. 2, c. 2."For Rent," *Spirit of Jefferson*, 3/28/1848, p. 4, c. 5. Company Treasurer Edward M. Aisquith put his Charlestown house and its contents up for sale, and brothers Isaac and Jesse Strider sold off the livestock and crops on the farm they leased. See: "Public Sale," *Virginia Free Press*, 1/11/1849, p. 3, c. 4; and "Public Sale," *Virginia Free Press*, 2/22/1849, p. 3, c. 3. J.J. Miller, local Penn Mutual Life Insurance agent, offered "those who leave families an opportunity ... of securing to them (in the event of their death while gone) a handsome sum, for a small consideration." See: "For California," *Virginia Free Press*, 2/15/1849, p. 3, c. 2.
[113] "The California Company," *Virginia Free Press*, 2/15/1849, p. 2, c. 3; "Charlestown (Va.) Mining Company," *Virginia Free Press*, 2/15/1849, p. 2, c. 5; "Constitution of the Charlestown Va. Mining Company," *Virginia Free Press*, 2/15/1849, p. 2, c. 6-7.
[114] California Emigrants' Tune "O! Susanna!" *Virginia Free Press*, 1/11/1849, p. 4, c. 1. 115 "Charlestown Mining Company," *Virginia Free Press*, 3/29/1849, p. 2, c. 4.
[116] "Off to California," *Virginia Free Press*, 3/22/1849, p. 2, c. 1.
[117] "Letter from Col. Fremont," *Virginia Free Press*, 3/29/1849, p. 2, c. 5.
[118] At Harpers Ferry, George H. Furtney was recruiting a company to be led by Col. Whiting, "late of the Texas Rangers." Members included Daniel Stipes, Jacob Vanvacter, Ebenezer Marlatt, John D. Stipes, Jonathan Russell, Charles Holt, David Potts and James Riley, of Harpers-Ferry; and Dr. Lambert and David McIntosh, of Loudoun County. See "Another Company," *Virginia Free Press*, 2/22/1849, p. 2, c. 3. At Shepherdstown, Dr. Richard Parran recruited thirty-one men from Jefferson, Berkeley, Frederick, and Hardy counties in Virginia, and from Washington County, Maryland. See "California Company," *Virginia Free Press*, 3/29/1849, p. 2, c. 4.
[119] "Close of the 30th Congress," *Virginia Free Press*, 3/8/1849, p. 2, c. 3.
[120] "The Post Office," *Virginia Free Press*, 4/19/1849, p. 2, c. 1.
[121] "Proscription," *Virginia Free Press*, 4/19/1849, p. 2, c. 2.
[122] "Virginia," *Virginia Free Press*, 4/19/1849, p. 1, c. 7.
[123] "Mr. Faulkner's Report," *Virginia Free Press*, 4/5/1849, p. 2, c. 5-7, p. 3, c. 1-3.
[124] "The Slavery Question," *Virginia Free Press*, 4/26/1849, p. 2, c. 5.
[125] A.H. Sanders, "High Water," Cairo Delta, 3/20/1849. From John McMurray Landsen, *A History of the City of Cairo, Illinois*, Chicago: R.R. Donnelley & Co., 1910, pp. 74-75
[126] J.H. Kelly, "Charlestown Mining Company," *Virginia Free Press*, 4/26/1849, p. 2, c. 6.
[127] Not an organized, incorporated territory until 1861, in 1849 it referred to the upper Mississippi valley and surrounding plains, then occupied by the Dahcota branch of the Sioux India tribe.

[128] "Cholera, Fire, and Civil War (1840s - 1865). The Tough Days of 1849." Accessed 5/6/2016.

[129] "The Champions of the Mississippi," Currier & Ives, ca. 1866.

[130] J.H. Kelly, "Charlestown Mining Company," *Virginia Free Press*, 5/10/1849, p. 2, c. 6. Thomas West Washington was a son of William Temple Washington and a second cousin of Frank Washington. See: Justin Glenn, *The Washingtons: A Family History*, vol. 7.

[131] "Correspondence from St. Joseph," *Baltimore Sun*, 6/5/1849, p. 1.

[132] "The State Elections," *Virginia Free Press*, 5/10/1849, p. 2, c. 1; "And Still Another!" *Spirit of Jefferson*, 5/29/1849, p. 2, c. 2.

[133] "The Cholera Town Ordinance," *Spirit of Jefferson*, 5/29/1849, p. 2, c. 1.

[134] J.H. Kelly, "Charlestown Mining Company," *Spirit of Jefferson*, 5/29/1849, p. 2, c. 7, p. 3, c. 1.

[135] J.H. Kelly, "Charlestown Mining Company," *Spirit of Jefferson*, 5/29/1849, p. 2, c. 7, p. 3, c. 1.

[136] J.H. Kelly, "Charlestown Mining Company," *Spirit of Jefferson*, 5/29/1849, p. 2, c. 7, p. 3, c. 1.

[137] At the time, "Indian Territory" referred part of what is now Iowa and the States of Kansas, Nebraska, and Oklahoma.

[138] Kelly, J. Harrison, "Charlestown Mining Company," *Spirit of Jefferson*, 5/29/1849, p. 2., c. 7, p. 3, c. 1.

[139] "Diary of Vincent E. Geiger," May 15, 1849 to May 18th, 1849, in *Trail to California: The Overland Journal of Vincent Geiger and Wakeman Bryarly*. David Morris Potter (ed.) New Haven: Yale University Press, 1945. For the Great Nemaha Indian Agency (Kansas), go to https://familysearch.org/learn/wiki/en/%20Great_Nemaha_Indian_Agency_%28Kansas%29

[140] According to the *WPA Guide to Kansas* (1939), Iowa Point "on the western edge of the broad valley, was once the largest Kansas town on the Missouri River. It was founded in 1855 on land given by the Reverend S.W. Irvin by the Iowa Indians. Within a year it had an estimated population of 3,000, but the intense partisan strife between Free State and proslavery settlers soon disrupted the town's commercial life. In 1857, it began an abrupt decline."

[141] Edwin Bryant published a detailed account of his 1846 journey to California by pack mule. See *What I Saw in California* (1848).

[142] J.H. Kelly, "Charlestown Mining Company," *Virginia Free Press*, 6/21/1849, p. 2, c. 6. Concerning Joseph Young's burial, Vincent Geiger's diary entry for May 25th notes: "The clear & shrill voice of our guide roused us early and we prepared for a start. At sunrise the remains of our late comrade, Young, was interred. He was wrapped in his blanket. Without shroud, sheet or coffin, he was laid in the silent grave. He was buried on a hill, commanding a beautiful country. After the performance of this sad duty we started on our march.

[143] "Fort Kearney," https://www.nps.gov/oreg/planyourvisit/site4.htm, accessed 5/7/2016; J.H. Kelly, "Charlestown Mining Company," *Virginia Free Press*, 7/5/1849, p. 2, c. 6.

[144] "Charlestown Mining Company," *Virginia Free Press*, 7/5/1849, p. 2, c. 6.

[145] "Sanatary Measures," *Virginia Free Press*, 6/7/1849, p. 2. c. 4; "For the Free Press," *Virginia Free Press*, 6/21/1849, p. 2, c. 4.

[146] "Rewards and Punishments," *Virginia Free Press*, 6/7/1849, p. 2, c. 1; "It Has Come," *Virginia Free Press*, 6/7/1849 p. 2, c. 2.

147 Vincent E. Geiger, "Journal of the Route of the Charlestown, Virginia, Mining Company from St. Joseph, Missouri, to California", June 1 and 2, 1849. In: *The Overland Journal of Vincent Geiger and Wakeman Bryarly*. David Morris Potter (ed.) New Haven: Yale University Press, 1945.

[148] B.F. Washington, "California Letter," *Virginia Free Press*, 10/25/1849, p. 2, c. 5-6.

[149] B.F. Washington, "California Letter," *Virginia Free Press*, 10/25/1849, p. 2, c. 5-6.

[150] Byarly, "Diary," June 7, 1849.

[151] Geiger, "Journal," 6/9/1849. Edwin A. Riely's private letters to his wife contained frequent complaints about the Directors' lack of experience. See Edwin A. Riely, *In Search of Gold As Told Through Riely Letters*. Herndon, VA, 1995.

[152] B.F. Washington, "California Letter," *Virginia Free Press*, 10/25/1849, p. 2, c. 5-6.

[153] From "Fort Laramie Photos." Accessed 12/20/2016.

[154] "Fort Laramie - Crossroads to the West."

[155] "The Devil's Gate," Wyoming State Historic Preservation Office, accessed 5/31/2016.

[156] J.H. Kelly, "Charlestown Mining Company," *Virginia Free Press*, 10/4/1849, p. 2, c. 3. Byrarly, Diary, 6/28/1849.

[157] "Fourth of July," *Virginia Free Press*, 7/5/1849, p. 2, c. 2.

[158] Delano, Alonzo, *Life on the Plains and Among the Diggings – Or an Overland Journey to California*, Miller, Orton, and Mulligan, 1854, p. 122.

159 Bancroft, *History of California*, p. 291, vol. 6; "The Fourth of July," *Placer Times*, 7/7/1849, p. 2, c. 1; "Independence," *Weekly Alta California*, 7/12/1849, p. 2, c. 4.

[160] "The Convention," *Weekly Alta California*, 7/2/1849, p. 2, c. 2.

[161] Byrarly, "Diary," 7/14/1850.

[162] "A Well Spent Day," *Spirit of Jefferson*, 8/7/1849, p. 2, c. 1.

[163] "Slavery," *Spirit of Jefferson*, 8/7/1849, p. 2, c. 2 ; "Who Shall Decide?" *Virginia Free Press*, 8/2/1849, p. 2, c. 2.

[164] "Our California Company," *Spirit of Jefferson*, 8/7/1849, p. 2, c. 1.

[165] W. Bryarly, "Journal of the Route of the Charlestown, Virginia, Mining Company from St. Joseph, Missouri, to California", August 1849. In: *The Overland Journal of Vincent Geiger and Wakeman Bryarly*. David Morris Potter (ed.) New Haven: Yale University Press, 1945.

[166] "Assembling of the Convention," *Placer Times*, 9/22/1849, p. 2, c. 1.

[167] "Our Office Building," *Virginia Free Press*, 9/6/1849, p. 2, c. 2.

[168] "Free Schools in Albemarle," *Virginia Free Press*, 9/13/1849, p. 2, c. 3.

[169] "Democratic Modesty," *Virginia Free Press*, 9/6/1849, p. 2, c. 1; "Magistrates for Jefferson County," *Virginia Free Press*, 9/20/1849, p. 2, c. 1.

[170] Edwin Bryant traveled to California in 1846 and published *What I Saw in California* in 1848. Bryant used pack animals on his journey rather than wagons when he left Ft. Laramie. While his detailed narrative was useful to the Charlestown Company in many respects, it did overlook many of the difficulties of using wagons for the rest of the journey. John C. Fremont had made the trek to California in 1842-1843 and published his account in 1845. Being an explorer, much of his account did not address the problems that wagon trains would encounter, and he did not visit several of the more dangerous locations frequented by emigrants. Thomas Hart Benton (1782 – 1858), a U.S. Senator from Missouri, began his political career as a Jacksonian Democrat, but by 1849 he opposed secessionist John C. Calhoun. At this time, he was a staunch advocate of Westward expansion but opposed the introduction of slavery into the new territories. His daughter Jessie was Fremont's wife.

[171] B.F. Washington, "Letter. September 9, 1849, Sacramento, California," *Virginia Free Press*, 11/15/1849, p. 2, c. 5-6.

[172] The Shepherdstown Company, headed by Dr. Richard D. Parran, left Shepherdstown, Virginia, shortly after the Charlestown, Virginia, Mining Co. set off in late March. It consisted mainly of men from the Shepherdstown area and from Washington and Frederick Counties in Maryland. Members included Thomas Binnix, James Boyer, John Cloth, _____ Davis, _____ Denoley, _____ Fay, two Fortney men, _____ Headrick, _____ Hendricks, _____ Jones, _____ Kennedy, _____ Larue, _____ Leopold, _____ Light, _____ May, _____ McKnight, _____ Mendinall, _____ Miller, Joseph Rinehart, Leander Luther Rye, _____ Schneilby, _____ Seymour, _____ Stewart, _____Waters, and Dr. _____ Wilder. They reached California a few days after the Charlestown Company.

A few of the members brought "servants" with them (i.e., slaves), a practice that was frowned upon by most Californians, even before their Constitution outlawed slavery.

After disbanding and arriving in California, the Shepherdstown men frequently crossed paths with the men from Charlestown, sometimes joining their "messes" to mine gold. See: "California News," *Shepherdstown Register*, 12/4/1849, p. 2, c. 5; "Letter from California," *Shepherdstown Register*, 12/18/1849, p. 3, c. 1; "California Letters," *Shepherdstown Register*, 2/19/1850, p. 2, c. 3-4; "Mr. Joseph Reinhart ... ," *Spirit of Jefferson*, 1/15/1895, p. 3, c. 3; "The Virginia Overland Company," *Baltimore Sun*, 10/24/1849, p. 2; "Virginians in California," *Baltimore Sun*, 2/14/1850, p. 1; "California Letters," *Virginia Free Press*, 1/24/1850, p. 2, c. 7 - p. 3, c. 2; "California Company," *Virginia Free Press*, 3/29/1849, p. 2, c. 4; "California Letters," *Virginia Free Press*, 4/11/1850, p. 2, c. 4.

[173] J.H. Kelly, "Our California Company," *Virginia Free Press*, 12/13/1849, p. 2, c. 6-7.

[174] "Proceedings of the Convention," *Weekly Alta California*, 9/20/1849, p. 1, c. 5.

[175] From James Mason Hutchings, "The Miners' Ten Commandments," San Francisco: O'Meara and Painter, printers, 1850.

[176] "Oppose It to the Bitter End," *Virginia Free Press*," 10/4/1849, p. 2, c. 1; "Elegant Extracts," *Virginia Free Press*, 10/4/1849, p. 2, c. 2.

[177] "Third Auditor of the United States Treasury," *Virginia Free Press*, 11/1/1849, p. 1, c. 1. John S. Gallaher served as Third Auditor through the terms of Presidents Taylor and Fillmore, but was replaced in April 1858 under the administration of Franklin Pierce. He accepted a position in the office of the Quartermaster General and remained in Washington until his death on February 4, 1877. He was buried in Edgehill Cemetery in Charlestown, WV. See: Charles J. Faulkner, "John S. Gallaher," in *Aler's History of Martinsburg and Berkeley County, West Virginia*. Hagerstown, MD: 1888, pp. 116-123.

[178] J.H. Kelly, "Our California Company," *Virginia Free Press*, 12/13/1849, p. 2, c. 6-7.

[179] B.F. Washington, "California Letters," *Virginia Free Press*, 1/24/1850, p. 2, c. 7, p. 3, c. 2.

[180] 1850 Census of Jefferson County, Virginia. See Theriault, "Profile of H.H. Gallaher," *West Virginia GeoExplorer Project*.

[181] "Changing the Tune," *Virginia Free Press*, 11/15/1849, p. 2, c. 1.

[182] J.H. Kelly, "From California," *Virginia Free Press*, 1/17/1850, p. 2, c. 5-6.

[183] "The Election Results," *Weekly Alta California*, 11/15/1849, p. 2, c. 1. Peter H. Burnett was one of the defense counsel for Mormon Joseph Smith, Jr. (1839), a member of the Oregon provisional legislature (1844 - 1848). He resigned the governorship of California in 1851 See: "Peter Burnett," Governors Gallery. http://governors.library.ca.gov/01-Burnett.html. Accessed 6/13/2016.

[184] "The Shepherdstown Register," *Shepherdstown Register*, 12/4/1849, p. 2, c. 1; "Shepherdstown Register," *Virginia Free Press*, 12/6/1849, p. 2, c. 2. Henry Hardy was an English widower who moved to Shepherdstown from the District of Columbia. His stint as an editor/publisher was short lived, for he sold his portion of the paper to Joseph Entler, Sr., in May 1850. Due to lack of public support, the paper ceased publication on December 3, 1850, and reopened on November 26, 1853 under the ownership of John H. Zittle.

[185] "Late from California," *Virginia Free Press*, 12/13/1849, p. 2, c. 7. Chivalry Democrats opposed the admission of new states that prohibited abolition.

[186] Leonard L. Richards, *California Gold Rush and the Coming of the Civil War*, New York: Vintage Books, 2007, pp. 193-194.

[187] J.H. Kelly, "California Letters," *Virginia Free Press*, 3/21/1850, p. 2, c. 5-7.

[188] Mr. Root of Ohio introduced a resolution to establish a territorial government for the land acquired from Mexico lying East of the Sierra Nevada mountains. The House adjourned before considering the resolution (*Virginia Free Press*, 1/3/1850, p. 2, c. 2). On January 4th, U.S. Senator James M. Mason introduced a fugitive slave bill. Most Southern legislators welcomed the initiative. Editors like the *Spirit of Jefferson's* James W. Beller, felt that "Some such enactment as the Bill proposed by our worthy Senator, is positively necessary to secure to us the most obvious demands of justice, and for which the South is determined to contend, as one of the plainest yet most sacred rights guaranteed her by the Constitution..." It also stalled. About a week later, Vermont's Governor sent resolutions to the other state legislatures,

arguing that Congress had the right to prevent the extension of slavery and the slave trade anywhere under its jurisdiction. Virginia promptly returned it to the sender, informing him "that the Legislature of Virginia understand their Constitutional rights and mean to maintain them." They also voted to boycott all products made in Vermont or in any other state expressing similar opinions. See: "An Important Bill," *Spirit of Jefferson*, 1/15/1850, p. 2, c. 5'; "The Proceedings," *Shepherdstown Register*, 1/22/1850, p. 2, c. 2; "The Vermont Resolutions," *Spirit of Jefferson*, 1/15/1850, p. 2, c. 3.

[189] Zachary Taylor, Special Message, January 23, 1850.
[190] See: "Congress Last Week," *Virginia Free Press*, 1/31/1850, p. 2, c. 3.

> Resolved, That California, with suitable boundaries, ought, upon her application to be admitted as one of the States of this Union, without the imposition by Congress of any restriction in respect to the exclusion or introduction of slavery within those boundaries.
>
> Resolved, That as slavery does not exist by law, and is not likely to be introduced into any of the territory acquired by the United States from the republic of Mexico, it is inexpedient for Congress to provide by law either for its introduction into, or exclusion from, any part of the said territory; and that appropriate territorial governments ought to be established by Congress in all of the said territory, not assigned as the boundaries of the proposed State of California, without the adoption of any restriction or condition on the subject of slavery.
>
> Resolved, That the western boundary of the State of Texas ought to be fixed on the Rio del Norte, commencing one marine league from its mouth, and running up that river to the southern line of New Mexico; thence with that line eastwardly, and so continuing in the same direction to the line as established between the United States and Spain, excluding any portion of New Mexico, whether lying on the east or west of that river.
>
> Resolved, That it be proposed to the State of Texas, that the United States will provide for the payment of all that portion of the legitimate and bona fide public debt of that State contracted prior to its annexation to the United States, and for which the duties on foreign imports were pledged by the said State to its creditors, not exceeding the sum of _____ dollars, in consideration of the said duties so pledged having been no longer applicable to that object after the said annexation, but having thenceforward become payable to the United States; and upon the condition, also, that the said State of Texas shall, by some solemn and authentic act of her legislature or of a convention, relinquish to the United States any claim which it has to any part of New Mexico.
>
> Resolved, That it is inexpedient to abolish slavery in the District of Columbia whilst that institution continues to exist in the State of Maryland, without the consent of that State, without the consent of the people of the District, and without just compensation to the owners of slaves within the District.
>
> But, resolved, That it is expedient to prohibit, within the District, the slave trade in slaves brought into it from States or places beyond the limits of the District, either to be sold therein as merchandise, or to be transported to other markets without the District of Columbia.
>
> Resolved, That more effectual provision ought to be made by law, according to the requirement of the constitution, for the restitution and delivery of persons bound to service or labor in any State, who may escape into any other State or Territory in the Union. And,

Resolved, That Congress has no power to promote or obstruct the trade in slaves between the slaveholding States' but that the admission or exclusion of slaves brought from one into another of them, depends exclusively upon their own particular laws.

[191] "The Vermont Resolutions," *Spirit of Jefferson*, 1/15/1850, p. 2, c. 3.
[192] "The Proceedings," *Shepherdstown Register*, 1/22/1850, p. 2, c. 2.
[193] "The President's Message," *Virginia Free Press*, 1/3/1850, p. 2, c. 1.
[194] "Abolitionism! Practice vs. Profession," *Virginia Free Press*, 1/17/1850, p. 2, c. 1.
[195] "Farmers' Repository," *Virginia Free Press*, 1/31/1850, p. 2, c. 1.
[196] "Farmers' Repository," *Virginia Free Press*, 1/17/1850, p. 2, c. 1.
[197] "Overflow at Sacramento," *Daily Alta California*, 1/11/1850, p. 2, c. 2; "From the Overflow Placer Intelligence," *Daily Alta California*, 1/24/1850, p. 2, c. 3; "Legislative Proceedings," *Daily Alta California*, 1/27/1850, p. 3, c. 2; Gov. Peter H. Burnett, "First Annual Message of the Governor of the State of California," *Daily Alta California*, 12/26/1849, p. 1, c. 1-4.
[198] "Washington is Dead!" *San Francisco Daily Examiner*, 1/23/1872, p. 2, c. 1-3.
[199] J.H. Kelly, "California Letters," *Virginia Free Press*, 3/12/1850, p. 3, c. 1.
[200] "Doings in Congress," *Spirit of Jefferson*, 2/12/1850, p. 2, c. 5.
[201] "Fragments of Mr. Clingman's Speech," *Shepherdstown Register*, 2/5/1850, p. 2, c. 3; "Thirty-First Congress," *Shepherdstown Register*, 2/12/1850, p. 2, c. 2.
[202] "The Attitude of Virginia," *Spirit of Jefferson*, 2/12/1850, p. 2, c. 6; "Virginia Legislature," *Shepherdstown Register*, 2/5/1850, p. 3, c. 2-3.
[203] "Doings in Congress," *Spirit of Jefferson*, 2/12/1850, p. 2, c. 5.
[204] "Fugitive Slaves," *Virginia Free Press*, 2/14/1850 p. 2, c. 1; "Dissolution of the Union," *Virginia Free Press,* 2/14/1850 p. 2, c. 1.
[205] "Bitterendism and Disunion," *Shepherdstown Register*, 2/26/1850, p. 2, c. 1; "The South and the North," *Shepherdstown Register*, 2/26/1850, p. 2, c. 2-4. The "Storting" is the supreme legislature of Norway (established 1814), located in Oslo.
[206] "Whig Meetings," *Virginia Free Press*, 2/28/1850, p. 3, c. 1.
[207] "California Letters," *Shepherdstown Register*, 2/19/1850, p. 2, c. 3-4.
[208] J.H. Kelly, "California Letters," *Virginia Free Press*, 4/9/1850, p. 2, c. 4.
[209] "California Letters," *Shepherdstown Register*, 2/19/1850, p. 2, c. 3-4; J.H. Kelly, "California Letters," *Virginia Free Press*, 4/9/1850, p. 2, c. 4
[210] John C. Calhoun, "The Causes by Which the Union is Endangered," 3/4/1850/ United States Senate.
[211] Daniel Webster, "The Constitution and the Union," 3/7/1850. United States Senate.
[212] "County Candidates," *Spirit of Jefferson*, 3/12/1850, p. 2, c. 2; "The Convention," *Shepherdstown Register*, 3/19/1850, p. 3; "The Democracy," *Virginia Free Press*, 3/21/1850, p. 2, c. 1.
[213] "County Candidates*,"* *Spirit of Jefferson*, 3/12/1850, p. 2, c. 2; "The Convention," *Shepherdstown Register*, 3/19/1850, p. 3; "The Democracy," *Virginia Free Press*, 3/21/1850, p. 2, c. 1.
[214] "Whigs of Jefferson County*,"* *Virginia Free Press*, 3/21/1850, p. 2, c. 1.
[215] "Light Still Beaming," *Virginia Free Press*, 4/11/1850, p. 2, c. 1; "Senator Mason," *Virginia Free Press*, 4/11/1850, p. 2, c. 1.
[216] "Let There Be No Bargaining," *Virginia Free Press*, 4/4/1850, p. 2. c. 2; "The Spring Campaign," *Virginia Free Press*, 4/4/1850, p. 2, c. 3; "The County Canvass," *Virginia Free Press*, 4/11/1850, p. 2, c. 4, p. 2, c. 2-4.
[217] "A Bill to Incorporate Sacramento City," *Sacramento Transcript*, 4/5/1850, p. 4, c. 1-4; "Municipal Officers," *Sacramento Transcript*, 4/5/1850, p. 3, c. 2; William H. Willis, *History of Sacramento County*, Los Angeles: California, Historic Record Co., 1913, pp. 50-53; "The Squatter Riots of 1850," *A Memorial and Biographical History of Northern California*, Chicago: Lewis Publ. Co., 1891.
[218] Sheriff Joseph McKinney was killed that October in the Squatters' Riots. See "Further California News," *Virginia Free Press*, 10/11/1850, p. 2, c. 5.
[219] J.H. Kelly, "California Letters," *Virginia Free Press*, 5/31/1850, p. 2, c. 6-7.

220 *Daily Alta California*, 4/19/1850, p. 2, c. 5; Act for the Government and Protection of Indians (Chapter 133, Cal. Stats., April 22, 1850). See also: Kimberly Johnson-Dodds, *Early California Laws and Policies Related to California Indians*, Sacramento: California Research Bureau, September 2003.
221 "The Compromise," *Virginia Free Press*, 5/24/1850, p. 2. c. 5.
222 "The Compromise Again," *Spirit of Jefferson*, 5/28/1850, p. 2. c. 2.
223 "The Compromise," *Virginia Free Press*, 5/24/1850, p. 2. c. 5.
224 The Constitution of the Company stated that: "Should any member of the Company die, either on the route to California or whilst there, the heirs of the same shall draw one full half share; and if he shall have been engaged in mining or other service for any time, there shall be awarded the heirs a full proportion for all such time that the member may have been engaged, together with a half share in all such sums as shall be gathered after his demise and before the date of dissolution of the Company; and the Board of Directors are hereby enjoined to see that this covenant shall be well and truly executed." See: "Constitution of the Charlestown Va. Mining Company," *Virginia Free Press*, 2/15/1849, p. 2, c. 6-7.
225 "Charlestown Mining Company," *Virginia Free Press*, 11/15/1849, p. 2, c. 3; "Charlestown Mining Company," *Virginia Free Press*, 5/10/1849, p. 2, c. 6; "Charlestown Mining Company," *Virginia Free Press*, 6/21/1849, p. 2, c. 6; "Death of E.A. Riley," *Virginia Free Press*, 1/24/1850, p. 3, c. 3; "California Letters," *Spirit of Jefferson*, 4/9/1850, p. 2, c. 4.
226 "The Election," *Virginia Free Press*, 5/2/1850, p. 2, c. 1; "The 'Unterrified Precinct,'" *Virginia Free Press*, 5/2/1850, p. 2, c. 1; "The Spirit of Jefferson," *Virginia Free Press, 5/2/1850*, p. 2, c. 1.
227 "Change effected in the proprietorship of the Shepherdstown Register," *Shepherdstown Register*, 5/28/1850, p. 2, c. 3.
228 "Municipal Officers," *Sacramento Transcript*, 4/5/1850, p. 3, c. 2.
229 "Compromise of 1850," *Encyclopedia of American History*. Accessed 5/18/2016.

> The Committee's recommendations included:
>
> The admission of any new State or States formed out of Texas to be postponed until they shall hereafter present themselves to be received into the Union, when it will be the duty of Congress fairly and faithfully to execute the compact with Texas by admitting such new State or States;
>
> The admission forthwith of California into the Union, with the boundaries which she has proposed;
>
> The establishment of territorial governments, without the Wilmot proviso, for New Mexico and Utah, embracing all the territory recently acquired by the United States from Mexico not contained in the boundaries of California;
>
> The combination of these two last mentioned measures in the same bill;
>
> The establishment of the western and northern boundary of Texas, and the exclusion from her jurisdiction of all New Mexico, with the grant to Texas of a pecuniary equivalent; and the section for that purpose to be incorporated in the bill admitting California and establishing territorial governments for Utah and New Mexico;
>
> More effectual enactments of law to secure the prompt delivery of persons bound to service or labor in one State, under the laws thereof, who escape into another State; and,
>
> Abstaining from abolishing slavery; but, under a heavy penalty, prohibiting the slave trade in the District of Columbia.
>
> See also: "The Compromise," *Virginia Free Press*, 6/21/1850, p. 2, c. 2; "The Debate in the Senate," *Virginia Free Press*, 6/28/1850, p. 2. c. 1.

230 "The Nashville Convention," *Shepherdstown Register*, 6/11/1850, p. 2, c. 2.

Jefferson County's Fourth Estate, 1840-1850

[231] "A Strong and Philanthropic Appeal," *Shepherdstown Register*, 5/2/1850, p. 2, c. 5.
[232] "The Position of the South and Ourselves," *Spirit of Jefferson*, 6/4/1850, p. 2, c. 2-3.
[233] "Destruction of a Relic," *Shepherdstown Register*, 6/25/1850, p. 2, c. 3.
[234] "Time for Speaking Out," *Virginia Free Press*, 6/28/1850, p. 2, c. 1; "The Nashville Convention," *Virginia Free Press*, 6/14/1850, p. 2, c. 7; "The County Court System," *Spirit of Jefferson*, 6/4/1850, p. 2, c. 5.
[235] "California," *Shepherdstown Register*, 6/4/1850, p. 2, c. 5.
[236] "A Dark Picture of California," *Shepherdstown Register*, 5/21/1850, p. 1, c. 2-3. The letter was written by Z.M. Chapman, of Ballston, New York (April 24, 1850) and republished from the *New York Express*.
[237] "California Letter, Weber Creek," *Virginia Free Press*, 8/9/1850, p. 3, c. 1.
[238] "The Anniversary," *Daily Union* (Washington, DC), 7/6/1850, p. 4, c. 2-4; "The Fourth of July," *Weekly National Intelligencer*, 7/6/1850, p. 5, c. 3.
[239] "Close of the Volume," *Spirit of Jefferson*, 7/2/1850, p. 2, c. 1.
[240] "Shepherdstown Register," *Shepherdstown Register*, 6/4/1850, p. 2, c. 1; "Fourth of July," *Spirit of Jefferson*, 6/4/1850, p. 2, c. 1; "Prospectus of the Shepherdstown Register," *Shepherdstown Register*, 7/9/1850, p. 3, c. 4; "The Fourth of July," *Shepherdstown Register*, 7/9/1850, p. 2, c. 2; "74th Anniversary," *Spirit of Jefferson*, 7/2/1850, p. 3, c. 1.
[241] "A Returned Gold-Miner," *Shepherdstown Register*, 7/2/1850, p. 2, c. 5.
[242] "The Celebration at Brighton," *Sacramento Transcript*, 7/6/1850, p. 2, c. 4; "Fourth of July Celebration at the Pavilion of Brighton," *Sacramento Transcript*, 7/4/1850, p. 3, c. 1; "Sons of Temperance on the Fourth," *Sacramento Transcript*, 7/6/1850, p. 2, c. 2-3.
[243] "The New Cabinet," *Virginia Free Press*, 7/19/1850, p. 2, c. 1; "The President and His New Cabinet," *Virginia Free Press*, 7/26/1850, p. 2, c. 6.
[244] "The Convention – Candidates," *Shepherdstown Register*, 7/16/1850, p. 2, c. 4; "Time to Speak Out!," *Spirit of Jefferson*, 7/2/1850, p. 2, c. 2; "Convention Candidates," *Virginia Free Press*, 7/5/1850, p. 2, c. 1.
[245] "Funeral Solemnities," *Virginia Free Press*, 7/19/1850, p. 2, c. 1, p. 3, c. 2; "The Funeral Solemnities," *Virginia Free Press*, 7/26/1850, p. 2, c. 6.
[246] "Congress Still Talking," *Virginia Free Press*, 7/5/1850, p. 2, c. 1; "Public Sentiment," *Virginia Free Press*, 7/12/1850, p. 2, c. 2; "The Debate in Congress," *Virginia Free Press*, 7/12/1850, p. 2, c. 2.
[247] "Death of General Taylor," *Daily Alta California*, 8/24/1850, p. 2, c. 1: "Mr. Gilbert's Correspondence," *Daily Alta California*, 8/24/1850, p. 2, c. 2-3; "The Spirit in New Mexico," *Shepherdstown Register*, 7/23/1850, p. 2, c. 1.
[248] J.H. Kelly, "Our California Company," *Virginia Free Press*, 9/13/1850, p. 2, c. 5.
[249] "The Passage of the Texas Bill," *Virginia Free Press*, 8/16/1850, p. 3, c. 2; "Affairs at Washington," *Virginia Free Press*, 8/30/1850, p. 2, c. 1; "The Fugitive Slave Bill," *Shepherdstown Register*, 8/27/1850, p. 2, c. 3.
[250] "Masonic Notice," *Virginia Free Press*, 7/26/1850, p. 3, c. 3; "I.O.O.F.," *Virginia Free Press*, 7/26/1850, p. 3, c. 3; "Cadets of Temperance," *Virginia Free Press*, 7/26/1850, p. 3, c. 3.
[251] "The Cholera," *Virginia Free Press*, 8/9/1850, p. 3, c. 3; "Cholera," *Virginia Free Press*, 8/16/1850, p. 3, c. 1; "Harpers-Ferry Again," *Virginia Free Press*, 8/23/1850, p. 2, c. 2.
[252] "The Election. Jefferson County," *Shepherdstown Register*, 8/27/1850, p. 2, c. 5. The candidates elected favored the state's number of Representatives to be calculated on the basis of eligible white males only. Proponents of the "Mixed Basis" wanted it to be based on both eligible white males and some proportion of the slave population. The Mixed Basis favored the eastern part of Virginia, where the majority of its slaves were located.
[253] "Further California News," *Virginia free Press*, 10/11/1850, p. 2, c. 5; J.H. Kelly, "From California," *Virginia Free Press*, 9/27/1850, p. 2, c. 3.
[254] "Further California News," *Virginia Free Press*, 10/11/1850, p. 2, c. 5.
[255] Daniel Jenks, Humbolt River Valley, 1859. Wikimedia Commons. Accessed 6/11/2016.

[256] "The Funeral Obsequies," *Daily Alta California*," 8/28/1850, p. 2, c. 1; "The Proceedings Yesterday," *Daily Alta California*, 8/30/1850, p. 2, c. 1-2.

[257] J.H. Kelly, "From California," *Virginia Free Press*, 9/27/1850, p. 2, c. 3.

[258] "The Compromise Bill," *Virginia Free Press*, 9/13/1850, p. 2, c. 1; "The California Members," *Virginia Free Press*, 9/13/1850, p. 2, c. 1; "Passage of the California and Utah Bills — The Effect," *Virginia Free Press*, 9/13/1850, p. 2, c. 3; "Passage of the Fugitive Slave Bill," *Virginia Free Press*, 9/20/1850, p. 2, c. 1; "Adjournment of Congress," *Virginia Free Press*, 9/27/1850, p. 2, c. 1.

[259] "California a State," *Shepherdstown Register*, 9/17/1850, p. 2, c. 4.

[260] "The Recent Outrage at Harrisburg," *Shepherdstown Register*, 9/10/1850, p. 2, c. 3-4.

[261] "Harpers Ferry — The Cholera," *Virginia Free Press*, 9/13/1850, p. 2, c. 2; "Harpers Ferry — No Cholera," *Virginia Free Press*, 9/20/1850, p. 2, c. 4; "The Convention," *Virginia Free Press*, 9/27/1850, p. 2, c. 1; "The Shepherdstown Bridge," *Shepherdstown Register*, 9/17/1850, p. 2, c. 5-6.

[262] Reed, G. Walter. *History of Sacramento County California*. Los Angeles: Historic Record Company, 1923, p. 65.

[263] J.H. Kelly, "Private letter from our correspondent," *Virginia Free Press*, 11/1/1850, p. 2, c. 3.

[264] Arriving in Sacramento in June 1849, Winn was elected City Councilman and then mayor in August. His career had included a stint as Colonel of the First Regiment of the Mississippi Militia — experience which prompted the California Legislature to appoint him Brigadier General of the California Militia. During the Squatters Riots of August 1850, he issued a Proclamation declaring Martial Law and brought 500 members of the State Militia to patrol streets of Sacramento City. During the following months, Winn helped raise a a force during the Coloma Indian troubles in El Dorado County.

Some of Winn's critics had accused the militia of being lazy or incompetent and the reports of Indian violence as highly exaggerated. Winn appointed Kelly his special Aid-de-camp for his trustworthy reputation rather than for his military expertise.

See: Kenneth Knott, "Californians and the Military: Major General Albert Maver Winn." http://www.militarymuseum.org/Winn.html. Accessed 6/19/2016.

[265] J. Harrison Kelly, "Official Dispatches," *Sacramento Transcript*, 11/20/1850, p. 2, c. 4.

[266] "Condition of Affairs in the Indian Country," *Sacramento Transcript*, 11/20/1850, p. 2. c. 1.

[267] "Latest from El Dorado Co. THE TRUE STATE OF THE CASE," *Sacramento Transcript,* 11/20/1850, p. 2, c. 4.

[268] "Latest from Col. Rodgers' Volunteers," *Sacramento Transcript*, 11/25/1850, p. 2, c. 1-2.

[269] Stephen B. Oates, *To Purge This Land With Blood*, 2nd ed., 1970, pp. 70-75.

Index

Aisquith, Edward M. , 62, 68, 72, 77, 81, 90, 142, 146, 155, 160, 169, 181, 186, 197, 210
Alburtis, John, 40
Allen, James R., 114
Allen, John, 155, 173
American River, 138, 147, 160, 169, 178, 199
American System, 4
Arbutis, John 3
Anderson, John, 59
Anderson, Robert, 162
Avis, John , 41, 62

Bank Bill of 1841, 8
Barley, Richard, 142, 155, 181
Barton, Richard W. , 7
Bedinger, Henry, 10, 19, 20, 26, 43, 51
Beller, James W., ix, 14, 15, 19, 20, 22, 25, 26, 29, 31, 36, 37, 39, 43-45, 47-49, 51-52, 53, 55, 60, 78, 95, 116, 118, 132, 133, 137, 138, 145, 154, 157, 162, 166-169, 172, 173, 176, 183, 191, 214
Bender, Jacob, 142
Benton, Thomas Hart, 119, 120, 212
Berkeley and Jefferson Intelligencer 3
Bigelow, Hardon, 173, 189
Binnix, Thom, 212
Blakemore, Robert M. , 129, 142
"Black Tariff," 33
Blessing, J.F. , 111
Boley, John L., 142, 181, 194
Boteler, Alexander R., 25
Bowers, John W., 142, 181
Bradley, Thornton C., 142, 181, 186, 194, 197
Bryarly, Dr. Wakeman, 62, 64, 117, 124, 133, 142, 184, 186, 189, 194
Broderick, Daniel C., 102, 114
Brown, John, 169
Burnett, Peter H., 144, 151, 153, 154, 168, 171, 174, 188, 203, 213

Burwell, Walter J. , 90, 142, 160, 182
Butcher, R. Hume, 13, 14

Cairo, IL, 70, 71
Calhoun, John C., 150, 151, 164-166, 168, 172
Carlyle, Thomas, i
Cass, Lewis, 52, 194
Cedar Lawn, 10
Chambers, George W., 138
Charlestown, VA, 3-8, 10, 13, 15, 18, 20, 22, 25, 31, 32, 36, 40, 47, 49, 51-53, 59, 61, 62, 65, 66, 79, 81, 111, 117, 124, 131, 134, 137, 187, 197
Charlestown, VA Artillery, 6, 13, 28, 31, 36, 38
Charlestown VA Mining Co., 62, 66, 67, 72, 86, 91, 93, 119-121, 126, 128, 133, 143, 145, 158, 181
Chimney Rock, 96, 99, 103, 104
Chinese immigrants, 116
Cholera, 67, 71, 72, 76, 78, 79, 81, 88, 89, 94, 108, 115, 116, 171, 183, 186, 188, 195
Clay, Henry, 4, 24, 26, 41, 46, 151, 157, 158, 160, 164, 165, 166, 172, 187, 194, 196, 197
Clevenger, Acy (Asa), 170, 186, 193
Cockrell, Daniel, 142, 181, 186
Constitutionalist, Harper's Ferry, 22
Cookus, John H., 44
Comegys, G.W., 142, 169
Compromise of 1850, 9, 150, 157, 172, 174, 176, 187, 193, 196, 197
Conway, Hugh, 142, 169
Crane, Smith, 62, 84, 141, 146, 180
Cunningham, Charles, 132
Cunningham, George, 132, 141
Cunningham, James, 42, 109, 132, 168
Cunningham, N.C. 172

Dallas, George M., 19, 25
Daugherty, Enos, 141, 154

Davenport, Braxton, 19, 39, 51
Davidson, James, 125, 171
Davidson, William Samuel, 100, 109, 185
Davis, Clem, 159
Davis, Joseph C., 141, 180, 193
Delano, Alonzo, 111
Devil's Gate, 106
Disunion, 15, 157, 164, 166, 167, 194, 204
Donnelly, Daniel, 141
Douglas, Stephen A., 113, 171, 173
Duke, F.W., 173
Duke, James W., 110, 141, 180
Duke, Talbot S., 78, 166
Dutton, Rev. Mr., 13

Education, 12, 30, 33, 37, 47
Engle, Jacob H., 141, 142, 180
Engle, Joseph, 154, 159, 171
Entler, Joseph, Sr., 172, 182, 212

Fagan, Danie, 89, 131, 141, 180
Faulkner, Charles, Sr., 68, 69, 78, 187
Faulkner, William, 204
Feather, River, 54, 134, 177, 185, 191
Ferrill, Milton, 141, 180
Foote, Henry S., 181, 193
Fort Hall, ID, 73, 76, 109, 114, 118, 125
Fort Independence, NB, 59, 91
Fort Kearney (Fort Childs), NE, 92, 93
Fort Laramie, WY, 76, 90, 91, 104, 105, 107, 111
Fort Leavenworth, KS, 61
Free Soil Party, 52, 53, 149
Fremont, John C., 66, 99, 104, 118, 144, 150, 152, 193

Gallaher, Adeline Beeler Hayden, 136
Gallaher, Horatio Nelson, ix, 6, 25, 26, 37, 46, 66, 136, 137, 144, 151, 156, 166, 167, 168, 171-173, 184, 187, 194, 195
Gallaher, John S., ix, , 2-5, 7-9, 11, 14, 15, 17, 22, 25, 26, 30, 31, 33, 36, 37, 39, 40, 43-47, 49, 51, 52, 54, 56, 59, 60, 66-69, 78, 94, 110, 115, 117, 130, 131, 136, 151
Gallaher, John W., 62, 141, 168, 185, 193
Gap View, Jefferson Co., VA, 29
Garry, Dr. James, 94
Garnhart, John H., 142, 145

Geiger, Vincent E., 62, 84, 95, 100, 141, 144, 168, 185, 193, 210
Gettysburg, PA, 14, 32
Gilbert, Edward, 150, 193
Gittings, Thomas, 141
Gold Rush, California, x, 61 ff., 171
Grant, Capt. Richard, 114
Great Kanawha River, 10
Gwin, William M., 101, 113, 116, 117, 128, 144, 150, 152, 193, 196

Hagner, Peter, 131
Haines, Peter, 14
Hamtramck, J.F., 31, 38, 41, 50, 51, 62
Hardy, Henry, ix, 143, 172, 182
Harper's Ferry, VA,, xiv, 3, 4, 6, 17, 22, 26, 31, 35, 36, 37, 40, 42, 47, 49, 67, 78, 94, 111, 136, 172, 186, 194
Harper's Ferry Guard, 6
Harper's Ferry Armory, 30
Harrison, Hamilton C., 89
Harrison, William Henry, 3-8, 130
Harrisonburg, VA, 41
"Harrisonburg Outrage," 194, 204
Hayden, Adeline Beeler (Gallaher), 137
Hayden, Charles A., 1141
Heiss, John, 207
Herbert, Noblet, 81, 89, 141
Hickey, John J., 23
Hodge, John Blair, 29, 30
Hoffman, Benjamin, 89, 111, 141, 168, 180
Hooper, Edward, 142
Howe, Henry, xi, 7, 13, 15, 16, 35, 77, 175
Humphreys, John,
Humphreys, Dr. Joseph D., 154, 172
Hunter, Andrew, 28, 31, 46, 52
Hunter, Henry Clay, 110
Hunter, Sen. Robert M.T., 171, 173, 186

Inauguration Day, 5
Independence Day Celebrations, 13, 19, 28, 31, 35, 44, 49, 50 , 110, 113, 181, 182
Irish Immigrants, 78

Jackson, Thos. A., Map of Cal., 99
Jefferson, Thomas ix
Jefferson Co., VA, background, ix
Jefferson's Rock x
Jewett, John M., 166

Jefferson County's Fourth Estate, 1840-1850

Johnson's Ranch, 197, 198, 199
Jones, Alexander, Rev., 6

Keeling, Robert H., 62, 84, 85, 88, 90, 141
Kelly, Jane Elizabeth, 47
Kelly, John Harrison, 72, 76, 81, 84-87, 89, 90, 92, 93, 108, 109, 125, 128, 131, 132, 137, 138, 142, 145, 147, 153, 158, 161, 162, 168, 177, 180, 185, 188, 190, 192, 193, 196, 197
Kelly, Margaret   25
Kennedy, Andrew   170
Kennedy, Anthony   7
Kloth, John H., 182

Ladies Garland, 3, 4
League of Gileadites, 204
Lenox, Walter, 181
Lewis, Joseph E.N., 62, 76, 84, 141
Long, William S., 116, 119, 141
Lucas, Robert, 25
Lucas, William, 7, 14, 18, 20, 22, 26, 28, 39, 187
Lupton, John M., 141, 180, 185, 194

Mackaran, William H., 180. 193
Manifest Destiny, 28
Manning, James M., 81, 141, 180, 191
Marcy, William L., 95
Marmion, Nicholas, 94
Marshall, James W., 49, 54
Martinsburg Gazette, 3
Mason, Sen. James Murray, 171, 173, 186
Masons, 62, 184, 186
McCurdy, James, 85, 87, 141, 162, 172
McDowell, James, 33
McDougal, John, 143
McIlhany, Edward W., 141, 143
McKay, Pilot, 100, 141
Mexican War, ix, 36, 37, 50, 52, 59, 62, 79, 86, 150, 188
Miller, Andrew R., 141
Miller. C.H., 172
Miller, J.J., 2102
Milton, Taliaferro, 125, 171
Moler, Daniel M., 85
Moler, John, Sr., 7, 206
Monroe Doctrine, 33
Monterey, CA, 54, 141
Moore, Henry H., 141, 146, 180, 185, 193
Moore, James H., 146, 149, 185, 193

Moore, Jesse, 172
Moore, John Jr., 193, 196
Moore, Samuel J.C., 49
Moore, Thomas C., 89, 100, 111, 141, 145, 180, 185, 193
Morgan, Jacob, 7, 141
Mormons, 104, 111, 114
Murphy, Dennis, 142, 180, 187

National Intelligencer (Washington, DC), 4
Native Americans, 84, 85, 87, 89, 92, 95, 96, 100, 103, 106, 111, 114, 116, 153, 170, 177, 190, 197-202, 204
Neuva Helvitia, 120
Niles Register (Baltimore, MD), 3
North, William D., 7

O'Bannon, A.J., 51, 61
Odd Fellows, 31, 34, 36, 37, 41, 62, 117, 136, 183, 197
Opie, Hierome L., 20, 30, 36
Oregon Territory, 20, 23, 30, 36
Oregon Trail, 67, 73, 83, 105, 110, 114, 171, 203

Palfrey, John G., 56
Parran, Richard, 157, 208, 210
Pen mightier than sword, ix, 1
Pleasants, John H., 10
Polk, James K., 19, 24, 25, 32, 36, 41, 43-45, 48, 49, 55
Potomac Rifles, 6, 36, 38
Prarie Schooner, 74
Purcell, John, 141, 168

Ranson, Georgiana Hite, 29
Ranson, James I.   28, 29
Richelieu, Cardinal, 1
Richmond, VA, 4, 33, 40, 46, 136, 167
Richmond Compiler, 4
Richmond *Enquirer*, 5
Richmond *Hawk,* 4
Richmond *Republican,* 60
Richmond *Times,* 171
Richmond *Whig*, 9, 69
Riley, Edwin A., 145, 172
Riley, James, 208
Rissler, William, 141, 168, 180, 193, 196
Ritchie, Thomas, 206
Roberts, Jonathan, 170
Rohrer, Elisha, 141, 180

Roland, John T., 141
Rowan, John W., 13, 20, 28, 31, 32, 36, 38, 40, 41, 51, 62, 110, 186
Rumsey, James, 175

Sacramento City, CA, 87, 95, 113, 117, 119, 121, 123, 126-128, 131, 132, 137, 138, 140-142, 144-146, 152, 153, 154, 159, 161. 162, 167, 168, 173, 185, 188, 190, 192, 196
Sacramento County, 168, 172, 187
Sacramento and Placer Intelligencer, 173
Sacramento River, 127, 141, 152, 178, 183
Sappington, George W. , 40, 49, 53
Scott, Winfield, 41, 43, 44
"See the elephant," 41, 57, 59, 60, 66, 79, 129, 176, 203
Seevers, Benjamin F., 141, 159, 168
Seevers, Nathaniel, 62, 86, 111,, 141, 168
Semple, Robert B., 113, 117, 128
Shannondale Springs, VA, 16, 27, 28, 36, 44, 115, 136, 182
Shepherdstown Register, ix, 143, 150, 157, 165, 172, 174, 175, 182, 194
Showers, John S., 141, 187, 193
Showman, P.B., 141, 180, 193
Simpson, Frances R., 146,
Slagle, Charles S., 141
Slavery, ix, xi, 19, 29, 30, 38, 45, 49, 52, 56, 69, 113-115, 140, 144, 148, 150-152, 156, 157, 164, 167, 170, 171, 173, 193, 207
Smith, S. Frank, 82, 83, 91, 92, 95, 127, 132, 141, 180
Smith, Joseph, Jr., 73
Smith, William S., 22 , 41, 128
Smithfield (Middleway), VA, 17, 26, 172
Smithfield Blues, 6
Sonoma, CA, 37
Spirit of Jefferson, ix, 20, 21, 22, 25, 26, 29, 31, 33, 37, 39, 42, 44, 45, 47, 53, 54, 60, 65, 68, 71, 78, 150, 153, 167, 171, 172, 175, 182
Squatters' Riot (Sacramento, CA), 187, 188, 191, 214
St. Clairsville, OH, 107
St. Louis, MO, 67, 70-73, 76, 79, 100, 116, 153

St. Josephs, MO, 72, 75, 76, 78, 80, 81, 84, 8-91, 93, 102, 104, 107, 108, 128, 132, 145, 176
Stewart, Charles S, 110
Stipes, Daniel, 109
Stipes, John D., 108
Strider, Isaac Keys, 141, 145, 159, 168, 180, 208
Strider, Jesse A., 208
Sullivan, John O., 28
Sutter, John A., 143, 183, 187, 191
Sutter;s Fort, 109, 154, 155, 169, 171
Sutter's Mill, 49, 54

Tavenner, Newton, 126, 171
Taylor, Zachary, 36, 41, 43-45, 48, 52, 53, 55, 56, 60, 68, 78, 115, 148, 149, 151, 156, 157, 172, 181, 183-186, 192
Texas annexation, 17, 19, 25, 28, 30, 33
Texas Boundary Bill, 186
Trinity Church (St. George's Chapel), 15
Tustin, Septimus, 110
Tyler, John, 4, 5, 6, 7, 8, 9, 12, 25, 131
Typhoid fever, 89, 115, 159, 160, 162, 172

Van Buren, Martin, 5, 7, 52
Varle. Charles, *Map of Frederick, Berkeley and Jefferson Counties*
Vaughan, Alfred J., 87, 88
Virginia Free Press, ix, 3, 4, 7, 15, 25, 31-33, 39, 41, 43-45, 47, 51, 54, 59-62, 68, 69, 78, 111, 130, 117, 131, 136, 137, 144, 151, 165, 167, 173, 180
Virginia Military Institute, 87

Wagner, Andrew, 141, 168, 180
Walper, John C., 141, 168, 180
War of 1812, 15, 28
Washington, Benjamin Franklin, ix, 10, 13, 14, 20, 25, 28-30, 38, 39, 40, 43, 45, 49, 51, 52, 60-62, 64, 81, 88, 97, 98, 101, 102, 111, 113, 116-118, 125, 132, 136, 141, 153, 158, 161, 165, 167, 169, 170, 172, 173, 183, 185-188, 192, 193, 196
Washington, George, 40, 131
Washington, Georgiana, 118
Washington, John Thornton Augustine, 11

Washington, Lawrence B., 62, 81, 141
Washington, Sally, 10
Washington, Thomas West, 76, 78, 81, 171
Washington, William Temple, 209
Washington, D.C. ., 3, 40, 47, 113, 149, 150, 156, 158, 171, 181, 183, 185, 192
Washington Medical University, 62
Washington Monument (DC), 181
Weaver Creek, CA, 138, 145
Webon Creek, CA, 153, 159, 162
Webster, Daniel, 163-165, 167, 183, 186, 193

Whig Journal, 9
Whig philosophy, 4
Williams, Richard, 59, 151
Willis, Edward J., 169
Wilmot, David, 38
Wilmot Proviso, 38, 52, 69, 115, 207
Winn, A.M., Gen., 188, 197, 199, 216
Wise, Henry, 150
Worthington, William C. , 78
Wright, George W., 151, 193

Yeoman, 5
Young, Joseph C., 89, 125, 171, 209
Zittle, John H., ix, 211